The Scourge of the Mission

NEW PERSPECTIVES ON INDIAN PASTS

Other Books in the Series:

THOMAS R. TRAUTMANN
Aryans and British India

A.R. VENKATACHALAPATHY
In Those Days There Was No Coffee:
Writings in Cultural History

DAVID N. LORENZEN
Who Invented Hinduism?
Essays on Religion in History

THOMAS R. TRAUTMANN
Languages and Nations:
The Dravidian Proof in Colonial Madras

HARLAN O. PEARSON
Islamic Reform and Revival in Nineteenth-century India:
The Tariqah-I Muhammadiyah

THOMAS R. TRAUTMANN
The Clash of Chronologies:
Ancient India in the Modern World

SAURABH DUBE
After Conversion:
Cultural Histories of Modern India

USHA SANYAL
Devotional Islam and Politics in British India:
Ahmad Riza Khan Barelwi and his Movement, 1870–1920 (Classic reissue)

CYNTHIA TALBOT (ed.)
Changing Conceptions of South Asia's Past (Forthcoming)

DAVID GILMARTIN
Civilization and Modernity:
Narrating the Creation of Pakistan (Forthcoming)

The Scourge of the Mission

Marco Della Tomba in Hindustan

DAVID N. LORENZEN

YODA PRESS

YODA PRESS
268 A/C Vasant Kunj
New Delhi 110070

Published in India
by YODA PRESS

First Published 2010

ISBN 978-81-906668-8-6

Typeset in Sabon 11/14
By Jojy Philip, New Delhi 110 015
Printed at G.H. Prints, New Delhi 110 020
Published by Arpita Das, YODA PRESS, New Delhi

Contents

Illustrations

Introduction

According to the first-century Roman historian Tacitus, the Caledonian rebel Calgacus harangued his British troops against the Roman army led by Agricola with this famous denunciation of imperial greed: "Brigands of the world, they have exhausted the land by their indiscriminate plunder, and now they ransack the sea. The wealth of an enemy excites their cupidity, his poverty their lust of power. East and West have failed to glut their maw. They are unique in being as violently tempted to attack the poor as the wealthy. Robbery, butchery, rapine, the liars call Empire; they create a desolation and call it peace."[1] There is, of course, no possibility that Calgacus spoke these exact words. Nonetheless, his speech continues to offer a vivid reminder of the predatory nature of the great empires of the past, present and future. It is particularly fitting, and ironic, as an epitaph for the conquest and plunder of India by the forces of the English East India Company in the second half of the eighteenth century. This was precisely the period when the Capuchin friar Marco della Tomba lived in north India, then called "Hindustan". Before proceeding with Marco's story, however, I want to say something about how the example of Tacitus's rhetorical device of an invented speech applies, and does not apply, to this book.

During the sixteenth and seventeenth centuries, European historians often wrote essays about the practice and art of writing history.[2] In them historians debated the proper methods and style to be employed in historical texts and the proper moral and practical messages that the historians should attempt to impart. In spite of the many differences of opinion found in these texts, known collectively as *ars historica,* the texts still share many of the same topics and presuppositions. At least two of these presuppositions stand in sharp contrast to what professional historians today think about the proper method and purpose of writing history. The authors of the *artes historicae* generally assumed, first, that history should employ the artifices and tropes of classical rhetoric in order to convince and entertain the reader. Second, they regarded the purpose of writing history to be not simply the reconstruction of the past but also the teaching of important lessons from the past useful for understanding the present and serving as a guide to men's moral and political actions, particularly the actions of kings and statesmen.

One of the rhetorical issues often discussed in these texts was the propriety of including in history texts the imagined speeches of persons from the past. Was it proper for the historian to attempt to recreate speeches that probably had been spoken, but had never been written down? Most of the *ars historica* authors in fact argued that recourse to such speeches was an acceptable and valuable rhetorical resource. Even though such speeches were invented, they could, it was claimed, be employed to render more vivid and convincing the views of past historical actors. In this view, invented speeches were quite proper so long as the historian followed the "decorum" of the historical actors and their historical context. In other words, the historian had to create speeches whose content, if not their rhetorical form, was historically plausible. Anthony Grafton translates the following comments in defense of such speeches from the *ars historica* of Giovanni Antonio Viperano (1535–1610):[3]

> Some deny that a historian may insert any speech, if he has to make it up; for history can admit no fiction. But events work in one way, words in another. The former can be described as they took place. The latter cannot possibly be reported as they were pronounced. And if it is acceptable to follow probability when recounting obscure events, why is that not permissible for words as well?

Carlo Ginzburg has noted that the inclusion of such invented speeches in histories written today "would be totally inappropriate…, not to say absurd."[4] Nonetheless, this is, in a more modest way, what I have done in this autobiography of the eighteenth-century Capuchin missionary to northern India, Marco della Tomba (1726–1803). I certainly have not attempted to insert any grandiose rhetorical speeches in Marco's story, but I have filled out the two autobiographical essays he wrote and several letters he wrote about his adventures with various passages written for him in the first person, as if I were Marco. I have also reorganized the materials used to create a continuous narrative of Marco's life as a missionary. In all of these added passages, however, I have strictly kept to the decorum of only giving information known from other sources or summarized from Marco's own letters and essays. This book is a biography and autobiography, not a historical novel. Only in the last chapter describing the events leading to Marco's death have I resorted to a more traditional third-person format.

Marco della Tomba was an amazingly intrepid Italian Capuchin missionary who worked mainly in northeastern India, the region called Bihar, during the second half of the eighteenth century. Marco was in India from 1757 to 1773 and again from 1784 until his death in 1803 as a member of what was then known as the Tibet Mission. He acquired the pejorative epithet "scourge of the mission" (*fléau de la mission*) near the end of his life in a vicious and foolish report sent to church officials in Rome by the proxy-visitor to the Tibet Mission, a French secular priest named Louis René Foulon. Soon after Foulon's report arrived in Rome, Marco's erstwhile protector and patron in Rome, the prefect of the sacred congregation of Propaganda Fide, Cardinal Stefano Borgia, picked up and repeated the epithet, calling Marco the "scourge of the mission" (*flagello della missione*) in an address to the executive committee of the Congregation made in 1804, after, as was later learned, Marco had already died.

Marco's life began in the mostly rural region of east-central Italy, known as The Marches or Le Marche. During the eighteenth century, Le Marche formed part of the Papal States, governed from Rome with the pope as head of state. Le Marche has a long coastline and one good port, Ancona. The land, however, is mostly mountainous and much less productive than the gentler hills of Tuscany or the rich plains of Lombardy. Nor could Ancona compete commercially with the great trading port of Venice further to the north. Le Marche could, however, boast of the artistic splendor of the Renaissance palace and court of the city of Urbino, the birthplace of the great painter Raphael (1483–1520). Nonetheless, by the eighteenth-century the region had become a political, economic, and cultural backwater and exported many of its more talented citizens. Some sought employment in cities like Rome or Venice while others joined the church and, in some cases, became missionaries in the distant lands of Asia.

The brightest light among the missionaries who traveled out

from Le Marche to Asia was undoubtedly the Jesuit, Matteo Ricci (1552–1610), a great scholar of Chinese language and culture. Ricci was born in Macerata, a small hill town in the region near Ancona and also near Loreto, the famous Catholic shrine of the Virgin and the Santa Casa (Holy House). Among the many Capuchin missionaries from Le Marche who belonged to Marco's own Tibet Mission, there were three (in addition to Marco) who made important early contributions to European knowledge about Asia: Domenico da Fano (1674–1729), Francesco Orazio da Pennabilli (1680–1745), and Cassiano da Macerata (1708–1791). The tradition of Le Marche sending out scholars to Tibet was revived in the twentieth century by the secular Orientalist Giuseppe Tucci, who, like Matteo Ricci and Cassiano, came from the town of Macerata.

The Capuchins form one of three branches of the Franciscan Order of friars founded by St. Francis (1181–1226) of Assisi of town in the neighboring province of Umbria. The Capuchin branch of the Franciscan Order was originally established in the sixteenth century by Franciscan friars from the Umbrian and Le Marche regions who wanted to follow a stricter regimen and rule than that of the other two main Franciscan branches, the Observants and the Conventuals. In the early eighteenth-century, in 1703 to be precise, the Sacred Congregation of Propaganda Fide assigned the newly created Tibet Mission to the Capuchin friars of the Picena Province, this being another name for Le Marche from the name of its early inhabitants, the Piceni. At this time the Capuchins remained very strong in the Umbrian and Le Marche regions, but they also had spread out from there and established centers throughout Europe, as well as in Asia, Africa and the Americas.

The history of the Catholic Church's interest in Tibet begins with an expedition by the Portuguese Jesuit António de Andrade in 1624 (Didier 2002). Andrade never reached the Tibetan capital of Lhasa, but he did explore parts of Ladakh and western Tibet and built a church at Tsaparang to the west of Lake Mansarovar. In 1633 the mission at Tsaparang became a casualty in a war between Ladakh and the kingdom of Tsaparang and was never reestablished. Another early attempt at establishing a mission in Tibet was made around the same time by two other Portuguese Jesuits, Estêvão Cacela and João Cabral. They approached Tibet from Bengal and Bhutan and reached Shigatse about 220 kilometers west of Lhasa in 1627–28. They were unable to establish a permanent mission there, however, and by about 1630 had abandoned the attempt.

Another event leading to the eventual creation of the Tibet Mission was the establishment, in 1622, of a new congregation or committee of the Catholic Church that was meant to coordinate and centralize control over all the Church's numerous missions throughout the world. This committee was the Sacred Congregation of Propaganda Fide, more often called simply Propaganda Fide or Propaganda, and now officially named the Congregazione per l'Evangelizzazione dei Popoli. Propaganda Fide soon ran into trouble with the Portuguese and Spanish governments, however, since the Church itself had earlier entrusted these governments with the duty and right to appoint and finance missionaries in Asia and the Americas. The evangelization of most of Asia had been assigned to Portugal under an arrangement known as the *padroado*. This gave Portugal considerable practical control over the missions in India, even though Portuguese political influence in the region was declining, and the Portuguese crown was reluctant to cede this control without receiving anything in exchange. As a result Propaganda Fide and Portugal came into conflict over who would be in charge of the missions in India. A rough modus vivendi was eventually reached in which the Portuguese controlled most of the missions in southern India, while Propaganda Fide controlled the Capuchin mission in Tibet, Nepal and Bihar; a Carmelite mission in Malabar (Kerala); and an Augustinian mission in Golconda (Andhra Pradesh). This division of labor did not prevent a dispute between the Jesuits and Capuchins in the early eighteenth century over who had a right to establish a mission in Tibet and another dispute in the 1760s and early 1770s over whether or not the Capuchins had a right to offer public Masses in the oratory attached to their hospice in Chandernagore. Marco himself played an important role in the latter dispute, but the whole affair became irrelevant in 1773 when the pope officially disbanded the Jesuits and their Society of Jesus.

The reports of the voyages of Andrade, Cacela and Cabral in Tibet circulated among Church officials in later years and helped inspire the initiative of a French Capuchin friar named François Marie de Tours to establish a new mission to Tibet. He petitioned Propaganda to establish this mission, and in 1703 Propaganda issued a decree that created the Tibet Mission and assigned it to the Capuchins of the Picena Province, who immediately set about recruiting friars for the mission. The first friars to reach Lhasa were Padre Giuseppe da Ascoli and Padre François Marie de Tours, who arrived there together in June 1707. François Marie returned to Kathmandu in 1709, but Giuseppe da Ascoli was soon joined in Lhasa by Padre Domenico da Fano and the lay brother Michelangelo da Borgogna. In 1710, however, Giuseppe and Michelangelo had to leave Tibet, leaving Domenico in Lhasa alone. In the spring of 1711, Padre Giovanni da Fano joined Domenico, but by the end of that year both of them had to return to India because of a lack of funds to maintain the mission. Lhasa was abandoned.

Meanwhile, Andrade's early expedition to Tibet had also inspired an Italian Jesuit named Hippolito Desideri to undertake his own mission to Tibet. He arrived in Lhasa in March of 1716. Without knowing this, the Capuchins had organized a new expedition to Lhasa, and in October 1716 the friars Domenico da Fano, Francesco Orazio della Penna and Giovanni Francesco da Fossombrone arrived in Lhasa and found Desideri already there. Although they all agreed to live together in the same house, the Capuchins sent protests to Rome against the presence of the Jesuit Desideri in Lhasa. Desideri also wrote to Rome to defend his mission, but eventually he received orders to leave Tibet and arrived in Kathmandu in December 1721. After Desideri's departure, the Capuchin mission continued to struggle to establish a Christian community in Lhasa but with very little success. When they finally did begin to win a few converts in the 1740s, this angered the Dalai Lama, and the Capuchins were definitively expelled from Tibet in 1745. Forty years of hardships, expense and diligent labor had come to naught.

Desideri and two of the Capuchin friars in Tibet were important scholars. During his time in Tibet, Desideri intensely studied Tibetan Buddhism and produced several works written directly in Tibetan as well as an important account in Italian of his studies and travels (Luca 1987). The Capuchin Domenico da Fano wrote an important medical treatise incorporating elements of traditional Tibetan medicine, and his colleague Francesco Orazio della Penna translated several apologetic Christian works into Tibetan and several Buddhist texts written in Tibetan into Italian (Petech 1954–56: Part 1, pp. lxxxvi–xciv).

After their expulsion from Tibet in 1745, the Capuchins' only remaining hospices were those at Kathmandu in Nepal, at Patna in Bihar and at Chandernagore in Bengal. The

Mission nonetheless continued to be officially called the Tibet Mission. A few years earlier, however, contact had been initiated between the Capuchins and the Hindu king of Bettiah in extreme northwest Bihar south of Kathmandu. The king became friendly with a Capuchin named Giuseppe Maria da Gargnano who had been in Lhasa but had then moved to Patna. In Marco's account, Giuseppe Maria is said to have used his medical skills to cure the Bettiah queen of a "gangrene of the throat." The king then sent a request to the pope to allow the Capuchins to set up a hospice in Bettiah, which they finally did in about 1750. From then until his death in 1761, Giuseppe Maria spent most of his time in Bettiah. For several years he was accompanied by his friend and biographer, Cassiano da Macerata, who returned to Europe in 1754.

Marco della Tomba's immediate predecessors in the Mission, Giuseppe Maria de Gargnano and Cassiano de Macerata, wrote important letters, memoirs, translations and essays about their experiences in India and their encounter with the Hindu religion. Giuseppe Maria, with the help of Cassiano and a Brahmin teacher, wrote a long "Dialogue between a Christian and a Hindu about Religion" in the Hindustani language and script and presented a copy of this dialogue to the King of Bettiah in 1751. Two manuscripts of this text, one dated 1751 and another 1787, survive in the Vatican Library. Giuseppe Maria is also said to have translated a number of Sanskrit and Hindi works in Italian and to have translated or directly written several other expositions of Christian doctrine into Hindustani. All these other texts are now lost. Cassiano, for his part, wrote in Italian an account of his own travels to and through Hindustan, a biography of his friend Giuseppe Maria, a book about Hinduism, and a translation into Hindustani (in Roman script) of the Gospel of Matthew. The biography was published in Verona in 1768, and the account of Cassiano's travels was published by Petech in 1954–56. The original manuscripts of Cassiano's travel account and the still unpublished book on Hinduism and his translation of Matthew are now preserved in the Biblioteca Comunale Mozzi-Borgetti in Macerata.[5]

Marco's own scholarly works are described in the course of this book, and all his known writings, including his letters, are listed in the bibliography at the end of this book. His scholarly works include his two autobiographical essays, a big book on Hinduism, a polemical essay against Holwell's views on Hinduism, and several translations from Hindustani to Italian, most notably a part of Tulsidas's *Ramcaritmanas,* often called the Bible of north Indian Hinduism. Marco's translation of this text precedes all others into European languages by at least 80 years. His other translations include a long text, the *Gyan Sagar*, associated with the heterodox Hindu sect known as the Kabir Panth.

Marco arrived in the French city of Chandernagore in Bengal on October 20, 1757, not long after the city had been captured by the English as part of a spillover into India of the European Seven Years War (1756–63). At this time, the Tibet Mission had hospices in Chandernagore, in Patna, in Bettiah and in Kathmandu. From Chandernagore, Marco moved on to Bettiah to join Giuseppe Maria da Gargnano. After several months in Bettiah, Giuseppe Maria sent Marco off to join the renegade French army of Jean Law (Marco's Monsieur Lassa) as a chaplain. After the saintly Giuseppe Maria's death in Bettiah in 1761, Marco retuned to the hospice there. Marco became the new superior of the Bettiah mission. In Bettiah, Marco began to seriously study Hindu religion, translated Hindu texts into Italian, and wrote several essays about Hindu religion and culture and about the history of north India and Nepal.

In 1773 Marco returned to Italy and brought with him at least the drafts of his scholarly works. He revised some of these in Italy and sent the whole lot to Monsignor Stefano Borgia, the secretary of Propaganda Fide. Borgia kept them in his private museum in Velatri and eventually they ended up in the Vatican Library where they are today. Marco spent most of the next 10 years in a Capuchin monastery in Senigallia near his home village of Tomba (now Castel Colonna). Soon after arriving in Italy, however, Marco began petitioning Borgia to let him return to the Tibet Mission. Exactly why Marco was so anxious to leave Italy is not clear from his surviving letters, but at one point he even asked to be sent to Brazil if it proved impossible for him to return to India.

Whatever Marco's motives may have been, his requests were held up for unknown reasons, and he had to cool his heels in Italy until 1783 when he was finally allowed to set sail to rejoin the Tibet Mission. By 1784 he was back in Chandernagore. He spent most of his remaining years in the town of Bhagalpur on the Ganges in eastern Bihar. As far as we can tell, Marco did little or no scholarly work after his return to India and spent most of his time caring for local Christians and engaging in a number of acrimonious disputes among the friars of the Tibet Mission. Most notable was the trial he organized in 1793 against his fellow friar, Giuseppe da San Marcello. The document of this trial, written by Marco and translated in this book, offers a remarkable look at the everyday conflicts of the common people of Bettiah in this period. The low point of Marco's life and career came in early 1803 when he was officially repudiated by the proxy Visitor to the Mission, Louis René Foulon. Marco died a lonely death in Bhagalpur in either March or June of 1803.

North India in Marco's Time

Marco's adventures in Hindustan took place in the historical context of the step-by-step consolidation of British colonial power in north India, first in Bengal and then in Bihar and regions further to the west. Nowadays, every schoolgirl and schoolboy in India, Pakistan, Bangladesh and Britain is expected to know something about this period, but among recent historians the narrative of the conquest of India between 1750 and 1820 has not attracted the interest it merits. In part, this neglect undoubtedly reflects the fact that for South Asians this is the story of a great political, economic, and cultural defeat, while for the British this is the story of a moral failure: a ruthless military conquest, the rape of Indian wealth, and a growing cultural insensitivity that led to the imperial arrogance and racism of the nineteenth and twentieth centuries. From either point of view, the conquest of India is, in the end, a story no one today wants to claim as his or her own, except perhaps in the rosy-hued, false versions of imperial nostalgia. The true story, however disagreeable, nonetheless merits retelling. It is a history filled with eccentric characters, political intrigues and thefts on a colossal scale, and the first serious cultural encounter—at least for North India—between Indians and Europeans on a daily basis. Marco was there and directly describes what he saw and heard. His perspective is that of a European and a Christian, but not the perspective of a person tied to the economic and political interests of the English or other Europeans.

If we skip over the institutional complexities, political undercurrents, and multiple motives behind the events leading to the English takeover of North India, the rough outlines of the imperial conquest are clear enough. In October of 1757 when Marco arrived in Chandernagore, the traders of the

English East India Company had recently avenged their ouster the previous year from their trading settlement at Calcutta by the nawab of Bengal, Siraj-ud-Daulah. The English had returned in force, retaken Calcutta, and moved on to defeat the Bengal nawab in a desultory battle at a place called Plassey or Palasi near the nawab's capital of Murshidabad in northern Bengal. Along the way, the English also captured the French settlement of Chandernagore, a little north of Calcutta, where the Tibet Mission had a hospice. When Marco arrived in Chandernagore, most of the Frenchmen of the settlement had been taken prisoner and the women had been left in a pitiable state, as Marco describes. Eventually, the British allowed the French to continue their trading activities at Chandernagore, provided that the settlement was not fortified.

The English East India Company then moved gradually to take over the direct administration of the territories under its control and to extend its military conquests further to the West. The main motive was evidently simple greed rather than power, glory or religion. Each new conquest led to enormous compensations being paid by the defeated Indian rulers to both the English Company and directly to its servants. The English clerk turned military general and chief administrator, Robert Clive, became unimaginably wealthy as did many of his subordinates. The Company gradually undertook a more direct collection of land revenues and, at the same time, established a trading system in which only the British traders and the East India Company were exempted from the many customs duties that had to be paid for transporting goods from one place to another.

In the first years after Plassey, the British had to accept a dual government shared between them and the nawab of Bengal, who continued to collect taxes and administer justice while paying enormous tribute to the Company and granting its officials the right to trade without paying any inland customs duties. The appointment of a new nawab of unexpected efficiency and ambition named Mir Kasim Ali Khan in 1760 led to a direct military confrontation between him and the Company. When the nawab decided to cancel the advantage held by Company traders by eliminating the inland duties on all trade by anyone, the Company officials decided that the nawab had to be replaced.

One of the first battles in the ensuing war was prematurely unleashed by the commander of the fortified English "factory" (or warehouse) in Patna on June 25, 1763. The soldiers employed by the factory overran the town but were thrown out the very next day by the forces of Mir Kasim, led by his Armenian commanders, Ghurgin Khan and Margar, as well as by their German subordinate named Samru. In the ensuing melee, the Capuchin friars of the Patna hospice were attacked by a mob and then paraded through the town in their shorts. The Armenian commander Margar finally rescued them. Marco tells this story through a letter sent to him by the prefect of the Mission, Anselmo da Ragusa, who was one of the friars in Patna.

Mir Kasim then allied himself with the forces of the nawab of Awadh, Shuja-ud-daulah, and those of the Mughal emperor, Shah Alam II. At this time, Marco was chaplain to the army of the Frenchman Jean Law, who was in the employ of the Emperor. The allied forces lost an important battle at the gates of Patna in which Marco was captured and then sent to Calcutta. Not long afterwards, a more decisive battle was fought on October 22, 1764 near the town of Buxar or Baksar, 120 kilometers further to the west. The Indian defeat at Buxar meant that the East India Company was now in direct military control of most of Bengal and Bihar. In 1765, the Company received the *diwani* or right of administration from the increasingly powerless Mughal emperor, and the responsibilities of the new puppet nawab were reduced to a minimum.

By 1765, the British had also taken control of Bettiah, where Marco was now stationed. Another important event of the period was the Bengal famine of 1770 in which as much as one third of the population died. Some of the effects of this famine are described in Marco's text. As has been noted, Marco returned to Italy in 1773 and was not back in India until 1784. By then, the English East India Company, led by its Governor-General Warren Hastings, was in full control of both Bengal and Bihar. The years of an undisciplined rape of the country by the Company "servants" had ended, and the era of a more disciplined exploitation had begun.

In 1786 the East India Company government, for reasons that are not entirely clear, officially confirmed a grant earlier made to the Capuchin Mission of land-holder rights (*zamindari*) over about 90 acres near the center of Bettiah town, over an entire village called Dossaya located quite near to Bettiah, and over the village of Chuhari some 20 kilometers north of Bettiah. Chuhari was where the Nepali converts of the Tibet Mission had settled after their exodus from Nepal in 1769.

The traditional duties and high-handed behavior of land-holders or *zamindars* were assumed with gusto by the Capuchin friar Giuseppe da San Marcello. Marco and three other friars finally put a stop to Giuseppe's excesses by submitting him to a private trial in 1793 and then packing him off in irons to Calcutta. Along the way, however, Giuseppe was apparently freed by an English friend and the whole episode ended in a rather unclear fashion.

By this time, the military campaigns of the British had

moved further afield and their main military enemies were Hyder Ali and Tipu Sultan in the south and the Marathas to the southwest. Tipu was defeated in 1799. The Marathas were defeated in 1800 and again, more decisively, in 1819, long after Marco's death in 1803. Administratively, the main changes in this period were an increasing control over the East India Company by the British crown and the introduction in 1793 of a permanently fixed, annual tax on agricultural land, a measure that led to considerable amounts of land changing hands as traditional *zamindars* found themselves unable to pay the revenue demand and had their lands confiscated and resold to other landlords, many of whom were urban bourgeoisie who often proved to be more ruthless exploiters of the peasantry.

The Financing of the Tibet Mission

The Tibet Mission was almost always in financial trouble. Propaganda Fide at first attempted to fund the annual subsidy of the Tibet Mission with money derived from a donation to the Church made by the heirs of Giovanni Domenico Spinola, a wealthy cardinal who had been Bishop of Mazara in Sicily from 1636 to 1646.[6] Most of this bequest, however, was tied up in the form of a debt that the king of Spain, Philip V (ruled 1700–46), owed to Spinola's estate. To recover the money, Propaganda Fide was obliged to request it from the king of Spain. The king of Spain, however, was short of cash and passed his debt on to the government of his Spanish colony of New Spain, what is now Mexico and California. The king also conceded to Propaganda Fide the right to collect alms for the Tibet Mission in Mexico. As part of the effort to collect both the debt and the alms, Propaganda Fide sent to Mexico a Spanish Capuchin lay brother (later ordained as a priest) named Fermín d'Olite, who operated as Propaganda's agent and conducted negotiations with the government of New Spain to recover the debt owed to Propaganda.

Propaganda also sent to New Spain several Capuchin friars to collect alms for the Tibet Mission. Among these friars were a Spaniard named Francisco d'Ajofrín (1719–89) and an Italian named Ilarione da Bergamo (died 1778). The ethnographic accounts of early eighteenth-century Mexico written by these two friars are now basic documents for Mexican history of this period. Their presence in Mexico probably also explains the publication in Mexico City in 1745 of a pamphlet about the history of the Tibet Mission written in Spanish. I serendipitously found a copy of this pamphlet in the library of St. Bonaventure University in New York State. Evidently it had been adapted from an Italian original into Spanish, possibly by Francisco d'Ajofrín himself, and then published in Mexico to facilitate the work of acquiring alms for the Mission among the wealthier residents of Mexico.

The difficulties of financing the Tibet Mission were compounded by the failure of the Mission to achieve the sought-after large-scale conversions among the populations of Tibet, Nepal, and Hindustan. As already noted, the Capuchins were forced to leave Tibet in 1745, just when they were starting to make a few converts. The Capuchins in the Kathmandu valley of Nepal were slightly more successful but had to abandon Nepal with 14 families of their converts in 1769. One or two missionaries returned to Nepal in later years, but had little further success in establishing a Christian community there. The only lasting success of the Mission was the establishment of a community of Christian converts in the city of Bettiah itself. This Christian community later grew and spread in the Bettiah region and beyond and today numbers about 15,000 persons.

Propaganda's frustrations with the small number of conversions—especially compared to the Church's massive success in Mexico and South America—evidently provoked a good deal of skepticism among the Propaganda officials in Rome about the justification for continuing to finance the Mission. This skepticism was vividly expressed in a personal letter of 1779 from the secretary of Propaganda Fide, Stefano Borgia, to Cardinal Antonelli, the new prefect of Propaganda Fide, about the efforts of Marco to return to the Mission from Italy. With a considerable dose of sarcasm, Stefano Borgia wrote:

> *Padre della Tomba, Capuchin—who no longer has anything to do with the Tibet Mission, to which for just reasons I believe he should not be sent, although he has wished it—continues to be generous with his letters to the Eminent Prefect [of Propaganda Fide] and to Secretary Borgia, who is writing this letter. A reply was given to him not long ago that he would be provided with all [he wanted], but this was not enough to make him keep quiet. He has too much interest for a mission that for too long has not made any progress. Some other Capuchins describe it as second rate* (mediocremente bene) *and others say that it is quite bad* (assai male). *In sum, what the Sacred Congregation does for Tibet serves to maintain as nominal Catholics twenty or thirty European scoundrels who have taken refuge in Bengal and four or six Indians who manage the kitchens of the missionaries.*

Marco's Autobiography

I first came across Marco della Tomba's name over 10 years ago in the context of my research into the history of the Kabir Panth, a heterodox Hindu sect founded in the name of Kabir, a fifteenth- and sixteenth-century poet-saint from the city of Benares. Marco, I learned, was the earliest European to comment on the practices and beliefs of this sect and had translated some Kabir Panthi texts into Italian, including, it was said, a Kabir Panthi version of a part of the famous Hindu epic, the *Ramayana*. These translations and abridged versions of several of Marco's Italian essays were published by Angelo de Gubernatis in 1878. After finding a copy of this book, I began to read Marco's autobiographical essay, "*Introduzione al viaggio per l'India*" with the help of a graduate student who knew Italian. This text convinced me to read more about Marco and the Tibet Mission.

In the following years, I set about learning Italian and acquiring all the available published studies of the Tibet Mission as well as photocopies and microfilms of the manuscripts of books, essays, reports and letters written by Marco, Giuseppe Maria da Gargnano, Cassiano da Macerata, and other friars and church officials associated with the Mission. Most of these manuscripts, I learned, were in the Vatican Library, in the archives of Propaganda Fide in Rome, and in the Biblioteca Comunale Mozzi-Borgetti in Macerata. Cassiano's early published biography of Giuseppe Maria, as well as some other difficult-to-find early published sources turned up in the library of the Franciscan Institute of St. Bonaventure University. Other hard-to-find published and unpublished sources were located in the Biblioteque National de France and the Capuchin Archives in Rome (San Lorenzo). The friars of a Capuchin School in Agra gave me some essential but difficult-to-find books written by the Capuchin friar Fulgentius Vannini. The Library of Vidya Jyoti College in Delhi provided access to some important unpublished papers on the Tibet Mission by Henry Hosten. Father Jose Kalapura of the Bihar Social Institute in Patna let me read his Ph.D. thesis on the Bettiah mission and provided me with a copy of Gottardo da Como's collection of the letters of Giuseppe da Rovato (1954), F. Vannini's *Hindustan-Tibet Mission* (1981), a large history of the Mission in an English language manuscript by the Capuchin friar Hilarion ab Abtei (1908), and other rare sources. The library of my own institution, El Colegio de México, luckily had all seven big volumes of Luciano Petech's collection of documents by Desideri and by the early friars of the Tibet Mission (1952–1956).

As noted above, the present book uses these varied source materials—most notably the essays and letters of Marco della Tomba himself—to construct a biography and autobiography of Marco's life from his recruitment into the Tibet Mission in Italy in 1755 until his death in Bhagalpur in 1803. At the heart of the text is his autobiographical essay, "*Introduzione al viaggio per l'India*", large parts of which are translated in this book (chapters 2–3, 5–6, and 8–12). Several other chapters are translated, in whole or in part, from other essays by Marco, from his big book on Hinduism, and from letters and documents written by him and by other friars of the Mission (4, 7, 15–16, 19). Still other chapters have been written mostly by me (1, 13–14, 17–18, 20–21). The main aim of this somewhat unusual procedure has simply been to give the book more continuity and to make it a more enjoyable read.[7] As noted above, the book is a biography and an autobiography, not fiction. The more scholarly reader who wants to know exactly who wrote what can consult the end notes where precise indications are given.

Throughout the book, the spellings of the names of persons and places have been modernized. Marco's spellings of Indian names are sometimes difficult to recognize, but the context usually makes them clear enough. In the translated sections, I have here and there added a word or two to clarify the sense. Otherwise the translations are as exact as I could make them.

Marco normally writes *gentile,* literally "pagan", instead of "Hindu", but I have used "Hindu" in the translations since Marco clearly distinguishes the *gentili* from the Muslims (also considered to be pagans). I have added footnotes to explain unusual words, locate little-known places, and give the background to important events. Brief biographical sketches of most of the persons mentioned in the book—including the friars and other clergy, Indian rulers and officials, and European officials—are provided in the "List of Key Persons" at the end.

Marco della Tomba knew how to tell a good story. He also had a fascinating life. He was an eye witness to the collapse of independent Indian rule in Bengal and Bihar, to the rise of the British colonial empire, and to the chaos and pillage that this transition brought with it. Through the long and perilous journeys from Europe to India and back, the endemic wars of the 1750s and 1760s, the 1769–70 famine, through his periodic bouts of fever and dysentery and the dangers of whirlpools, bandits and tigers, Marco somehow survived and prospered. He was always a bit of a gadfly and rather vain about his abilities and courage. He undoubtedly felt, and with reason, that his efforts on behalf of the Mission were never given the recognition they deserved. It seems likely that Marco's rough vitality and his persistence were what provoked the wrath of the proxy visitor Foulon and of Cardinal Borgia. Notwithstanding Marco's sad end as the "scourge of the Mission", he persevered in his chosen vocation for almost 50 years and has left us a vivid account of what he saw and heard.

Chapter 1

From Tomba to Pondicherry

Why did I choose to live and die in Hindustan? Are there not enough poor souls in Italy who need us Capuchin friars to lead them into the arms of Christ and His Church? When Cardinal Hugolino asked St. Francis why he had sent his friars off to distant provinces, our Seraphic Father replied: "*My Lord, do you think or believe that the Lord has sent the friars solely for these provinces? I say to you in truth that the Lord chose and sent the friars for the profit and salvation of the souls of all men in the whole world, and they are to be received not only in the lands of the faithful but also of the infidel.*"[1] I have always done my best to follow this path, but I must also confess that the daily routine in our Italian monasteries could never satisfy me. The temptations of adventure and my curiosity about strange lands were too strong. Wanderlust has been my weakness, but I, Marco della Tomba, have always dedicated heart and soul to the service of our Holy Church and our poor Tibet Mission. Over these many years, Hindustan has become my home and soon it will become my tomb.

Our Mission was established by the Sacred Congregation of Propaganda Fide in 1703. Originally the Mission had hospices in Tibet, Nepal and Hindustan. Now only those in Hindustan remain. Our Mission was expelled from Tibet in 1745, and the hospice in Nepal was abandoned in 1769 (although we did later move back to Kathmandu). Our chief hospices are now in the towns of Patna, Bettiah, Chuhari and Bhagalpur. From time to time we have set up residences for our friars in other towns, but we have always been too few in number to maintain these new stations for long. Nowadays, I am left here alone in Bhagalpur.

Providence blessed me with a strong constitution, but old age and the climate of Hindustan have taken their toll. Fever and dysentery come and go, while caring for my small flock of Christians in Bhagalpur often demands more effort than I can manage. Every day I pray that the prefect of our Mission will send me a companion to help in the task of saving souls. Until then the local Christians and I are cast adrift in a sea of idolatry.

I will surely pass the rest of my days in Hindustan. My ties to Europe and Italy are nearly all broken, and my few remaining friends and relatives never write. I am confident, however, that I have honorably served God, our Holy Church and the Christians of this, my adopted land. Even on the day in 1757 when I first arrived at our hospice in Chandernagore, I knew that Providence had chosen this destiny for me. In 1773 I returned to Italy to plead the cause of our Mission to my superiors in Rome. Ten years later I was back in Hindustan. I am writing this in the year 1797 and have now been in India for a total of 30 years. I am 71 years old and my mortal life is drawing to its close. May God have mercy on my soul.

Before my trip back to Italy in 1773, I wrote many essays about my experiences in Hindustan and my studies in Hindu religion for the instruction of future missionaries, to teach them about the country and people of Hindustan and to help them avoid the errors that Europeans so often make. For many years our poor Tibet Mission has been left abandoned by the Sacred Congregation, and little chance remains that Rome will send the new missionaries that we so desperately need. Who now will read my essays and for what purpose? Why write anything more? No reason I suppose. But what harm is done if an old man holds fast to a small amount of hope and vanity? I am telling the story of my life in Hindustan for myself and for whoever might want someday to read about it. I have forgotten much that happened so many years ago, but I still have copies of my essays and of the letters I sent to my superiors in Rome. I will use them to cobble together the things that I have seen and done and to revive my memories as best I can. If someday somewhere some reader will find amusement or edification in my story, I wish him well.

At this point it makes little sense to go back to the beginning. It is too long ago and far away. For the record, I was born in 1726 in the village of Tomba near the town of Senigallia on the Adriatic coast. My father was Crisostomo Agresti and my mother was Vittoria Luzietti. May they both be with God in Heaven. My name before entering the Capuchin order was Pietro Girolamo Agresti. I was received into the order by the Very Reverend Padre Giacomo da San Giovanni, in Marignano, the Provincial of Le Marche, in Marignano and was invested with the Capuchin habit in the house of the novitiate at Camerino by Padre Felice da Cagli on April 25, 1745. Padre Felice, the guardian and teacher of all us novices, accepted my profession of the vows for a perpetual simple life exactly one year later in the house at Camerino.[2] Over nine years after this, on October 9, 1755, I passed the exam given by Propaganda Fide for acceptance into the Tibet Mission with the highest commendation (*optime*) and changed my life forever.[3]

These towns are located in the region called Le Marche, once a border area of the Roman Empire. Today the Marches form part of the Papal States. In late Roman times, my village of Tomba was called "Castrum Tombae." In the time of Charlemagne, the Castle of Tomba became the seat of an important earldom (*contea*). In the sixteenth century it was an important residence of the Colonna family including the famous patron of the Capuchin order, Vittoria Colonna, Marchioness of Pescara. Vittoria Colonna saved our Order from the attacks of Paolo Pisotti and other enemies, but she also defended the celebrated preacher and renegade friar Bernadino da Ochino, who disgraced the Order and fled to join the heretic reform in Geneva.* During my return stay in Italy from 1774 till the end of 1782, I spent most of my time back in Senigallia and in the towns of Rimini and San Marino, a day's journey to the north.

As I said, all this was long ago and far away. Here my story will begin with my first voyage to Hindustan in 1757 as missionary in the Mission to Great Tibet:[4] I will not dare [...] to note anything that I did not see or hear or at least

* In the early sixteenth century Paolo Pisotti was the head of the Observant branch of the Franciscans. Although the then newly founded group of Capuchins were also considered to be Franciscans, Pisotti was opposed to them, mostly because many Observant friars were joining the Capuchins. Although Pisotti managed to convince Pope Clement VII to issue bulls in 1529 and 1530 canceling their privileges, the Capuchins paid little attention to these bulls. Meanwhile, the famous aristocratic patron and humanist, Vittoria Colonna, and others defended the Capuchins to the pope. By about 1535 the Capuchins were back in papal favor. Bernardino da Ochino was elected Vicar General of the Capuchins in 1538. He fled to Calvinist Switzerland in 1542 when he feared that he would be arrested for heresy by the Church authorities in Rome. See Cuthbert 1929 and Iriarte 1982.

judge to be true. I left for this Mission not moved by any mundane reflection, but only with the desire to do good [....] With this spirit, then, I began my journey by order of the Sacred Congregation, under the auspices of the blessed eternal Virgin Mary and of our Seraphic Father, Saint Francis. I endeavored to hold as my model and example our Saint Fidelis of Sigmaringen, the first martyr of Propaganda and my particular defender.* [...]

Armed with the appointment by the Sacred Congregation of Propaganda and with the permission of our Superiors, I departed from my Province of the Marches of Ancona on October 29, 1755. I went first to Livorno and there joined Padre Odoardo da Cingoli who had come to Rome from the Hindustan Mission and was returning to Hindustan. Together we left Livorno for Marseilles on a French ship. From there we went by the Languedoc Canal to Bordeaux** and from there to Hennebont and Lorient where the ships that sail to the Indies are found. I will not write down the details of this journey, because it is well known and almost all the missionaries will have had to endure the same inconveniences of this journey through France. The journey is difficult both because of the cold and because of the poor hospitality that one receives in

* St. Fidelis of Sigmaringen was a German Capuchin who was appointed by Propaganda as the superior of the mission to the Grisons canton in Switzerland early in 1622. He was battered to death by a crowd of Calvinists at Grusch on April 24 of the same year.

** In 1755, the Languedoc Canal, also known as the "Canal du Midi", was still one of the engineering marvels of Europe. It was built between 1666 and 1681 and used 103 locks to raise boats to a maximum of 190 meters above sea level and then lower them back down again. It saved people and goods traveling from the Mediterranean to the western coast of France from having to brave the dangers of brigands on the land route or dangerous seas on the long trip around the Iberian Peninsula and through the strait of Gibraltar.

some of our monasteries and the laity's lack of piety. For this reason the missionaries are often obliged to resort to using money for both transport and food during the trip. Padre Odoardo and I were forced many times to sleep outside on a little straw, or to be more precise, to cover ourselves with straw to protect ourselves from the December cold. [...]

We finally arrived at Lorient, the chief port of the French Company of the East Indies, on February 30, 1756. We arranged our voyage with the captain of a ship. We fixed our passage at the rate of one rupee for each day that we remained on board. We also acquired the necessary provisions: a heavy blanket, cushions, a thin blanket, some shirts and pants, napkins, handkerchiefs, sugar, tea, and some liquor. One should note that after Lorient the first port of call is the Island of Mauritius to the east of Madagascar, usually a four-month journey. On board ship, morning and evening meals as well as medicines are provided by the captain. All this is truly abundant unless some ruinous accident occurs which might cause a lack of food. For the rest, however, each passenger has to provide for himself. One should change one's clothes every three or four days, not only to be able to live together with those others who hate all filth but also to avoid the irritations that accumulate everywhere and that the ship's officers, with whom one absolutely needs to get along, do not on any account want to endure. For this reason it is necessary to change one's clothes often. At sea one's clothes cannot be easily washed since those wet with salt water never get dry. Before embarking one must pack three or four sets of linen garments in order to change clothes in hot places, and at least a dozen shirts and trousers, a dozen table napkins, cushions enough to be able to change them often, handkerchiefs as needed [...], an amount of sugar sufficient for one's tea in the morning and when one is indisposed, and also some liquor, since the captain does not supply any of these things. It is often said on board ship: Each man for himself and God for all. [...]

Once we had acquired all we needed we boarded the ship in order to depart, but a contrary wind kept us in port for 17 days. During this time some English ships were also seen. These would lie in wait for our ships in order to attack and capture them.* On this news our ships received orders to stay in port and not to depart that year. We returned to shore and disembarked in order to wait for the coming year.

In Lorient we encountered five Chinese youths who had arrived recently from China in order to attend the College of Naples.** They were guided by a Franciscan padre who died in those same days in Lorient. We also met three Chinese priests who were returning to China from the College of Naples and were also guided by a Franciscan padre. This padre died in those same days at Lorient. This left five Chinese

* The Seven Years War between France, Austria and Russia, on one side, and Britain and Prussia, on the other, lasted from 1756 to 1763. The fight between France and Britain for colonies in North America, the West Indies, and India was the most important phase of this war. By its end, the possibilities of a French Empire in India were dead, although the English allowed the French to continue to hold a few commercial ports.

** The College of Naples was founded by the secular priest and missionary to China, Matteo Ripa, in about 1724 as a school to train Chinese men, brought directly from China, to become priests. The school was officially recognized by Pope Clement XII in 1732 as the *Collegio dei Cinesi* (see Fatica 1997). The five Chinese youths who Marco took to Naples can be identified. They were Joan Ev. Tai (1735–?), Jacobus Jen (1736–62), Cassius Jos. Tai (1737–85), Simon Car. Lieu (1742–1820), and Lucius Thoms Hoan (1741–72). The three Chinese priests mentioned below can also be identified. They were Jos. Lucius Li (1717–76), Pius Conf. Lieu (1718–86) and Pius Mart. Lieu (1718–85). I thank Gianni Criveller of Holy Spirit College in Hong Kong for this information (see Criveller 2005).

youths without any guide to Naples and three Chinese priests without any guide to China. Since at that time I was no longer about to depart that year for India, Monsignor Gualtieri, the apostolic nuncio in Paris gave me orders to pick up the five Chinese youths and guide them to Paris. I did so and from there he ordered me to guide them to Naples. For me this journey was a great consolation and pleasure since it gave me a chance to learn something of the world. Before this I had been sent on my journey direct from my studies and had very little experience. In Naples we had a great welcome from all the gentlemen of the College and even from the king himself, Dom Carlos. The king wished to meet the youths and sent his own carriages to pick us up.

From Naples I returned to Rome where I received orders to pick up the other three Chinese priests who were delayed at Lorient and to guide them to India in order to turn them over to Monsignor Maton in Pondicherry.[5] Since he was procurator of the missions to Siam and China, he would find a way to send them home, and so it was done. I was especially happy to have spent less money traveling from Lorient to Naples with five youths than the Franciscan father had spent traveling from Naples to Lorient with only three priests. I finally arrived back in Lorient and arranged passage on a ship of the [French East India] Company named the Duque de Borgogne commanded by a Monsieur Duprès. The Chinese and I made use of the supplies acquired the year before and also the money saved for the captain, at the same rate of one rupee per day counting only the days that we were on board. Everything was agreed with order and success and we departed for the Indies on December 16, 1756.

One thing I forgot to mention is that as I was departing from Lorient for Paris with the five youths, Padre Odoardo, my companion, remained at Lorient in the house of a certain

Mademoiselles Danó. One day while walking along the coast in order to go to say a mass in a country chapel, he was caught in the rain, got wet, and then contracted a fever. A few days later he died in that place, so that when I arrived in Paris I received the news of his death.

We departed from Lorient for the Indies with six escort vessels, but a few days later near Cape Land's End we got caught in a squall that separated the vessels and we kept only two of them for the journey to the Island of Mauritius. We were pursued by three English ships but our ship made headway at up to 15 miles per hour and this superior speed defended us. When one crosses the line of the equator, it is the custom to hold a ceremony called "*Battesimo*", which finishes with a payment made to the crew. The sailors dress themselves as devils, climb down the masts,[6] and throw great buckets of water on whoever they find. They tie up with a cord anyone who has not crossed the line before and do all sorts of other ridiculous things. At the end they demand some money as a tribute to the line.

The Cape of Good Hope is a difficult passage, always stormy, especially from May to September, with seas so big that the ships' crews sing the *Te Deum* after they sail past it. Thanks to God, however, we sailed past easily and arrived at the Island of Mauritius on the fifth of May. We stayed in the house of missionaries who are called Lazarists, or followers of St. Vincent de Paul, who are the missionaries and curates on those islands of Mauritius and Bourbon.* They received us

* The Lazarists were founded by the French saint, Vincent de Paul (1581–1660). They were prominent as missionaries in North Africa and Madagascar. In his text, Marco has written the saint's name as Francesco Paoli, but this is clearly a mistake. The Isle de Bourbon is now called "Réunion" and is still a French territory. Mauritius has been independent since 1968.

with much courtesy. We stayed with them for 53 days without paying anything other than a few masses that we dedicated to their project.

Mauritius is an island belonging to the French. It is small but well fortified. The inhabitants are Frenchmen settled there for many years. They are served in the fields [...] and in every other task by blacks, their slaves. They go to buy them in Madagascar, a nearby pagan island, or in Mozambique, or also in Bengal. This island is conveniently located for the passage and shelter of the ships, but otherwise is quite sterile. They bring their food supplies from Madagascar or from the Isle of Bourbon, about 30 leagues away. Bourbon is bigger and more fertile, particularly for coffee, but has no port to receive the ships. It has a rocky roadstead, difficult for landings. The ships cannot stay there for long and have to weigh anchor at the first sign of any wind and sail away.

In Mauritius all the French ships armed themselves for war in the Indies. We departed for there on August 1, 1757. The convoy included seven warships and four of transport. We all arrived at Pondicherry on the September 8. From Mauritius to the Indies the sea is very beautiful, the seasons are orderly, and there is little else to fear except unexpected violent storms when the ship must quickly lower its sail or risk capsizing. This recently happened to a Dutch ship which had on board the children of Monsieur Renault, the commander of Chandernagore.* Our journey, however, was excellent and without any problems.

In Pondicherry the French Capuchins are missionaries and

* Chandernagore, the French city and trading port on the Hooghli River in Bengal, was founded in 1676. The town and its fort were attacked and overrun by the British in 1757, but afterwards allowed to continue as a French settlement. As is noted in Chapter 2, Marco arrived in Chandernagore soon after the British attack.

parish priests of the French, called "the Whites", in contrast to the Jesuits, who are missionaries and parish priests of the blacks, called "the Malabars". As soon as we had disembarked we went to our hospice and a few hours later took the three Chinese priests and turned them over to Monsignor Maton, to whom they were directed by the Sacred Congregation. I then stayed in our hospice until I left for Bengal on September 26 on a Portuguese ship since the French were not then traveling to Bengal because of the war with the English.

Chapter 2

Chandernagore

I arrived in Chandernagore on October 20, 1757. There I found our padres, who had remained after the wars of the previous month of March between the English and the French. The French were all taken prisoners.[1] The English transported most of the French men outside the city, but left the women there. Women of all conditions were dying of hunger and were hanging on the arms of our padres. The English were in arms against the Moors, or people of the country. Our hospice had been sacked, in part by the English troops, while our padres were away from the hospice for some time in order to serve in the French hospital. Meanwhile, the Jesuits had been banished from Chandernagore, with orders to hang the first of them who reappeared there. Their church was knocked down to the foundations. The poor inhabitants were overwhelmed by the pillage suffered in the war. Large numbers of English workers were employed to demolish the fort and the factories belonging to the French East India Company.* All the English

* In eighteenth-century India, several countries—most notably England, France, Holland and Denmark—operated joint-stock corporations known as "companies." These companies had royal charters that granted them monopoly privileges for trade with the Orient. The "factories" of these companies were essentially fortified warehouses used by traders to store

endeavored to transport the movable goods of the French from Chandernagore to Calcutta, their principal city some six leagues distant from Chandernagore.

It was on this occasion that I, following the advice of Padre Daniele da Morciano, requested from the English admiral the big bell, weighing 1900 pounds, that was in the French fort and that the English were going to carry off to Calcutta with the other things.* I obtained it and now it is in our hospice in Chandernagore. The Jesuits have pestered us often for this bell, but they have not been able to succeed in their aim to recover it in order to put it in the new church which they constructed after they had obtained permission to return to their former site.

When my colleague (and later the prefect of our Mission), Giuseppe da Rovato, arrived in Chandernagore in December of 1762, over five years later, conditions were not much better than when I first saw it. In a letter to his friend in Italy, Padre Alessandro da Bergamo, Giuseppe wrote:[2]

> *Chandernagore was a quite beautiful city. In terms of European taste it was in every way the equal of Calcutta. But now it is all in ruins, a pitiful sight. Our hospice and the church were saved from the pillage by the goodness of the English admiral. In this year there has been a sort of pestilence in all Bengal. In Chandernagore alone more than thirty French persons of both sexes have died among the roughly two hundred that are still prisoners there.*

---

goods before shipment out of the country. They were not places to manufacture goods.

* The English East India Company official who commanded the capture of Chandernagore was the famous Robert Clive (1725–74). The capture took place on March 23, 1757. He was aided in this task by Admiral Charles Watson. Since Watson died in August, 1757, he cannot have been the admiral who gave Marco the bell.

Here I should note that after the capture of Chandernagore by the English, the Jesuits who were exiled because they were French went to stay in Shrirampur, a Danish colony.[3] There they erected a house and church made of straw and resumed all their parochial functions since many of the Frenchmen from Chandernagore were staying there. The chief vicar, namely the local Portuguese vicar who held title to the mission in Shrirampur, then appointed as the parish priest a Capuchin named Padre Onofrio in order to take away all title [from the Jesuits]. After he received this title, Padre Onofrio constructed a house and church in the Danish colony and established a baptismal font there. Padre Daniele da Morciano, also a Capuchin, had been made parish priest of Chandernagore by the same vicar of the bishop of the diocese. Padre Daniele held this post for a period of five years. The Jesuits opposed all this and continued to perform parochial functions in Shrirampur. In addition, they went every Sunday and Feast Day to say a second mass in Chandernagore in the house of a private person (since their church had been demolished). In this house they performed all the parochial functions and as far as possible hindered the residents from coming to our church.

These problems about parochial functions lasted four or five years. Unfortunately, our problems with the Jesuits were not completely resolved until the pope finally dissolved their Company in 1773. Even then we Capuchins were obliged to take in many of the disbanded Jesuits. Otherwise they would have starved to death. In a later chapter I will say more about our disputes with the Jesuits and my own role in helping to save our public church in Chandernagore from their attempts to close it. For now, however, I will return to the story of my arrival in Chandernagore.

Once I had arrived in Chandernagore, I announced myself to the Very Reverend Padre Prefect, at the time Tranquillo d'Apecchio, and requested him to give me my orders.[4] He instructed me to accept the command to go to the Bettiah Mission where Padre Giuseppe Maria da Gargnano would be my companion. I departed for Bettiah on January 29, 1758.* [...] But first let me describe Bengal.

Bengal is a flat country, sparsely inhabited. Apart from the parts that lie along the Ganges River, the rest is deserted, full of tigers, bears, etc. The Bengal Mission belongs to the Portuguese Augustinians, who were established there during the first conquests of the Portuguese and protected by the king of Portugal himself. The king never gave his consent for other missionaries to carry on their activities in that region. [...] We established a hospice in Chandernagore in 1704. Our church was made a public one from 1720, or perhaps, as Padre Tranquillo asserts, from 1713. Our rights, however, do not extend beyond the four walls [of the church]. We hear confessions and preach in our church, but only with the permission of the diocesan bishop, to whom every new padre is obliged to present himself to ask permission. [...]

The Portuguese Augustinian padres have 10 or 12 churches in various parts of Bengal. They are dependent on the Provincial of Goa for their ordinary management and in canonical matters are dependent on the bishop of Saint Thomas or Meliapur,**

* The city of Bettiah is today located in the northwest of the Indian state of Bihar near the Nepal border and south-southwest of Kathmandu. Marco spent much of his time in India in the mission station in Bettiah. The Christian community that Giuseppe Maria da Gargnano and Marco established in Bettiah has since survived and grown. Several thousand of these Bettiah Christians now live in Bettiah and others have migrated to major cities like Patna and Delhi.

** Saint Thomas (San Thomé) or Meliapur was a Portuguese settlement on the southeastern coast of India just south of the land that after 1640 became the city of Madras, now called Chennai.

to whom the entire vast province of Bengal belongs. The bishop's diocese is in Meliapur, and [the surrounding region of] Malabar is immense.* In addition, from his residence in Saint Thomas to Bengal there is usually a 20 days' sea journey, one that is impossible to make during six months of the year. For these reasons, this bishop has appointed a Vicar in Bengal, who is ordinarily the Steward or Commissary of that mission of the same Order of Augustinians.

In Bengal there are very many Christians. In the city of Calcutta alone there are about 25,000, of whom about 15,000 take the sacraments. Others are in a state of public or private concubinage [and cannot take the sacraments]. The city of Calcutta contains a mixture of all sorts of people, Catholics, heretics, schismatics, etc.** Many keep Hindu or Muslim women. These women, once they have eaten with people from outside their nation, immediately lose their caste and can no longer return to their families. They have children and want to be served by others. They cannot be accepted as anything other than Christians and are usually baptized when they are about to die or at some other particular time. There exist more than 10,000 of these women. In every house of a heretic or bad Catholic there is a seraglio. Among the troops, every [foreign] soldier has his woman, and all are Christians. I believe that this is because of the readiness of the Portuguese padres to baptize such people. I said "Portuguese padres," but one should note that they are usually padres native to Goa,

* Malabar is more correctly the region along the southwestern coast corresponding to the modern state of Kerala. Apparently Marco takes Malabar to mean the whole southern part of the subcontinent.

** By "heretics", Marco undoubtedly means Protestant Christians. By "schismatics" he may just mean the same, but he also may be referring more specifically to the Anglicans (who technically maintain the Catholic apostolic succession) or to Armenian and Syrian Catholics.

either whites or brown-skinned. The education and studies in Goa do not amount to much. Shortly after finishing their novitiate and some studies, they are sent off to the missions, where they usually live alone. For this reason they are more liable than others to make mistakes. But it is not my task to talk about this more than is necessary to give an idea of what Bengal is like.

Turning from the spiritual to the mundane situation of that place, I should note that the entry into Bengal is very dangerous. The mouth of the Ganges River, where the ships enter, is very wide, beyond the sight of land. Its depth is barely more than is necessary and is very uneven. There are many sandbanks that are invisible to navigators. The ships that run aground on them are usually lost because the flux and reflux of the current is so strong that the ship immediately capsizes. Even good swimmers then have great trouble in saving themselves because the currents always form whirlpools that swallow up everything that gets caught in them. Those who manage to reach the shore without being eaten by crocodiles are usually devoured by tigers that abound in the forests.

To get some idea of the force of the current of the Ganges, it is enough to know that the flow of the ocean tide, particularly during the three days before and after the new and full moons, travels 60 French leagues in just six hours, with so much speed that it seems to be a sheet of foam that pushes back all the water of the river. Woe to those boats, big or small, that then get caught near the shore or in those places where the water is not deep enough. [...]

Boats cannot enter the Ganges unless they are guided by professional river pilots who are paid by the various companies and always stay near the entrance in order to guide each ship that arrives. Before each ship enters, a pilot goes on board, arranges his payment, and then takes command of the ship. [...] Some of the pilot's assistants go ahead in the pilot's boat and constantly measure the water's depth and signal the fathoms to the pilot. Other assistants on the entering ship throw cords tied to lead weights and shout out the number of fathoms. This is how they enter and exit. Ships must enter the Ganges during the six hours that the tidal current goes upriver. Those that exit must do so during the six hours that the current goes out to sea. [...]

As I said, I arrived the first time at the mouth of the Ganges on a Portuguese ship. Once we had arrived we had to wait for five days for a pilot since the pilots could not stay there because of the wars. From time to time we fired cannons and during the night we shot off fireworks so that someone might hear us or see us. Finally a Dutch pilot appeared. He spoke to us, came on board ship, and [guided us upriver] for a payment of 800 rupees, which is the usual payment for ships from other nations. For ships of the same nation, the pilots are paid by their respective trading companies. In the end it was necessary to pray to God that during the four or five difficult days [in which we moved upriver] we would experience none of the storms that frequently occur since there would be nowhere to take refuge. Along the route the canal is so narrow in many places that the ship cannot turn about and risks being lost in any sudden strong wind.

Chapter 3

Patna and Bettiah

In Chandernagore, then, I received the command to go to Bettiah. I left for there on January 2, 1758.[1] From Chandernagore to Patna the journey is easy since it is by boat. But it is necessary to hurry to load the boat with a month and a half's provisions since nothing is available along the way except rice and sometimes fish. During the first 10 days one travels on the small Chandernagore River where the only risks are thieves and tigers.* But once one enters the great Ganges one risks the winds that cause many boats to perish. This is particularly true during the months of April and May, and September and October, when storms are frequent and unexpected. If they hit in places where the boat cannot come to shore, one risks disaster. The whirlpools are even more dangerous than the winds. From time to time the water opens up like a well and if the boat enters the well it is usually lost. If this happens, you must keep your wits and row as hard as you can in order to keep the boat caught in the whirling water from following the spinning water down to the bottom. Unfortunately, the local boatmen more often

* Chandernagore, like Calcutta and Shrirampur, is located on the Hugli River, but Marco never refers to this river by this name.

drop their oars and commend their fate to the Ganges, and thus they seldom escape.

Once I myself was caught in one of these whirlpools, called *virvire.* My boatmen abandoned their oars and my companion, Brother Liborio da Fermo, could do nothing except call out "Jesus and Mary".* I alone grabbed an oar and rowed as hard as I could for about a half hour. Finally the boat reached the calm water and I collapsed unconscious. The Dutch had sent a boat with ropes to help us, but by the time it arrived we were already in the calmer water. Because of these *virvire,* the journey on the Ganges is not feasible in the months of June, July, August, and also September. In 1752, our Padre Giambattista da Bergamo attempted the journey in July and perished in one of these whirlpools near Rajmahal.** [...] The route by land is nowadays no longer feasible because of the jungles, the assassins and the tigers. Those who know the country well can travel by various routes, but without practice and knowledge of the local language this is very difficult.

I reached Patna on the February 26, without any special mishap. [...][2] I stayed for several days in Patna with the Reverend Padre Giovanni da Brescia,# who received me and treated me with great fraternal charity. He took me to make the visits necessary in that city and also took me to see the curiosities of the country and the then pompous splendors of the rich and powerful residents. I saw the wedding cortege

* Padre Liborio da Fermo (1708–69) arrived in Chandernagore in 1738. He was in Nepal from 1740 to 1769 and died in Bettiah.

** Rajmahal (Marco's Ragmol) is located on the south bank of the Ganges about half way between Bhagalpur and Murshidabad.

\# Giovanni da Brescia arrived in Chandernagore in 1753. He died at Patna in 1770.

of the daughter of the nawab of the city.* The nawab spent an amount equal to 50,000 Roman *scudi* on this wedding.** I saw the pompous processions of the feast day when the Muslims celebrate the memory of two Muslim brothers who were killed by the Hindus in a religious war. At this time the Muslims make public processions of penance for eight days. On the last day they make grand processions in which they carry certain trophies,[3] usually made of flowers and papers, outside of the city.#

I departed from Patna for Bettiah on March 5. By land this is a journey of five days. It is easy and secure except for a stretch of two leagues near Bettiah where one has to travel through a forest filled with tigers. In the period before my journey from time to time one met a certain type of guards, called *caukis*,## who were very impertinent. They harassed our padres as much as they could. Besides the money they took, they also treated them very badly. But the above-mentioned Padre Giovanni da Brescia had earlier made an appeal [against them to the king of Bettiah] at a good time and in good circumstances. As a result the *caukis* were well punished so that afterwards they never bothered our padres.

* The nawab of Patna was a subordinate of the nawab of Bengal. At this time (1758), the nawab of Bengal was Mir Jafar.

** The *scudo* (plural *scudi*) is an Italian "crown", a common monetary unit of the period.

\# Here Marco is apparently describing the Shi'ite celebration of Muharram. This commemorates the martyrdom of Imam Hussain, the Prophet Muhammad's grandson, at the Battle of Karbala in Iraq in A.D. 680. Hussain's victorious opponent was the Umayyad Caliph, al-Yazid. Despite Marco's comment, the Hindus of India obviously had nothing to do with Hussain's defeat.

\#\# The Hindi word *cauki* (Marco's *cioki*), in fact designates the highway-toll and customs stations themselves and not the guards employed in them, who were called *caukidars*. See also the note on p. 58, below.

After arriving in Bettiah, I met the Reverend Padre Giuseppe Maria da Gargnano, the very worthy superior of that place.* He was a true apostolic missionary, the founder of that hospice, and ever diligent in his ministry. Twice a day he taught the doctrine to Christians and catechumens. He talked about religion with everyone he could and welcomed without distinction everyone who came to the house, whether they came for medicine or to argue with him. He endured persecutions admirably. Just the other day he buried two Christian children near to the wall of the church. A rumor arose among the people that the padres had cooked these two dead children in order to prepare medicines, and the rumor spread so much that it was necessary to appeal to the king to stop it and vindicate us. The king holds this padre in such esteem that the king always keeps him close and never does anything important without consulting him.

On Holy Saturday, which fell a few days after I arrived in Bettiah, Padre Giuseppe Maria gave me orders to baptize 10 catechumens. I gave the first of them my own name, Marco. The example of Padre Giuseppe Maria encouraged me. I worked hard to learn the language. I immediately copied out both a grammar and a dictionary, and with the aid of Padre Giuseppe Maria and of a scribe, or teacher, I began to preach in the church within a period of six months. In my spare time I built an armillary sphere and a terrestrial globe in the language of the country. This earned me the constant company of learned Brahmins. From them I learned many things about their books and about their religion. I carefully

* In a letter dated December 26, 1758, Giuseppe Maria says this about Marco: "I have been alone for three years. Now, however, I have Padre Marco dalla [*sic*] Tomba as a companion. He arrived here in Bettiah this year. He is an excellent friar (*Religioso*) who has an ability for languages, so I hope he will be a success."

noted down all this in a separate book. In this way, Padre Giuseppe Maria had the possibility of going out of the city to talk about religion while I remained at home and taught the catechism to Christians and catechumens twice a day. With them I also learned my catechism in their language. I attended the school of the young boys, and with them I learned to read and write [in their language]. This situation lasted for a period of two years.

During this period, Padre Giuseppe Maria was appointed Vice Prefect by Reverend Padre Tranquillo d'Apecchio, who had received written permission to return to Rome. Since his successor, Padre Antonino da Monte Alboddo, was not yet there, Padre Tranquillo turned over the seals to Padre Giuseppe Maria so that he could govern the Mission in the interim. This was accepted by the common consensus of the missionaries. Padre Tranquillo then departed for Europe, but when he arrived in Pondicherry he found a letter from the Most Reverend Padre [Amato da Lamballe], procurator [of the Capuchin Order]. The Procurator, thinking that Padre Tranquillo was still in the Mission, begged him to continue to govern the Mission until the election of the new padre prefect. On the basis of this letter, Padre Tranquillo returned to the Mission. Once there, however, he found that the padres were opposed to his resuming the government of the Mission. For this reason he remained in Patna as an ordinary padre. When he was presented with the necessity of his presence in Nepal, he returned there, to his credit and merit, in order to resolve various conflicts that had arisen in the time of Padre Anselmo da Ragusa.

Chapter 4

Alexander and Didame

It is quite true, although many of our historians may deny it,[1] that Alexander the Great conquered this Hindustan in the year 3675.* Leaving aside the reasons that other historians adduce for this conquest, I should state that in this kingdom of Bettiah I myself have seen two columns erected in two different provinces: one to the east of the city of Bettiah and the other to the south.** The two columns appear to have been constructed by the same artisan. Without counting whatever part of the columns that may be underground, they are 27 cubits high from ground level to their capitals, above which there is a lion sculpture that looks quite natural. The circumference of the column is seven cubits. I myself

* It is not clear why Marco chooses this strange date. Perhaps it is the date from either the Creation (according to the Christian Bible) or from Noah's flood. Alexander the Great (356–323 B.C.) was in the Punjab of modern Pakistan from about 326 to 324 B.C.

** These two columns Marco saw must be columns set up by the Buddhist king, Asoka Maurya (ruled ca. 273–232 B.C.). The inscriptions on them would then be in the Brahmi script and the language would be Asokan Prakrit. Marco's description of these columns has been discussed in detail by Henry Hosten (1912). Hosten could identify only one of the columns as still existing.

have measured it. The column appears to be constructed from a single stone. I hit it several times with an axe and shot some bullets at it, but I could not notice any difference. The two columns are partly covered with some writing that I transcribed onto paper and then sent to the Hindu Academy in Benares and to some lamas in Tibet. Not one of them could read the letters or understand a single word of it. Not even one of the people of the country knows how to explain it. The characters may represent the ancient Greek language since some of them seem similar to the Greek alphabet. At the end of this inscription there is a line in Arabic characters and language that says: "This column has been erected by Id... (the name cannot be made out), minister (*vigir,* i.e., *wazir*) of Alexander the Great." I cannot affirm, however, that the Arabic characters have been carved by the same artisan. The main characters of the two columns are the same, only the words are different and one column is fuller than the other. The line in Arabic is found only on the eastern column. This column is erected in an isolated area where there are also some ruins of a fort.

The educated inhabitants claim that the column was put there by Alexander the Great, known in these parts under the name "Maha-Sikander". In a book by Kabir many things are written about him. Kabir in fact boasts that Alexander was his own spiritual disciple.* There are also found several places called Sikandar that the inhabitants say were constructed by Alexander's men. From this, one can infer that Alexander was in Hindustan. It also seems undeniable

* Kabir, who lived about A.D. 1500, is associated in legend with the Muslim king Sikandar Lodi (ruled 1489-1517), but not with Alexander the Great. The followers of Kabir do claim that Sikandar Lodi became Kabir's disciple. The name Sikandar is in fact derived from Alexander.

that Alexander was probably in Benares. [One can infer this] from the several dialogues that he had with the Brahmins of the University of Benares and from a letter that I transcribe here to prove this claim.

Alexander was curious to learn about the religion of this country and about their way of life. He spoke to the head Brahmin of the University of Benares, the only person who would instruct him about what he asked. The Brahmins usually prefer to excuse themselves in such situations and did not want to offer him any explanation. Finally, Alexander tried to convince them by promising to become their disciple. It is the custom in these regions that disciples are made by mutual choice and by taking from a teacher a *mantra,* namely a *Tibisoli.*[2] This consists of some written words that should be recited every day. They believe that this is enough for them to be saved. Didame, the head Brahmin of the University of Benares, accepted Alexander's promise and wrote to him the following letter:*

> *O Alexander, the desire you have shown to know wisdom makes me believe that you can become one of the wise. The only thing that makes me doubt that you can do this is the desire you have in your heart to subjugate that human race and govern the whole world. The true philosophy teaches us to submit to the law without any rebellion. But your heart*

* Several versions of this famous apocryphal letter from Didame—sometimes called Dindimus or Didamus, etc.—to Alexander were circulating in eighteenth-century Europe (*Upright Lives* 1981; Stoneman 1991). I have not been able to identify the source of Marco's version. De Gubernatis (1978, 41) suggests that the presence of several gallicisms in Marco's text shows that he probably took his version of the letter from a French source. All of the versions praise the moderation and simplicity of the life led by the Brahmins. Marco's interest in this letter reflects his *relatively* sympathetic view of Hindu religion.

and desire cannot accept this and therefore pose for you an invincible obstacle.

You asked to be instructed in our customs and habits. I do not dare to do it. I have no talent for words, and your concerns and activities prevent you from hearing what I say. Since you have made a request, however, I cannot refuse it. Nonetheless, I beg you not think that I can flatter you. We are always sincere and do not understand human politics.

The life of a Brahmin is as pure as it is simple. They have no trace of the concupiscence that deceives most men. Reason alone is the guide of our desires, which always submit to circumstances. Our mouth never expresses complaints nor worse things. We are indifferent about nourishment. We have no knowledge of voluptuousness apart from its name. We eat only plants and vegetables that the earth produced without care or culture. We know no diseases, except from the lamentations of others.

The fact that we are all equal makes us all independent. This drives out from among us any envy, jealousy, ambition or quarrels. We have no tribunals because we do nothing that requires punishment. The just lives we live have not produced the harsh laws with which the crimes of others are punished. In addition we fear that accepting such laws would open our minds to the evil that they defend against. Our only law is to not corrupt the law of nature.

Being far from blame we are not liable to pardon others so that the others may pardon us, and much less [are we liable] to purchase pardon or impunity. Since such mercy (grazia) *is usually conceded from avarice, it renders the judge guiltier than the criminal. Among ourselves we rigorously chastise idleness. Among ourselves we regard cupidity as the origin of all evils. We love hard work for the sake of exercising the body, but we reject it when it leads to cupidity. All our concerns are directed toward what is necessary, and we hate other concerns as the beginning of evils.*

In our fields one sees neither boundaries nor limits that indicate property. We say that such things are usurpations and contrary to nature. The earth produces for everyone, and each one can take its produce wherever he likes. We allow the birds to fly peacefully in the air, the animals to graze in the fields, the fish to swim freely in the water. We possess only the things that are necessary and the rest we leave for whoever has need of it.

Nothing gives us such pain as the desire to possess for oneself, [a desire] that never stops putting in a man's heart thousands of necessities. In proportion as a man's riches increase, his necessities increase. The sun warms us, the rains and the dew refresh us, the rivers quench our thirst, the plants and roots of the fields nourish us. The earth is our bed. Concerns do not keep us awake. Peace of heart renders our spirit free. Our independence frees us from the fear of anyone. We receive each other as brothers, whom nature has made equals, and as sons of the Supreme God, our common Father, who should divide the inheritance to his children equally.

We do not know what it is to cut down forests or break stones in order to build houses, since nature has given men caves in which we feel safe from heat, from cold, from rain, from wind, from storms. Their walls serve as shelter in life, and burial places in death. We expel from our habits both luxury and sensuality. The leaves and bark of tress cover the parts of us that nature does not want to be naked. Our women are not free to adorn themselves as other women do, but even if they had this freedom, their principles are contrary to it, given that they are convinced that such pompous ornaments require more effort than they decorate and that such mundane art cannot add anything to natural beauty nor cover up defects. For this reason not only is so much diligence superfluous, but even worthy of blame since it pretends to reform the work of the Creator. Just like this are our women. We have for them reciprocal love. The sin of infidelity is unheard of among us. It violates both nature and the conjugal bond.

Our society is a society of peace and gentleness. Our nature hates the mere thought of homicide. We do not provoke strangers, nor do we know anything about carrying weapons. It is gentleness alone that allows us to keep peace with strangers.

Luck alone is our enemy. It always fights with us, but it usually loses, even if we do not act against what happened. Thus lamentations are rarely heard. Death is painful for us when it arrives before old age, and when a father goes to his own son's funeral. In any case, someday it will arrive. We do not erect monuments since they seem to insult the humility of the soul. What thing can be more monstrous than the corruption of the body. We therefore burn the corpses in order to not sully the earth.

I do not mean to offend you, o Alexander, if with this portrait of our lives I chastise yours. But what subversion have you not put in the world? And all for the sake of cupidity and ambition! How many murders by your hands? Or by your orders? You seize children from the hands of their fathers, and deprive them of the death rites they are owed. You violate mausoleums. You run impetuously toward the place where the sun rises, as if you wanted to grab [the sun] with your own hands. You overthrow thrones. You force kings to honor your triumph. By mere whim, you force free men to become slaves and give freedom to slaves. You claim to have taken forts by force of arms when you have bought the governor with money. Without doubt corrupting the guards, you corrupt even the God of hell.

I will stop looking at your image in comparison with our customs and continue the instruction. We are unfamiliar with the tumultuous competitions, games, and spectacles that you delight in. What use do performances have for a people that completely scorns them? Such performances are only to be laughed at. Scenes that represent cruelty to us are for you an object of recreation. The Brahmins would suffer great anguish if they were to see men exposed to ferocious beasts or watch strong men, men in their prime, oppress each other in cold blood.

The sky is our spectacle, full of delights. In it we see order, economy, regularity and movement. We look with great pleasure at the sun, which flies on a crimson car with shining horses and travels through the celestial regions and at the end of the year returns to the place of its first departure. Then there is nature, its works each day are equally beautiful, admirable and incomprehensible: the birds singing, the springs flowing forth, the flowers, the leaves. Any one of these can fill our reflections and revive our spirit.

Whatever our earth produces is enough for us. Nor do we desire rare things that the heavens produce in other climes. We are content with whatever can be said to be ours. We scorn even your flowery words. We especially condemn the pernicious art of making falsehood appear plausible, of protecting crimes, of condemning the innocent, and sometimes of even justifying parricide. All our eloquence tends toward sincerity, and never goes against proper knowledge. The Brahmins' maxim is to never be cruel to nor sacrifice innocent victims. It is to never adorn temples with gold and silver, nor with stone slabs or precious gems. This is because they would be afraid to correct divinity, if they were to add something to what it has in itself. God should be honored with a pure cult and not a cruel one and should be petitioned with prayers and humility. By his word alone, he created all the visible world, conserves it, and directs it and nourishes it. This God is a pure spirit and, as a consequence, does not want anything except good actions, virtues, and thanks.

After hearing this exposition of our religion, you should compare your own, or at least allow me to make this comparison. I am not willing to endure your stubbornness in not wanting to recognize that your origin comes from heaven, and that it intrinsically unites you to the Divine or Supreme Being. You do not recognize anything except birth from illustrious blood, and thus you scorn your first origin. You relate everything to the flesh and in it are all your delights. This you cherish, this you care for, this alone you love. That which is most guilty, you judge worthy of being presented as a sacrifice to the immortal spirit.

You do not worship the true God, who exists, and you search for countless others gods. You admit some of them to heaven and assign to them the care of parts of your body. * *You say that Minerva resides in the brain as the seat of consciousness. Juno restrains the impetuous movements of the heart. Mercury, your god of eloquence, resides in the lips. Hercules gives strength to your limbs. Cupid gives tenderness to your senses. Bacchus gives savor or taste. Ceres gives digestion, Venus fecundity. Jupiter opens the organs of breathing. The industrious Apollo* ** *directs your fingers in making music and other delicate works. But think about it. What sort of divinity is it, whose power is limited to only a few things? In fact, it is so restricted that not even you could change anything. The objection is manifest in each cult that you render to them.*

You cannot offer to Jupiter anything other than a bull. Only the peacock to Juno. [A pig, a sheep and a bull] to Mars.[3]

* In what follows, Didame mentions several Greek and Roman gods. Minerva or Athena is the daughter of Zeus, born directly from him without a mother, an important goddess associated particularly with the city of Athens. Juno or Hera is Zeus's wife. Mercury or Hermes is a son of Zeus, Zeus's speedy messenger. Bacchus or Dionysus is a son of Zeus and the Theban princess Semele. He is the god of wine. Ceres or Demeter is the goddess of grain.

** Marco here writes the name "Epolone". The Greek Apollo is a god of music and Marco undoubtedly meant to write his name.

Only a swan to Apollo, a goat to Bacchus, a dove to Venus, a falcon to Minerva, cats to Ceres, some honey to Mercury. Hercules does not accept anything other than branches of palm on his statues and altars. Cupid loves only roses.

You cannot even change this order without falling into their bad graces. Look, please, at the contradictions of their characters. They appear to be truly united in causing you trouble at the same time and in the same way. One calls you to war. The other to pleasures. This one demands you to take care of commerce. That one calls you to the table. Each one pulls you to whatever he loves. They call you. They petition you. They never give you any rest until you have carried out their will.

And these are the gods that ought to be the joy and the delight of humanity. You should admit this and recognize for once that these gods are nothing but your own passions, which you convert into divinities.

You should recognize them. Fill the hells with them, and you will easily find your delights in honorable symbols. The Eumenides are your filthy thoughts. Tisiphone is nothing but the remorse of your criminal conscience. Tantalus is your insatiable cupidity. Cerberus expresses the punishment of your gluttony. Hydra is your senses that are reborn daily. The crown of vipers is your bad actions. Pluto himself descends from heaven and explains his own degeneration, as well*

* In this paragraph Didame mentions several malevolent Greek and Roman gods and monsters. The Eumenides are the Erinyes or Furies transformed into protectors, but here Marco seems to refer to their original malevolent character. Tisiphone is one of the three Erinyes or Furies. Cereberus is the three-headed dog that guards the gate to the underworld. Hydra ("Hider" in the Italian text) is a creature with nine heads that is killed by Hercules. The crown of vipers is presumably a reference to Medusa, a Gorgon killed by Perseus. Tantalus is a mortal son of Zeus who killed his own son and tried to feed him to the gods. Pluto is the Greek god who ruled the underworld kingdom of the dead.

as yours. You do not recognize the single origin, that from which you have your being. O unfortunate populace! Your religion causes crime in life and torment after death.

This, then, was the letter that Didame, the doctor and head of the Brahmins of Benares—the holy city and university, unique and universal for all India—wrote. It seems that this was the true religious system of the Brahmins in those times. How it later changed into idolatry, I have explained in another book which describes the religious system of these people. For now, it is enough to know and conclude that Alexander the Great conquered this India, passed almost though the center of it, was to fight Porus in the kingdom of Burma, then embarked toward Pegu,* then returned to Persia, and from there to his own country, where he died.** India remained in the hands of its legitimate masters. This information is collected from the third book of Kabir, entitled the *Mulpanji*, where Kabir says many things about Alexander, and claims to have been his spiritual teacher.

* Pegu is a former capital and region of lower Burma.

** What Marco says about the route of Alexander is obviously wrong. Alexander met King Porus somewhere in the Punjab of modern Pakistan and never got as far as Benares, much less to Burma or Pegu.

Chapter 5

Chaplain to a French Army

After the English had taken Chandernagore, it happened that a certain Monsieur Lassa, the chief of the French Company in Kassimbazar, became a fugitive with a few of his local followers.[1] They took with them whatever they could carry. In order not to fall into the hands of the English, he advanced inland toward Delhi, little by little assembling all the French who had escaped from the English and were dispersed in the provinces. It also happened that our Padre Onofrio da Monte Cassiano was in Chandernagore Fort when it was about to surrender to the English.

The French were in a desperate plight and begged the padre to take charge of two trunks full of documents from the Chandernagore archive, carry them to Kassimbazar, and turn them over to Monsieur Lassa, this being the only means to save them from the hands of the English. Padre Onofrio took it upon himself to render this great service to the French and had the pleasure of submitting the documents to Monsieur Lassa in Kassimbazar at precisely the moment when he was about to flee from that place.

Monsieur Lassa was very pleased with Padre Onofrio and enlisted him to go with him to serve as chaplain to his little army. At the time the army consisted of only about 100 persons. Padre Onofrio accepted the post and accompanied Monsieur Lassa to Delhi. Padre Onofrio was with him in all the battles he had to fight [on the way to Delhi]. Most noteworthy was the battle with the raja of the Jats.* Monsieur Lassa fought with him for three days and three nights while attempting to pass through his country against his will. Monsieur Lassa finally reached Delhi, where he had been invited by the son of the emperor in order to help him in a battle against his own chief minister or wazir. [...] By the time Monsieur Lassa arrived in Delhi the battle had already finished and the emperor's son had lost.**

The expedition had failed, and Monsieur Lassa retreated to Chhatarpur.# He stayed there for some time waiting for the arrival of new French forces in Bengal. Padre Onofrio, when he saw that the campaign was going to last a long time, wanted to take his leave and return to Bengal. Monsieur Lassa was thus left without any chaplain, while his army was growing every day with the arrival of members of the dispersed French forces. Monsieur Lassa was also on the point of departing from Chhatarpur in order to join up with the Imperial forces that were heading toward Patna where

* The Jats (Marco's *Giatti*) were and remain an ethnic group and caste cluster that is numerous in the Punjab and adjoining regions. They are traditionally peasants and have strong martial traditions. Most Sikhs belong to Jat communities.

** The Mughal emperor at this time was Alamgir II (ruled 1754–59). The wazir in question was Imad-ul-Mulk, a ruthless grandson of the first Nizam of Hyderabad, Asaf Jah. Alamgir II was murdered by Imad-ul-Mulk in 1759, the year of the events narrated here. The son of the emperor was Ali Gauhar. He succeeded his father and took the title Shah Alam II. His reign lasted from 1759 to 1806 although he never controlled much territory and eventually became a puppet of the English.

The town of Chhatarpur or Chatarpur (Marco's *Ciatrepur*) is located in northern Madhya Pradesh in Central India.

they would probably make an attack on the English. For this reason Monsieur Lassa wrote to Padre Giuseppe Maria in Bettiah begging him to please send him a chaplain for at least a few months. Monsieur Lassa sent a military escort with the letter in order to bring the chaplain back. Padre Giuseppe Maria, then vice prefect of the Mission as I have noted, sent me to Chhatarpur with orders to stay there until I was recalled.

I departed for Chhatarpur on January 27, 1759, a journey of about one month. I will not write down here all the difficulties that I had to endure on the journey. [...] I will say, however, that as a general rule journeys in Hindustan are very difficult because of the already mentioned *chaukis*, or guards, who stand in the road when they see strangers coming and do everything possible to rob them. They usually lie in wait in deserted places. They demand from them large sums as a fee for passage and take as much as they can. Then they run ahead by another road and again stop the strangers in another place. There the guards take more from them. This continues as long as the guards see that the strangers still have something. If the strangers defend themselves, they risk their lives since the guards are many and usually stop them in deserted places. If the strangers complain to the guards' chiefs in the city, the chiefs will promise justice but will never find the criminals since they themselves are in league with them. Our Padre Onofrio, on his journey from Chhatarpur to Bettiah, had many such difficulties and in one place was arrested for 25 days. In the end he was obliged to leave everything that he had with him and escape at night, which is just what the *chaukis* wanted. In my case, however, I was not bothered much on the same road from Bettiah to Chhatarpur since I had nothing with me and could speak the language.

When necessary, I mentioned the name of the *chaukis'* chiefs as if I knew them.* [...]

I arrived in Chhatarpur on February 19, 1759. My arrival immensely pleased Monsieur Lassa and the army since they were surrounded by Hindus, had to have their guns always at the ready, and hadn't had a priest for eight months. I stayed with them in that place until March 5. During this time I tried to prepare them spiritually for the imminent war they were getting ready for. I made some apostate heretics renounce their error, even after 30 years. I baptized a Jew and five others who were prepared [to convert].

Finally on March 5 we all set off for Patna in order to join the Imperial troops that were waiting for us near that place. Our journey was very difficult because of the big mountains we had to cross with carriages and artillery pieces being carried on the backs of the men, who also had to always keep their own guns at the ready because every chief of the country tried to rob us. The lack of money for our expenses and projects obliged the commander to move from one country to another. For example, we went to Panna in the mountains of the diamond mines, but the king sent us off without offering much help.** We moved on to Benares where the raja detained

* The highway tolls and internal customs duties collected at the *chaukis* or toll-stations by the *chaukidars* were at this time major income sources for provincial and local governments. The English East India Company had forced the Mughal Emperor, the Nawab of Bengal and local governments to grant free passes through these toll stations for shipments of Company goods and also the goods of the private trade of Company servants. This loss of income may partly account for the rapaciousness of the *chaukidars* that Marco and Onofrio encountered.

** The town of Panna about 100 kilometers to the east of Chhatarpur is, as Marco notes, famous for its diamond mines. Today the mines are largely exhausted.

us for eight days, not to give us the money he promised us but to take possession of our artillery, something he tried to do but without success. We then went to Bhojpur,* but that raja, instead of giving us the troops we had agreed upon, tried to get our own troops to desert us. All this was the result of the intrigues of the English who were quite afraid of Monsieur Lassa, not because of the forces he controlled but because of the advice that he could give to the people of the country.

Finally we reached Patna. At that time the city was opposed to the French since it was controlled by the English who were encamped in it. Monsieur Lassa prepared for the assault of the city, but the war council resolved to not risk the assault for the time being but rather to first join together with the Imperial troops who were three days away. We then moved off along the road and three days later met up with the Imperial troops. This was a very large army, but it included only about 30,000 combat soldiers. Monsieur Lassa then instructed his little army of 150 Europeans and 250 native soldiers, called "sepoys" (*sipai*), to join with them. Monsieur Lassa had good officers and good artillery. All this was more than enough to take Patna, a city that was the capital of the province and the key to Bengal. We met with the emperor's son and even I went to the audience.** He and Monsieur Lassa agreed to the attack on Patna and the army immediately moved off in that direction.

The city was attacked, but the project failed—either because the English had received help, or because some of the Imperial troops received money from the English, or because

* Bhojpur (Marco's Bogpur) is the town by this name to the east of Buxar (Baksar) in the Bhojpur District of Bihar.

** This was Prince Ali Gauhar, who became Emperor Alam Shah II the following year (1759).

in the end they did not manage to come to an agreement about the mode and hour of the attack. Monsieur Lassa, who was the only one to come close to scaling the defenses, ended up the victim. He lost 50 Europeans and some native troops. He finally had to retreat because they had not managed the proper measures and none of the other chiefs advanced to support him. In this affair, a Monsieur Carrione, an officer of Monsieur Lassa, acted with distinction. He disguised himself and in person visited the defensive ditch and identified the most appropriate place to assault the city. The attack would have succeeded if the Imperial army had advanced as had been agreed. Since he was in charge of everything, Monsieur Lassa had earlier been begged to not to participate in the assault. The project failed the first and second nights, and they were obliged to retreat.

I was put in charge of all the sick and wounded. I left the next day to transport the hospital to Suan, another city 10 leagues distant from Patna.* I stayed there until the wounded had either died or recovered. Afterwards I rejoined the army. It was moving from one place to another in order to capture several little forts. Padre Giuseppe Maria wrote to me from time to time begging me not to leave the army until he called me back. Thus I continued performing my duties with the French and other Christians. From time to time I performed baptisms. On Christmas day I baptized six adults and eight children.

Besides all this, I tried to exercise my office [of priest and missionary] in the Imperial army with those chiefs and nobles

* Marco writes *Ansua,* but this is probably a mistake for Suan, a city located about 55 kilometers south-southeast of Patna. Suan is apparently the same as the present-day Asthanwan, located about 10 kilometers to the east of Bihar Sharif.

and with the emperor himself.* I often went to his private quarters in the evening accompanied by one of his Muslim religious functionaries. Normally no one is allowed to visit him there except the confidants with whom he speaks privately. In public no one can speak with the emperor, not even when he has them questioned by his own Master of Ceremonies. The campaign ran from place to place in this fashion for almost two years. Several forts were captured and various interesting events happened that would be worth noting, but since they are not directly relevant to my purpose of giving instruction for new missionaries, I will not describe them here.

In the essay about my journey to India,[2] I wrote a history of the beginnings of the wars between the English and the peoples of the country, including such events as the arrival of the European traders; the military forts they built; the disputes between the English and the nawab of Bengal, Alivardi Khan; the defeat of the English by Nawab Siraj-ud-Daula, the son of Alivardi Khan; the death of many English prisoners in a warehouse; the revenge of the British and the execution of Siraj-ud-Daula; the above-mentioned English capture of Chandernagore in March 1757; the appointment by the English of Mir Jafar as the new nawab; the repayment by the English of the losses suffered by the inhabitants of Calcutta in the war; the intrigues and fights among Emperor Alamgir II, his wazir Imad-ul-Mulk, the emperor's son Ali Gauhar, and the nawab of Lucknow Shuja-ud-Daula; the attack on Patna by a raja allied with Shuja-ud-Daula and the treacherous capture of the raja's fort by the latter; the above-mentioned attack on Patna by the son of the emperor and Monsieur Lassa in 1759; the murder of Emperor Alamgir

* Most historians place the emperor in Delhi at this time. Probably Marco is referring to the emperor's son, Ali Gauhar.

by his wazir in the same year; the murder of Miran, son of Mir Jafar, by the English; and their replacing of Mir Jafar by his son-in-law, Mir Kasim. This history is now well known and I myself did not directly witness the events.* Here I will describe only a few later occasions when I was present and took part in what happened.

When Abdali, the emperor of Sam or Tartaria and protector of the crown of the Great Mughal, heard about the murder of Emperor Alamgir II by his wazir Imad-ul-Mulk in 1759, he immediately set off on the road to Delhi to avenge the emperor's death.[3] When Abdali approached the city, the wazir fled and abandoned the city. Abdali entered Delhi and elected Ali Gauhar, the son of the emperor, as the new Emperor Shah Alam II. Since Shah Alam II was then situated near Patna, Abdali put one of the emperor's sons who had remained in Delhi on the throne. After putting the court and government in order, Abdali crossed the Jamuna River in order to confer with Shuja-ud-Daula, the nawab of Lucknow and, it is said, to discuss the activities of the English.

Meanwhile the rainy season arrived, a season that lasts for four months and causes the rivers to flood. For this reason Abdali was unable to cross back across the Jamuna. The Marathas took advantage of the situation to go to Delhi, sack the city, depose the emperor's son, and put another of their choosing on the throne. When the four months of rains ended, Abdali crossed back across the river and gave battle to the Marathas. Some 80,000 dead were left on the battlefield. Abdali retook Delhi and put back on the throne the same

* The statement that "this history is now well known" is less true now than in Marco's own time. It is only very recently that the writing of narrative histories of the early colonial period has begun to make a comeback among professional historians and a comprehensive modern account of these events is much needed.

son of the new Emperor Shah Alam. Once he had done this, Abdali sent certificates to the emperor, who was then situated near Patna after having failed in the assault on the city.

The emperor welcomed Abdali's people with certificates and *sirpaos*. The *sirpao* is an imperial garment that serves as a crown.* A beautiful ceremony was held on the fields of Bhojpur. All the army was in arms. Monsieur Lassa, together with all his people in arms, stood in front as the emperor's bodyguard. The emperor mounted the throne. All the chiefs stood around him to pay him court. I myself was in the row near Monsieur Lassa. Abdali's ambassadors then entered. After the usual ceremonies, they presented the emperor with the imperial garment, certificates and various letters. He received these items with great respect. He read the letters, descended from the throne and withdrew into an apartment. There he put on the garment and returned to the throne, where he had his own election as the emperor of the Great Mogol proclaimed.

After this all the armies, corps by corps, presented themselves to offer their obeisance. Then the drums were beaten and all the army shouted: "Long live Emperor Ali Gauhar, or Shah Alam." These were the two names he took, one given by Abdali and the other chosen by himself. He immediately had money struck in his name. A few days later he sent back Abdali's ambassadors with the usual ceremonies and with letters of thanks and decrees for his son who sat in his place on the throne of Delhi. He said that he would not return to Delhi until he had conquered Bengal. This he really intended to do and he stayed a whole year moving

* A *sirpao* (more correctly "*sirpav*" or "*siropav*") is a garment that covers a person from head (*sir*) to foot (*pav*). They were traditionally given in royal audiences, or durbars, as a mark of esteem.

through the provinces both to make alliances with the rajas and to sustain his army. This army had 500,000 persons counting the women, servants, vendors, thieves, etc. They all lived on the things they pillaged in the villages and then sold to the army.

The English feared their own ruin, especially since Monsieur Lassa was with that great army which he and his councilors directed. The English prepared as well as they could to leave Patna, put themselves in the field and engage a decisive battle. This they did. On January 12, 1761 they left Patna, marched toward us, and on the 15th the battle was declared. I should note that they did not have more than 500 Europeans and 3,000 native sepoys, with another 10 or 15,000 people who accompanied their army. The English did not trust these people, however, and feared that they might betray them. They turned their cannons toward them and separated them [from their army]. The English then advanced against the Imperial army. They began the attack with big cannons. These dispersed the Imperial army without its offering any defense. The Imperial army was counting on Monsieur Lassa's cannons, but these were too small and unable to counter those of the English.

To the great advantage of the English, one of their cannonballs struck the throne of the emperor that was mounted on an elephant. The throne fell and the emperor jumped to the ground. The driver of the elephant had died and the furious animal, without its driver, ran about everywhere. This caused great confusion among all the troops who thought that the emperor had died. As a result they all fled, and I fled ahead of them. Only Monsieur Lassa remained on the field with his people. He wanted to make an organized retreat as well, but during the retreat found himself in a ditch that he couldn't cross with his artillery. He was unable to flee since his horse had been killed by an English cannonball. He was forced to let himself be taken prisoner together with those of his people who were unable to save themselves by flight.

I considered it unwise for me to return to the scene since the English army spies[4] had advanced to kill or plunder the fugitives. Taking advantage of the head start I had, I continued to flee with the fugitive Frenchmen until we reached the mountains where we finally rested around midnight since we were by then too tired to even stand. The next morning the remaining Frenchmen decided to depart for Pondichéry in the south. I was left in charge of 15 boys, the chapel, and the money and silver that various officers had entrusted to me. I had no idea what to do. It was impossible for me to go to Patna, five days journey away, since the roads and countryside were full of assassins, as is common after such defeats. I finally chose to go and join up with the English army that was somewhere else running after the fugitive emperor.

With my small cortege I set off on the road. The peasants of one village wanted to rob us, but I defended myself with the help of a horseman who was with me. On the third day I managed to reach the English army and found General Carnac. He received me with courtesy, and assigned one of his palanquins to me so I could travel with them. They pursued the emperor, who crossed one mountain after another, for eight days. In the end, the English saw that they couldn't catch the emperor and wrote him a letter telling him that since he was the emperor it was wrong for him to flee from the English who had declared themselves to be his servants. The war, they claimed, had been started because of their enemy, Monsieur Lassa, but now, since Lassa was their prisoner, the emperor could safely join them. This promise was signed by both sides and the emperor halted and joined the English who put him on the throne and had him recognized by the whole country. Finally, they made him confirm their privileges. They accompanied him with proper honors outside the Patna territory. The emperor then went to join Shuja-ud-daula in Lucknow where he stayed for some time.

Chapter 6

Back to Bettiah

As I said, I then stayed with the English army.[1] They asked me to go to Bengal with the French prisoners. I did not object to this at the time, but the next day a letter arrived for me from Patna announcing that Padre Giuseppe Maria had died in Bettiah [on January 15, 1761], the very same day as the above-mentioned battle. After I got this news I asked the general to excuse me from having to go to Bengal and allow me to go directly to Bettiah in order to take charge of that Mission which was now without any padre. The general was sympathetic but felt that since he had already declared that I was to go to Bengal he could not excuse me. But he offered to allow me to travel directly to Bettiah from Calcutta. I was thus obliged to go to Calcutta where I arrived on February 5.

I then presented myself to the English governor, Mr. Vansittart, and asked him to give me permission to return to the Mission. He politely replied that he had no objection, but warned me that the roads were full of thieves and army spies (*currori*) and advised me to wait for a while since one of his colonels was about to depart for that place with a detachment of troops. With him I would be well-protected. For this reason he told me to stay in Chandernagore with our padres and said that he would have me informed when they were ready to depart. Thus it was done.

Also around this time some letters arrived about the imminent arrival in Bengal of Padre Serafina da Como with two companions. For this reason, Padre Daniele da Morciano, at that time the Superior of Chandernagore, advised me to wait for them in order to be able to escort them to Patna. The padres' arrival was delayed, however, and news spread that their ship had been lost. I therefore decided to take advantage of the departure of the colonel and left for Patna, where I arrived on July 17, 1761, after a risky rainy-season journey on the Ganges.

From Patna I traveled on to Bettiah where I found Padre Anselmo da Ragusa. He was preparing to leave for Europe, but just at that moment received an order to become the Prefect of the Mission. A few days later he departed for Patna, leaving me in Bettiah as superior. After a campaign of two years with the army of Monsieur Lassa, I was back in Bettiah! There in Bettiah I was left all alone in charge of the Christians, the house, and the church. I tried to preserve the same methods and the same customs followed by the late Padre Giuseppe Maria. His body had died but his merit and prestige lived on among the people of the country, both big and small. The king himself told me how much he regretted the loss.

I remained happily in charge of those Christians until the month of December, when the city and fort of Bettiah was besieged by the men of the new nawab, Kasim Ali Khan, who not only attempted to take the king prisoner but also to take away all his money. At that time Padre Anselmo and the new padres also arrived on their way to Nepal. All of us together were besieged for more than three months. Usually we had to stay in the medicinal dispensary, since the other rooms in the house were liable to be hit by the enemy's bullets.

On April 20, 1762, after three months of siege, an agreement was made between the nawab's men and the king of Bettiah, Dhrub Singh. The king and his men would leave the fort, and the Muslims, as a symbolic victory, would enter by one gate and exit by the other, without ever stopping or causing any damage to the city. In exchange the king agreed to pay the expenses of the war. The king also agreed that after his death he would give half of his kingdom to his grandson, Jugal Kishore Singh, and the other half to a claimant named Shri Kishen Singh. All this was agreed and sworn to on the most sacred objects that they have among them.

Once the king had left the fort, however, he was taken prisoner and forced to go with them to Patna and present himself before the nawab, Kasim Ali Khan. The nawab received him as a prisoner and condemned him to pay 5,200,000 rupees. This caused the wars that I will describe shortly.

This king of Bettiah was named Dhrub Singh. It was he who had invited and admitted the missionaries into his kingdom. Since there was something unusual about the establishment of the padres in Bettiah, I will tell the story here. From the beginning of the Tibet Mission, our padres were established in Patna, a way-station for going on to this Mission. In about 1743, it happened that the wife of the king of Bettiah got sick with a disease that was unknown to those people. It also happened that the king [who is a Brahmin] had killed his brother with his own hands near a tree not far from the palace. One should also know that the Hindus believe that there is a rule that the killing of a Brahmin is an unpardonable sin and causes a family's destruction.

Given this supposition, the Brahmins did not fail to confront the king with his sin, assuring him that the soul of his brother had entered into that tree and that this brother would cause as much trouble as possible to the king's family. For this reason they convinced the king to make a great pagoda near that tree and to make houses for various Brahmins in which they would make daily sacrifices for his brother's soul, so that the brother would not disturb the tranquility of the king's kingdom and family. The king did this to placate his brother's soul, without any consideration of the expenses involved.

In the end, however, the queen got sick, and the doctors were unable to cure her. The Brahmins, always on the lookout for their own welfare, claimed that the brother's soul was tormenting her. The sacrifices were increased and the most famous Brahmin exorcists were brought from faraway countries. No effort was spared, but in the end all was in vain. The queen suffered more every day.

The raja was then told that in Patna (five days' journey from Bettiah) there were some European padres. Many things were said about them including that they had the power to expel demons. The raja immediately sent his palanquin (a comfortable bed that men carry) together with men and letters asking that the padres do him the favor of coming to his country. He assured them that their journey would not go unrewarded. At that time Padre Antonino da Montalboddo and the above-mentioned Padre Giuseppe Maria da Gargnano were in Patna. Since they both were newly-arrived and did not yet know the language, they refused the king's first and second invitations. The third time, however, Padre Giuseppe Maria decided to see for himself. He brought an interpreter and presented himself to the king, who received him and embraced him with the greatest affection possible for such persons when they have need of something.

The king told Padre Giuseppe Maria about the case of his brother, the claims of the Brahmins, and his queen's state. He begged the padre to use his powers to free the queen of this unhappy situation. Padre Giuseppe Maria asked to see the queen and to personally examine her discomfort. It was very difficult for the king to agree to this request, since it is the custom in India that such persons are never seen. For all that, in the end the king was reduced to having to allow the queen to come into the padre's presence so that he could hear from the queen's own mouth the state of her illness. In the end he made a secret exorcism for her, and, seeing that her only visible problem was some cankers on her throat, he frankly told the king that the queen was not possessed and that his brother's soul was not tormenting her in any way. Rather, she had a simple illness and, if the king wished, he would make a remedy for her and within a few days would cure her.

The raja, happy to hear this news, gratefully begged Padre Giuseppe Maria to make the remedy. He did so and within 15 days the queen was cured, to the indescribable delight of the king and all his family, although this caused great consternation among the Brahmins.

The king invited the padre to remain permanently with him. He promised to give the city and villages to the padre so he could live in grand style (a common promise in such situations). Padre Giuseppe Maria thanked him for the offer, but explained to him that his situation [as a Capuchin] was such that he could not take even a farthing. Rather it was his duty to preach the Gospel. The king begged him to at least establish a house in Bettiah, as had been done in Patna and Nepal, and then the king pledged to help him succeed in all that he desired. In the end it was agreed to write to Rome to obtain permission to construct a hospice in Bettiah. The king himself wrote to Benedict XIV, who replied with the permission to have two missionaries in the kingdom.[2] Thus it was that Padre Giuseppe Maria became the founder of the present-day hospice in this kingdom and of the Bettiah Mission.

This king always held all the missionaries and Christians in special esteem, but particularly Padre Giuseppe Maria. The king always wanted him near and never did anything important without his advice. The king came to visit him at home from time to time, a home that is not far from the palace. He ordered his grandchildren to pass by twice a day to greet the padres. Each day he sent the padres something to eat like meat, fish or fruit. He never listened to any petition or complaint by the Brahmins against the padres or the Christians, and always told them that the padres knew more than them and were worth more than them. The king learned much about our religion and claimed that he wished to die a Christian. He procrastinated in this sentiment until his final days.

The end [came soon after Kasim Ali Khan's attack on Bettiah in 1762]. Being a prisoner of the nawab and an octogenarian, Dhrub Singh saw that his death was near. Padre Anselmo and I went to wish him a good journey to Patna and encourage him to have patience and to resign himself to God's will. Finally, we reminded him of the many good promises he had made to God in the one thing that matters more than the kingdom itself. He wept and entrusted to us his grandchildren, who were in the mountains with their mother. He asked that one of us go with him in order to assist him in the death that he saw was imminent. Padre Anselmo went with him, but for some unknown reason he left him half way there. The king remained a prisoner for four months, and a few days later he died still a prisoner. He kept asking for the padres, but since they were not there at that time, he died without becoming a Christian, unless God had already accepted his good intentions.

One of his grandsons, Jugal Kishore, remained with him and assisted him until his death. Nawab Kasim Ali Khan, seeing that the raja had died without having paid any of the money he had promised, and not knowing where it was nor how to get it, called the king's grandchild, that same Jugal Kishore, and offered him his uncle's kingdom if he agreed to pay the money. The young man, who was still a prisoner, accepted to pay the indicated sum. Once this was agreed, he was brought back to Bettiah accompanied by 20,000 of the nawab's horsemen, who kept him prisoner and in dire straits so that he would be forced to pay the sum. He paid—bit by bit and in various ways—2,000,000 and 400,000 rupees, and was to pay the remainder also bit by bit. Then the nawab's men began to press him and threatened to abuse his mother if he did not send the money quickly.

Begging them not to abuse his mother, the young Jugal Kishore replied that the next day at noon he would finish paying all the debt. Expecting to receive the sum, the Moors calmed down, and in fact they received it. While the young raja was agreeing to this, 30 of his bravest and most trusted men, who had hid themselves in a pagoda, came out with their sabers in their hands after the Moors had eaten at midday and were sleeping. Swinging their sabers to the right and left, they entered the palace, took the young raja and brought him outside, fighting their way until they were outside the city gates. They killed 3,000 persons without any of the 30 having received any wound. The Moors were so surprised that they no longer knew where they were.

Hearing the noise, I looked out through the window. I saw wounded men running in all directions. I ran quickly to close all the doors and locked myself in, trying to see what was happening and how was it going to finish. At this point I saw about 50 persons run up and pound on our door. I replied through the window, asking what they wanted. They told me to run quickly to give medicine to various leaders who were seriously wounded. I told them that frankly I did not know any of them, but if someone I knew came I would go. They left without saying anything and soon a gentleman who was a friend of mine arrived. I took a bag of medicines and went with him. Passing by many bodies, I reached those leaders for whom they had called me. For several of them I patched up their wounds and made poultices, for others, who were without hope of recovery, I only gave them some plasters for appearance's sake. The whole day passed in this way without any of the further bad consequences that I feared.

The next day the armed men left to track down the fugitive raja, but within five days he had assembled 6,000 men to help him and soon forced the Muslims to retreat within the fort. Things were headed toward the long haul and the dangers were obvious. I therefore managed to transport all the Christians, big and small, outside the fort and placed them in a safe place. I then returned to take care of our house and the furniture. I hid the latter in such a way that it would not to be discovered. In fact the young raja returned several times during the year and many battles were fought there. Twice the city was sacked, but I did not lose anything and managed to save myself from all dangers either by flight or by hiding. When things had calmed down a little, Padre Michelangelo della Tabiago, who had accompanied the Christians to Selempur,* a place outside the Bettiah territory, returned from that place.

I then received orders from the Prefect, who was in Patna, to go to Nepal. I left for there on the October 15, 1762, but I found that an army of the nawab, Kasim Ali Khan, was on the road in order to take possession of Nepal. For this reason

* This Selempur is modern Salempur located southeast of Bettiah and on the south bank of the Gandak River.

all the routes to Nepal were blocked. I then accompanied a military detachment of Bengali Christians who were traveling to join that army and cross the mountains together with it. The army's passage was blocked at a mountain post called Makwanpur* and they stayed there for a month trying to capture it. They lost more than 3,000 men, without being able to take it. In the end the army was forced to abandon the effort and retreat from those mountains where all 20,000 of their troops were in danger of being lost. I was likewise forced to return to Bettiah, where Padre Michelangelo had been elected superior.

Nawab Kasim Ali Khan then came to Bettiah. He came to see our house and made many promises to us. He assigned four men to me at his expense in order to accompany me for several months on a tour of the Mission that I was about to undertake. But since the wars were coming near to Bettiah once again, Padre Michelangelo called me back, and I returned on March 20, 1763.

In one respect, Nawab Kasim Ali Khan's attack on Bettiah in 1762 proved to be, for me at least, a blessing in disguise.[3] At that time, the city was besieged for three months, at the end of which it was decided that the raja would go out to parley and make an agreement between them. Before going out, the raja of Bettiah, our friend Dhrub Singh, fearing the betrayal that in fact befell him, sent to our house four big trunks containing all his books, asking me to please conserve them with all diligence until he had arranged his business with the nawab. [...] Once he had consigned his books to me, he went out and what he feared in fact happened to him. He was made prisoner and was taken to Patna, where he died after

* Makwanpur (Marco's *Macuampur*) is a town in Nepal to the south of Kathmandu.

four months of captivity. The Muslims took possession of the city of Bettiah, of his palace, and of all that it contained.

For that reason, the books stayed in my hands for three years, during which I lost no time, nor spared any effort or expense in translating them, at least the most essential and mysterious ones. In addition, I was given another excellent opportunity. The same Doctor who before had explained the same books to the king had remained in Bettiah under my protection (because all the others and the inhabitants themselves had fled). This Doctor was a capable man who had studied at the University of Benares. He was also a good man and my friend. He had lost all his belongings in the pillage of Bettiah, and I found myself at that time in a condition of being able to maintain him. He thus stayed in our house for the whole three years, during which time he explained to me all the most difficult books, books that I by myself would not have been able to understand. I got from him translations of all of these books. It should be noted that I knew the language well enough to make it impossible for him to deceive me, since I was able to read [the words of] the same books.

In addition, he was a good man, and towards the end [of our time together] he resolved, through the impact of all that he had learned, to become a Christian. He was already about to receive his baptism, and I had written to Rome asking for permission to bring him with me when I would return to Europe. However, before receiving his baptism he wanted to go to Benares in order to make some arrangements in his family. Precisely on the road to Benares, there was an army that was sacking the region around Ghazipur.* He was killed

* Ghazipur is a city on the Ganges River about 65 kilometers east-northeast of Benares (Varanasi).

on the road, although I have never been able to find out exactly in what encounter. I have thought that perhaps it was other Brahmins [who did it] because of their hatred towards him for having explained their books to me and for his having wished to become a Christian, and because he, with arguments taken from us, debated everything they claimed and spoke openly against them. However the case may be, he died without ever receiving his baptism with water. If his will was correct—as he made me believe and as I hope—God will have granted to him the baptism of desire.

I made a collection of all the books [that we] translated and of [the details of] the systems of their religion, with an adequate compilation of their histories, texts that I hope will be absolutely useful and, I believe, necessary for new missionaries. From these texts, they will be able to learn all that is indispensable for their office, particularly with regard to this kingdom (since it is very true that in different places the Hindus have different systems of their religion and have different books, which are known and followed in one kingdom and not even known in another. [...]

In addition, the Doctors and the Brahmins are deceivers; they read some book and explain it as something completely different, and thus different accounts of it are carried to Europe, not from malice, but for the reasons just stated. What they do wrong in these accounts is to say, once and for all: "This is the religion of the Indians (*indiani*)." Instead, what they should say is: "This is what has been explained by so and so, a doctor in such and such a system, and is accepted in this particular book."

Chapter 7

The Kabir and Nanak Panths

Among the books I read with my Brahmin friend from Benares were two books regarded as particularly sacred by the Kabir Panthis, the followers of a curious Hindu sect known as the Kabir Panth.* These two books were the *Mul-panji*, or *Register of the Root*, and the *Gyan-sagar*, or *Ocean of Wisdom*.[1] In 1762 I wrote out interlineal translations of these two books into Italian, giving the original text and translation side by side. These translations I sent to Monsignor Borgia in Rome so scholars in Europe could also study them. During my years in Bettiah I got to know many of these Kabir Panthis and learned much about their beliefs and practices.

[The followers of this sect regard Kabir as] a great saint and miracle worker.[2] They say that he was the spiritual master of Alexander the Great.** About this sect I could say a great deal,

* Marco calls the followers of this sect Cabiristi. The Kabir Panth still maintains an important presence in the Bettiah region and elsewhere in the northern Indian states of Bihar, Chhattisgarh, Uttar Pradesh, and Madhya Pradesh. Kabir lived in the period ca. 1450–1520. Marco's descriptions of the Kabir Panth and the Nanak Panth are evidently the oldest in any European language (see Lorenzen 2002).

** Marco is wrong about Alexander the Great. What the Kabir Panthis claim is that Kabir met with the Indo-Afghan sultan named Sikandar (i.e., Alexander) Lodi (1489–1517).

because they are in great esteem and number. [...] The Kabir Panthi fakirs are secular.* They wear a necklace of small beads of wood, this being their distinctive mark, and some other symbols drawn on their foreheads. They eat neither meat nor fish, being rigorous followers of the opinion that all animals belong to the same species. For this reason they do not even kill their lice and take care not to step on the ants in their path, etc. They have permission to eat greens and pulses, in spite of the fact that these plants bear fruits, because, they say, need supercedes rules.

They do not believe in any particular god, but argue that God is nothing other than the power (*la Virtù*) that produces all things of the world. In order to prove this principle they are obliged to say abominable things. When they make their profession of faith, they swear to retain their semen (*in materiam decidentem*) and keep it in hand, promising not to release it, and, if released, to eat it. They have, however, wives and children. This type of fakir is not insolent. [...]

Their visible God is a certain Narayan.[3] In addition there is another named Niranjan, who is the instrument by means of which this God wished to create the world. But Niranjan, not finding himself capable of doing this, requested (as the book the *Mul-panji* says), as a favor from Narayan or God, one of His 16 sons. God granted him one of these 16 sons named Kurma. God ordered Kurma to give to Niranjan the egg to create the world. This Kurma had four heads, and his body

* The Kabir Panth in fact includes both *sadhus* (i.e., ascetics or fakirs), who are celibate, and *bhagats* (lay persons), who can marry. Marco is apparently confusing the two categories since he claims below that the Kabir Panthi "fakirs" marry and have children. Although the retention of semen plays an important role in yoga, Marco's claims about Kabir Panthi practices in this regard have not been noted by any other observer. The Kabir Panthi sadhus do have monasteries (against what Marco claims).

measured 16 *palang* (a *palang* is 90 Italian miles). Niranjan himself measured 9 *palang*. Before they came to an agreement, they waged a great battle between themselves and Niranjan cut off three of Kurma's heads. Then with these three heads he formed the five elements, namely the four elements plus the void. With these elements he then created all the rest of the things of this world. During their combat, Niranjan sweated a great deal and with his sweat he formed the ocean and the fish; and with other drops of sweat he formed the other 94 crores [of things] of this earth, etc.* He made the sun and the moon and the 900,000 stars. All these things are of the essence of God himself since they originated from the three heads of Kurma, the son of God. [...]

Having done this, Niranjan remained there thinking, not knowing how to populate the three worlds, that is, heaven, earth and hell. Then he went to God and performed penance for 768 years. God told him to go to Mansarovar,** where he would find a virgin with eight arms, whose name was the eternal Bhavani. This virgin contained in herself the root of 84 lakh souls (one *lakh* is 100,000), from which creatures of different sorts would be produced. For this purpose, Niranjan went there and saw the virgin. Fearing that they would lose her, he swallowed her alive. God became angry because of this and punished Niranjan, forcing him to eat 125,000 souls every day for as long as the world endures, and decreed that even then he would not be satisfied.

Then God, being inclined against Niranjan, agreed to a request by Kurma who demanded vengeance for the loss of his three heads and created a certain Jogajit to go and kill

* A "crore" (*karod*) is 10,000,000.

** Mansarovar (in Sanskrit, Manasa-sarovara) is a lake sacred to Hindus and located in Tibet.

Niranjan. They fought a great battle, but Kurma threw Niranjan down and removed the swallowed virgin, Bhavani, from his belly. Afterward Niranjan meditated seriously on his deeds, and from his thoughts arose Kal, the king of death. This sect of Kabir Panthis does not establish monasteries. These Kabir Panthis are rather like secular persons.

Another type of fakir, also numerous, who have monasteries and make secular disciples, forms the sect of Nanak Panthis, disciples of a certain Nanak.* About him there are very many stories, as is usual among the Hindus (*Gentili*).[4] They say that Nanak was in the world during the first age of the world. He was then called Ain Marvan. After having made various disciples, he returned to heaven. In the second age of the world he was called Arcan and, having made disciples, he went back to heaven. In the third age of the world he was called Janak. In this fourth age he is called Nanak. They make him the servant of God, and almost as eternal as He is.

These Nanak Panthis have a book of their religion, but it cannot be read by anyone who does not have the key to the way in which it is written.** The characters are clearly Indian ones,

* The Nanak Panthis are today more commonly known as Sikhs, or followers of the Sikh Panth. Guru Nanak (1469–1539) was the first of 10 founder gurus of the movement. Sikh beliefs are in many ways similar to those of the Kabir Panthis, but the Kabir Panthis consider themselves to be Hindus while the Sikhs now claim to form a separate and independent religion. One of the principal Sikh temples, or gurdwaras, is located quite close to the Capuchin hospice and old church in Patna. This gurdwara, named Patna Sahib, marks the birthplace of the tenth and final Sikh guru, Gobind Singh. Marco must have visited this gurdwara and spoken with the Sikhs he met there.

** This book is the *Guru granth sahib* or *Adi granth*. The script in which this text is normally written is called *Gurmukhi*. This script is related to the Devanagari/Kaithi script that Marco knew but is sufficiently different to have made it impossible for Marco to read.

and the language is also the same, but the difference is that, for example, "b" is called "a", and other letters also transpose their names. One time, I had an explanation of this book, and I confuted it chapter by chapter. These books of confutation are now found kept in Bettiah so they can be distributed. The book [of the Nanak Panthis] is full of fables, but ones so crude that one has to be quite a fool to believe them.

However, the cleverness of these fakirs consists in having accommodated things that exist among the Muslims and among the Hindus (*Gentili*), unifying the dogmas and customs of the former with those of the latter. Thus they have written: "*Nanak fakir, hindu ka guru musalman ka pir,*" that is to say, "The religious [leader] Nanak is the teacher of Hindus and the saint of the Muslims."[5]

When they receive novices into the religion, they put a little water into their hand and make them recite some mysterious words, called a *mantra*, in other words a *tibisoli*, by virtue of which they hope to be saved.

Today, in the year 1766, they count 350 years since Nanak came into the world for this fourth time.* They claim that before the end of the world the whole human race must become Nanak Panthis, in other words, followers of his religion. The religious leaders do not offer sacrifices to idols, but they do have temples for their religious ceremonies. They are also much respected and make many disciples. They wear a white monkish habit and over this they wear a long garment like a cope, sewn from various patches of various colors. They wear a pointed little cap like a white hood.**

* Given that this passage was originally written in 1766, this would place Guru Nanak's birth in 1416. Scholars now date Nanak's birth in 1469 and his death in 1538 or 1539.

** This cope-like garment sewn from colored patches is a traditional garment of Hindu sadhus and Muslim fakirs known in Hindi as a *kantha,*

These then are the sects, or the reforms, of the Hindus that are most known in these regions. The missionary needs to be well instructed about these reforms in order to be able to confute their proponents whenever the occasion presents itself.

Because the stories of the Hindu gods are so incredible, a large part of the Hindus are convinced of the falsehood of these same gods. Such Hindus often voluntarily embrace these reforms since they do not admit gods. The Hindus can easily enter these reforms without losing their castes and tribes, and they don't have to stop performing the general ceremonies that are required and cannot be dispensed with. And this is the reason why Hindus often voluntarily become followers of one of these reforms rather than becoming Christians, since when they become Christians they no longer can observe those things that are required for them to live harmoniously among the Hindus and among their own relatives.

---

kathari, gudadi, or *alapha*. The white, pointed cap that Marco describes seems to indicate the traditional cap worn by some Muslims. Kabir is often depicted wearing such a cap, and they are sometimes worn by Kabir Panthi sadhus. Such a cap is not normally used by Sikhs. It is curious that Marco does not mention that most Sikh men, namely those initiated into the Khalsa brotherhood, wear turbans and leave their hair uncut.

Chapter 8

Some Unfortunate Encounters

It would be a never-ending task for me to write about all the things we suffered during that revolutionary time.[1] I will limit myself to three events that were among the most important that happened in the year 1763.

First, one day when we were at home in Bettiah some Christian women ran crying to us to ask us to go free a certain Christian who was in the hands of some army men. According to the women, the army men were killing him. I went out and saw the Christian who was fighting off several army soldiers. I approached them, took the Christian by the hand, and led him to our home. I shut him up in a room and did my best to persuade those military men that I would take the Christian to the nawab who would punish him if he deserved it. More than 500 of those military men gathered there with guns, spears, and arrows. They all wanted to kill that Christian, but they were unable to come up since I had closed the door to the stairs. They remained in the courtyard below and threatened us with their guns at the ready.[2] While they were trying to find some way to climb up to us, Padre Michelangelo, seeing that things were getting out of hand, snuck out of a window and went off outside the city. At the beginning of the fracas, I had sent word to an important person who was my friend, asking him to come and stop the impertinence of those men. I expected him to arrive at any moment.

Meanwhile, from the upper veranda I spoke in friendly fashion to those men, telling them that it was for the nawab to exact justice and not for them as individuals. There was no way to placate them, however, for the only thing they wanted was either to grab the Christian and kill him or to shoot me. I knew how they did things and wasn't much afraid that they would shoot me, but I saw that they had found some ladders and were beginning to climb up. By then I thought that the Christian was surely finished. I told them not to climb the ladders, but that I would come down and open the door for them. This I did. I went down the stairs and opened the door. But God does not abandon us in such situations. Just as I went out and those men ran at me with their weapons raised to strike me, my friend, the local chief to whom I had sent a call for help, arrived on horseback and entered the gate with his unsheathed saber in his hand. He was accompanied by his own men and rode up at full speed. He shouted the "Who goes there?" Everyone turned towards him and I remained free, having barely felt contact with the weapons of those people. The local chief came forward and asked what was happening. He listened to their arguments and made them sit. Then he gave them two rupees as a settlement and sent them outside of our house and the thing was finished. Some events that seem insignificant when told, however, seem like much more when one is caught up in them and such events happen to us missionaries every day.

The next thing I want to write about was that of the consequences of the wars that the fugitive raja from time to time led against the nawab's men, who were dispersed in various parts of the country. The raja tried to surprise them, first in one place and then in another. On March 28, 1763, the raja prepared his men and more than 1,000 fakirs, or naked ascetics. He crossed the River Gandak at night and surprised a camp of the Muslim army. He slaughtered many Muslims and continued on the road towards the Bettiah fort. The army in the fort, frightened by what had happened at the other camp, decided not to hold the fort but to flee immediately. That same night, therefore, the fort became empty and we did not know what to do: whether to flee or to stay on almost alone inside the fort. In the end we decided to stay and not abandon our house and church thinking that when our friend, the raja, arrived we would not suffer any harm from him nor from his men.

Unfortunately we did not know anything then about the fakirs who were with the raja.* In the morning the raja's army arrived in front of the fort and prepared to pursue the fugitive Muslims. About 200 fakirs entered the fort in order to see if any of the enemy were hidden there. They came into our house and looked through it. Not finding anything, they left. I thought that it was all finished and around evening time I went out to visit the raja, who was staying outside the fort in the countryside, and entrust our house to him. While I was outside, around nightfall, about 500 fakirs returned to our house. They grabbed Padre Michelangelo and demanded either 5,000 rupees or his life. The poor padre did not yet understand their language and was in danger of being killed. When a fakir raised his spear to open up the padre's head, he accidentally broke a pot of rice that another fakir was

* The large bands of warrior-ascetics that Marco calls "fakirs" were important actors in the wars of Hindustan in this period. In fact most were Hindus (not Muslims as the term "fakir" implies) associated with the Dasnami order of sannyasis. The best historical account of their activities is a recent book by William Pinch (2006).

carrying on his head. The two fakirs argued about this among themselves and this gave the padre time to escape and hide himself among the bulrushes of a nearby pond.

At this moment I arrived, returning from my visit to the raja. At the gate I met that mob of fakirs who jumped on me and grabbed me. They demanded from me the same 5,000 rupees or my life. I knew their language well, however, and knew how those men acted. Jesting with them, I told them I would give them not only the 5,000 rupees but also wished to give them everything in the house. I told them that they should enter the house with me and I would open up all the coffers and desks so they could take all that they wanted. I knew, however, that there were only 19 rupees in the house. The fakirs accepted my proposal and entered with me. I, however, had secretly sent someone to inform the raja so that he would intervene with the fakir chief in order to stop these men from pillaging our house. Meanwhile I placated the fakirs, telling them to take whatever they wanted and opened up for them anything that they asked. They put to one side everything they liked, but they did not find many such things and I think that in the end they would not have been satisfied. Meanwhile, around the second hour of the night the chief fakir arrived at the house, accompanied by the raja. They entered the house and made all the fakirs leave, preventing them from taking whatever was there. The fakirs were very respectful to their master or chief and left without saying a word. We escaped that time and it only cost me a small carpet that I gave to the fakir chief as our thanks. I had them call Padre Michelangelo and he came out, all wet, from the bulrushes but was so frightened that that same night he wanted to flee from the house and went out into the jungle, having more trust in the tigers than in the fakirs. He departed for Patna, and I remained in charge of the house.

I was accompanied by two fakirs whom the fakir chief had assigned to me in order to defend the house from the others should they return.

Everything remained calm enough until the third day when they were about to depart. I suspected, and was not mistaken, that the same fakirs would return as they were leaving in order to do what they had hoped. I did not have a chance to get away from the house as I had hoped to, but I hid myself in a hole where they could not find me. The very same fakirs returned and looked for me everywhere. They seized the servants and the young boys and tried to force them to tell them where I was, but fortunately no one knew. I saw the fakirs carefully search most of the possible hiding places in the house and the church, but they were unable to find me and I managed to escape them that day.

The king pursued his enemies, who finally set up camp on a plain in order to give battle. It should be noted that only about 500 men accompanied the raja in pursuit of his enemies, who were about 15,000 men. The king, by then accustomed to victory, advanced against the enemy army at midday. He fought against them and put them to flight. He killed their commander called Ramachandra and brought back the victory.[3] He was now the boss of his country, but he foresaw that he would not be able to stay there for very long since the forces of the nawab, Kasim Ali Khan, were quite superior to his own forces. He therefore returned to the fort, dug up his hidden treasures that the Muslims had been unable to find, and, with everything finished, he crossed the River Gandak and departed towards the territory of Shuja-ud-Daulah. He left, *pro forma*, some people inside the fort, but they immediately fled at the first reappearance of the Muslims. I fled with them into a dense jungle and spent the night there. The Moors were again the bosses of Bettiah and the country remained calm for some months. Two days later I re-entered our house without finding any damage.

For some days all was calm. Meanwhile Padre Michelangelo, who had fled to Patna because of the fakirs, returned. Padre Giuseppe Alfonso da Palermo, who had recently arrived from Europe, also came to Bettiah. Our tranquility did not last for long. On July 3, 1763, we were suddenly arrested by the commander of the region, who came to our house with more than 50 men. He arrested us in the name of the great nawab, Kasim Ali Khan. He surrounded the house with sentry posts and then shut up all the rooms and the church putting his seal on each door. He then put us three padres in an empty room and assigned to us a guard of 30 soldiers and ordered us to give them 10 rupees per day. Once this was done, he left without telling us anything more.

We were astonished because we had no idea of the reasons for this action. We were more astonished when the soldiers who guarded us demanded that the 10 rupees be paid immediately. I said to them: "I have money in a coffer. Allow me to open it, and I will give you the 10 rupees." "No", they replied, "everything is sealed in the name of the nawab". "Then what can I do?" "See to it yourself (*tu videris*)".* "Please allow me," I replied, "to go to some person I know and borrow the rupees and I will pay you." "No, you are under arrest. You cannot leave this place." "Then bring here some of my Christians, or some boy whom I can send to request the money. Then I will pay you." "No," they replied, "no one is to approach this place." "Then what can we do? We have no money with us."

* The Latin phrase "*tu videris*" that Marco uses here apparently comes from Matthew 27.4. It is the reply of the chief priests and elders to Judas when he came to them to request that they take back the 30 pieces of silver that he had received for betraying Jesus.

"See to it yourself (*tu videris*)" was their reply. They gave us nothing to eat or drink and refused to allow us to stand up if we were seated or to sit down if we were standing. This went on until the third day. We felt desperation, especially since we did not know the reasons for our situation. We thought that they wanted to starve us to death and offered our souls to God. By the night of the third day I don't know what we would have done if God had not intervened to help us.

On the third day around four o'clock in the afternoon, seven native soldiers appeared at the door, armed in European style. We soon learned that they had come from Patna and immediately thought that the nawab had sent them to take us to Patna. We remained calm, knowing that nothing worse could happen to us. They stopped in the middle of the courtyard and said: "Where is the Superior?" I spoke up and replied: "What do you want?" "We have a letter," they said, "from your padre prefect of Patna." We breathed a sigh of relief at his name and told them to come up. I took and read the letter.

[Padre Anselmo da Ragusa's letter told us about the third unfortunate encounter.] Before I quote from this letter, however, I have to explain the political situation. [...] The English had deposed Nawab Mir Jafar after the death of his son Miran because they were suspicious of him. They then chose Mir Kasim, or Kasim Ali Khan, as the nawab. A while after he had been appointed, Kasim Ali Khan began to think of ways to get rid of the English. On some false pretext, he began to increase his army, and seized and robbed all the biggest and richest men of the country. For all this he made use of the policies of a certain Armenian named Gregory, or Khojah Gregory, whom he declared to be his prime minister. In two or three years, Kasim Ali Khan had collected all the money of the country. He kept the English happy with some gifts, and even managed to get some support from among the English. The thing, however, was too open for the consequences not to be guessed. The English guessed them quite well, but since their own forces were weak, they didn't dare say anything nor make known their suspicions. They waited for forces to arrive from Europe, to where they had written about the situation.

Kasim Ali Khan, however, also knew about all this and tried to finish off the English before their forces arrived. He openly declared himself to be an enemy of the English and obliged them to take some action. Finally, in a secret meeting he fixed a date on which he would attack the English throughout the country, wherever they had their factories and men.

The English who stayed in the factory outside the city of Patna were warned about the date. For this reason they assaulted the city without waiting for the nawab's own assault. They ran through all the streets of the city continuously firing their artillery and muskets. Within a few hours they had become masters of the city, a city that is very big and well fortified. To their disgrace, however, due to a lack to discipline, once they saw that the enemy had fled and the city was in their hands, they failed to fortify themselves there by putting men in the bastions and at the gates. In addition, they did not think to shut the gates nor put men on guard in case the enemy returned. They all set about a general pillage of the city, which, as I have said, is very big and very rich.

It happened that there was an expedition of the nawab near the city with 15,000 Arab, Armenian and Mughal soldiers, men all armed in European style, well trained and commanded by an Armenian named Margar. The expedition had been sent to make a surprise attack on the English factory. This army was not far from the gates and met the people who were fleeing from the city, which had already been taken by the English. The commander, Margar, forced all those who were fleeing to return, and he then followed the road until he was within the gates and did not encounter any resistance on the part of the English. He advanced into the city and found the English scattered here and there, loaded down more with money than with weapons. The English were unable to reunite themselves and immediately began to flee in order to get out of the city and retreat into their factory. Margar's army, however, both the re-entering cavalry and those who had remained hidden inside the houses of the city, did not give them time to escape. Many Englishmen were killed here and there throughout the city, and those who retreated inside their factory were unable to resist the cannons of the city. By the second day they were forced to escape on some boats, hoping to escape into the territory of Shuja-ud-Daula. By the third day, however, Margar's forces had caught up with them, both by river and by land. All of them—a total of about 250, including officers, gentlemen, and soldiers—were made prisoners and were taken in irons to Monghyr,* the residence of the nawab. I will tell what happened next shortly.

Let us first return to our imprisonment and to the letter sent by the padre prefect, Anselmo da Ragusa, from Patna. In this letter he describes the progress and circumstances of the war and then writes the following:[4]

> *It was about two hours after midday where we heard a rifle shot fired into our rooms below. This made us think that the Moors were coming against our house. Terrified, we went off to the church in order to commend our souls to God, our Lord. About a half hour later, the nawab's irregular troops*

* The town of Monghyr or Munger (Marco's *Mongher*) is located on the Ganges about 120 kilometers to the east of Patna.

arrived. Some of them entered the house through the lower window and some through the wall. They entered with such fury and anger that we believed that we were about to be killed. We retreated into the sacristy, absolved ourselves for the last time, and exhorted ourselves to face death. In fact, once the sack of the house had begun, some of them entered the church with their swords and guns at the ready, thinking that we would defend ourselves. They arrived at the door of the sacristy and got ready to kill us. But then, by the will of God, our Lord, they did not do it. Instead, with the most unimaginable barbarity, they began to pillage the church and the sacristy. We, meanwhile, were expecting at any moment that this tragedy would end in our deaths, for, after the first ones had taken away everything they pillaged, a second group arrived, and then a third. All of them had weapons in their hands and threatened to finish us off. Some held us at bayonet point and told us to confess where we had our money hidden or die. Others simply menaced us, reviled us and insulted us.

The pillage was almost finished when a group of about twenty soldiers entered. Raising their naked sabers against us, they ordered me to take off my clothes. I tried to explain the impropriety of leaving me naked, but one of them violently grabbed the front of my habit and tried to tear it off me. When I saw this, I myself pulled off my habit, together with my shirt, hoping to avoid a blow from his saber. Both Padre Giovanni and Padre Giuseppe did the same, * *as did the young men Bartolomeo, Domingo and Francisco. Their only pity was to leave us our shorts. We stayed in that sad state for almost an hour, in front of so many people that it seemed that the whole city of Patna had come running to undress us.*

* These two friars must be Giovanni da Brescia and Giuseppe da Rovato.

Then other wilder men entered with their sabers unsheathed. They wanted to cut us into pieces, but one of them, as far as I could tell, stood against them and somehow parried the blows they directed against us with his sword and his arms. He effectively suggested to them that the nawab had issued no orders to kill us. They then left, still threatening and insulting us.

Finally, we decided to leave in that state, as we were, and see if in the middle of that mob we could reach the gate in order to go to the Dutch lodge. In fact, either because all of them were intent on finding booty and on pillage or because there was such a crowd, we were allowed to pass through the people and leave through the gate.

While we were in the midst of such a crowd of people, no one stopped us. But when we left there, some soldiers were seen coming towards us as we were walking on the upper road that goes to the Dutch lodge. Stepping forward, they threatened to kill us right there if we did not go back. We finally got them to bring us to the nawab, so that he could condemn us if we were guilty or could absolve us if we were innocent. They were happy to do this. We then set off for the bazaar (the public square). [...] I cannot express the great confusion that we saw when we entered the bazaar that was full of cavalry and innumerable people. They shouted abuse and curses against us, pushed us, beat us with sticks, and gave us all sorts of insults. Everyone, big and little, shouted against us. They said they wanted us killed since we were guilty of thousands of deaths. In fact they would have massacred us many times over if the soldiers who were leading us had not stopped their attempts. They, in fact, hoped to receive some good reward for bringing us alive to the nawab.

We were forced to walk a good mile from our house up to the western gate of the city while suffering pains almost worse than death itself. Finally we reached the presence of the nawab, who was returning with his cavalry. When he saw us in so deplorable a state that even the tigers would have taken pity on us, he indicated to us that it was not his intention to reduce us to this state and gave orders that no one should continue to treat our persons badly. He told the same soldiers who had brought us to bring us back to the nawab's fort that was three miles distant.

Thus we were again forced to go from the western gate of the city to the eastern gate in the middle of that great crowd consisting of cavalry, irregular soldiers, and the people. We were naked and barefoot and had to walk through mud that reached up to mid-calf. They forced us to walk forward, shoving us, sticking the barrels of their rifles in our backs, and hitting us with their rifle butts. It was impossible to stop the people and almost all of them directed insults against (us) from the shops and the balconies. We finally arrived at the fort where they seemed to have all the Europeans in their hands. We again received many distressing abuses that I will not write about.

We remained in this situation in the middle of a crowd of soldiers and other people until about 23 hours by our Italian clock. We looked for someone who knew us and might tell the nawab that we were here in the fort in this ridiculous situation, but we found no one. Everyone wanted our blood. Finally the nawab arrived, and luckily for us Margar, the Armenian commander, was with him. Margar was pained by the spectacle of our situation. He made us come before the nawab and convinced him to free us and end our troubles. The nawab left us in his care. He consoled us and gave us seven brave soldiers from his garrison to take us home again with orders for them to kill whoever might wish to insult and harm us and to stop the people from sacking our house.

We then returned to our house, but we found it so badly sacked that it was a miracle that the main walls were still standing. If we had arrived a day later, not a single brick of the hospice would have been left. Since we could have only thrown ourselves down naked on the naked earth, we appealed to the Dutchmen to give us some used clothing in order to cover ourselves and asked them to send us something to eat to restore us. In fact, Mr. Bacheracht sent us three tunics and caps, shorts, and handkerchiefs, and, in the evening, a loaf of bread with a piece of meat.[5] *In addition, the poor local Christians got us some cots and some cushions. To sum up, downhearted and troubled we threw ourselves down to rest.*

I remain the devoted servant of Your Reverend Padres,
Brother Anselmo, Capuchin, your unworthy Prefect.
Patna, June 30, 1763.

When we three padres in Bettiah had read this letter, we understood why we were still kept as prisoners. [...][6]

The seven soldiers who came from Patna with the prefect's letter had been sent by the prefect himself, without him having known about our imprisonment, so that they could bring back to Patna some implements for saying Mass. The seven soldiers made themselves our protectors. They told the men who were guarding us about everything that had happened in our house in Patna. They explained that this had happened because of the inadvertence of the nawab, but that when he learned what happened to us he had ordered that whoever had taken something from the padres' house should return it immediately. Otherwise he would have to return 20 times [the value of what he had taken]. The nawab warned them to take care not to make him angry against them.

When the men in Bettiah learned all this, they began to give us something to eat and to drink and allowed us to speak with someone in order to pay them their 10 rupees per day. I asked them to tell us what orders they needed so that they could set us free. They replied that an order from Margar, the

Armenian commander in Patna, would be enough for them. I immediately wrote to that gentleman, who immediately sent his orders to set us free. But then the men in Bettiah said that this was not enough, and that they need orders from the nawab of Patna, Mehndi Ali Khan. I wrote again and immediately sent to Patna a request for his order to free us. When the order came, however, the men still did not want to acknowledge it. Now they said they needed an order from the great nawab at Monghyr, Kasim Ali Khan. I wrote to that nawab and within 10 days the order came, not only to set us free, but also to return everything to us and, in addition, for them to give us 400 rupees of their own money as restitution for the suffering they had unjustly caused us. The men then set us free and gave us back the keys to the house and its rooms. As for the 400 rupees, however, they procrastinated for several days and finally fled without giving us anything. In the end, we had lost the 220 rupees that we had had to pay them for 22 days at the rate of 10 rupees per day, rupees that they had told us that they would return if the nawab's reply was in our favor. Nonetheless, their flight was payment enough. I say their flight, because I need to tell here what happened to the Englishmen that the Moors captured in Patna.

Chapter 9

A Massacre, a New Caste, Buxar

The same day that these events took place in Patna, the English were attacked in all their other factories in the country.[1] They only managed to hold Calcutta, the strongest of their settlements, and the armies ran towards it from all sides. The English in Calcutta, however, did not wait for the Moors to arrive there. As soon as they heard what had happened at Patna, they marched out of Calcutta. Their army had only about 300 Europeans and 3,000 native soldiers. It seemed impossible that so small an army could go up against the nawab's army, which had more than 80,000 men including Europeans, Armenians, Arabs, Mughals, and native soldiers, all of them armed and trained, for some time, in European style, with good artillery and confident because of the victory reported in Patna. The English moved against them all this notwithstanding. They met for the first time near Plassey.* The English almost lost the battle, but eventually reported a victory either by means of a counterattack or by means of their shrewdness.

* Plassey, or Palasi, is the place where the English fought one of their first important battles against Siraj-ud-Daula, the nawab of Bengal, in 1757. As has been noted, that victory was won mostly by bribing Mir Jafar, the nawab's main general.

The English advanced and the Moors withdrew to Sakrigali or to Ruanalà, a very difficult route.* There the Moors positioned themselves and the English did not dare to attack. They both remained there 15 days, each army defying the other. Two hundred Frenchmen, who were in the service of the English, requested their commander, Adam[s],** to let them go around some hills at night and then attack the Moor army from the rear. They did this and succeeded marvelously. They sowed terror among the Moors who didn't know where to turn. Meanwhile the English forced their way forward and together the English and French slaughtered many Moors, who could only defend themselves by fleeing.

When the news of these two English victories was reported, the English began to believe that they could succeed in their endeavors. Their army increased in size as those who had dispersed throughout the territories joined it. The frightened nawab began to foresee his ruin. He summoned the English prisoners from Patna into his presence. He proposed that they mediate a settlement, but they replied that they had been too much at fault for having allowed themselves to be captured in Patna and for this reason their compatriots would not want to listen to them.

The nawab wrote to the English, telling them that if they advanced further against him, he would have all the prisoners killed. The English did not reply to this but continued advancing on the road until they reached the fort at Monghyr. They attacked it and captured it. The nawab, who was three leagues away at the time, left his armies behind and withdrew

* Sakrigali or Sakrigali Ghat (Marco's *Sacrigali*) is a town on the Ganges about 75 kilometers to the east of Bhagalpur. Marco's *Ruanalà* could not be identified.

** This officer is probably Thomas Adams (1730–64).

finally to Patna with the intention of making his last stand in that city. Patna is a large city, a good three leagues in circumference. On one side is the Ganges River, which makes it unapproachable. The rest of the city is surrounded by a great trench with double bastions placed at intervals. It has a castle with a double enclosure and is well fortified. Here then, his forces assembled, and he resolved to wait for the English. They arrived and attacked the castle with big cannons of 36 [pound balls]. Within eight days they made a breach [in the walls]. On the ninth day they attacked with the fire of hell and captured it. On that same day the city began to be depopulated. The English advanced through the streets where their artillery had caused great carnage. In the end, the Moors all fled and the English became the masters of the city. They were, however, much more attentive to their duty than the English who had earlier taken the city in the month of June. Our own padres, having learned from their own example, did not remain in our house, but in those dangerous days always stayed in the Dutch factory.

While we have been following the march of the English up to Patna, however, we left the poor English prisoners in leg irons in the hands of the nawab. He was so furious because of his own ruin that he couldn't wait for their death. In fact, when the English advanced on Patna, Nawab Kasim Ali Khan gave the order to kill all the prisoners. At the time they numbered about 250. The nawab's subalterns protested to him that to do this was against the law and that the English would never pardon such an act. For these reasons none of his officers wanted to take charge of this operation. Only one German European, named Samru, presented himself to the nawab and asked him to give him the commission. Once he obtained it, Samru killed those prisoners with unheard of barbarism. Some of them were cut to pieces and others killed with musket shots within the prison. Then he threw all their corpses, almost 250 of them, into a well.*

The English, once they had taken the city of Patna, pursued the Moor army up to the river Karamnasa,** which was the border between the lands of the region [and the territory of the kingdom of Awadh]. The nawab, Kasim Ali Khan, then took refuge in the city of Lucknow with the nawab of Awadh, Shuja-ud-Daula. The Mughal emperor was also there.# These three great personalities—the emperor, the wazir Shuja-ud-Daula and Kasim Ali Khan—then began to prepare their return together against the English.

Meanwhile, back in Bettiah the Moors who had made us prisoners heard the news about what had happened in our hospice in Patna and about the flight of Nawab Kasim Ali Khan, their own sovereign. They then fled from Bettiah and immediately afterward the raja himself, Dhrub Singh's grandson Jugal Kishore, re-entered the kingdom from the other side of the Gandak River where he had remained a fugitive. Once he entered the city, Jugal Kishore wrote to the English who replied that he should look after his kingdom and remain friends with them, etc.

During the wars in Patna, many Christians from there had come to stay in Bettiah. They settled in a small town called Salempur.## The padre prefect then wrote to me to go there to

* Although this 1763 massacre of English troops at Patna is now largely forgotten, for many years it was a great scandal among the English and other Europeans, rivaling the fame of the 1756 incident known as the "Black Hole of Calcutta." See Firminger 1909 and Brown 2006.

** The Karamnasa (Marco's *Carmnasà*) is a small river that feeds into the Ganges from the southwest near Buxar (Baksar).

This was Shah Alam II (ruled 1759–1806).

Salempur (Marco's *Selampur*) is evidently the town by this name on the south bank of the Gandak River about 45 kilometers to the southeast of Bettiah.

assist them. Padre Michelangelo and Padre Giuseppe Alfonso remained behind in our Bettiah hospice. I left for Salempur in the company of Padre Tranquillo and Brother Lorenzo. They were coming from Nepal and were on their way to Patna and from there to Bengal. From Bengal they hoped to leave for Europe if they found an opportunity. I remained in Salempur for only a few months. In December Padre Michelangelo left for Nepal with the padre prefect and Padre Giuseppe da Rovato. Padre Alfonso left for Chandernagore since he had been elected Superior and Agent of that place. I was recalled to Bettiah in order to care for the Christians distributed in various places of the kingdom.

The turbulence of the wars by then had calmed down somewhat. Insofar as possible I reassembled the Christians. I tried to rekindle their former fervor, weakened by the many events of the wars. For this purpose I established a brotherhood composed of all the important men so that they could take charge of ensuring that all the religious customs introduced by our former padres were observed. In addition, they were to judge and punish the delinquents. I encouraged them to form together a single caste, namely a body of Christians who would eat together without keeping any allegiance to their Hindu castes. Formerly, each person stayed in his own caste and they only assembled together in church. This was because they were more concerned not to offend or disgust their castes than their own religion. By means of these assemblies, over which I presided, however, they accommodated all their differences. The raja has never wanted, nor wants, to be involved in the affairs of the Christians. Rather, he turns everything over to the missionary, who does not always have at his disposal the means necessary for the punishments. But the assembly of all the Christians together condemns the guilty persons without their being able to protest. The procedure is customary for all castes, each of which makes their own judgments, except in criminal cases which are the business of the king.

Things were going quite well. The young king governed the country peacefully and he was a friend to us. The Christians were submissive to religious things and there was an adequate number of catechumens. Then in the month of March, 1764, almost all Hindustan armed itself against the English. The Emperor, the wazir, Shuja-ud-Daula, and Kasim Ali Khan, all joined together and set out for Patna with a very big army. This caused great consternation among the English, who supposed that they were lost. They all withdrew to Patna and fortified themselves as well as they could.

Leaving the English for now in their preparations, I want to tell the story of how news reached us here in Bettiah on March 15, that the padre prefect and his two companions had been arrested on their way to Nepal and were prisoners at Nuwakot.* This rumor upset me more than the news of the war against the English. I sent people to various places to find out what they could. In the end I learned that only 25 bearers had been arrested and had been held for 20 days. I wrote to the raja of Nuwakot, sending him some gifts, and they were freed.

Meanwhile, the big Moor army was advancing. They claim that it had 300,000 combatants including the service of 500 Europeans and 500 cannons, both big and small ones. With these troops was the German, Samru, who commanded 30,000 sepoys of Kasim Ali Khan. Also present was Monsieur Gentil, a French officer, who commanded the European troops

* This Nuwakot (Marco's *Novocot*) is a town about 20 kilometers to the northwest of Kathmandu.

of Shuja-ud-Daula.* Shuja-ud-Daula himself commanded 80,000 cavalry. Things, in short, were such that the English were quite frightened. The great army approached Patna. It attacked the city, but at a distance because the English army was stationed outside the walls somewhere near the city. Shuja-ud-Daula twice advanced against the English but both times he was driven back. He stayed there in this project for three months. Then, with the coming of the rainy season, he retreated to Buxar in Bhojpur.** His aim was to resume the siege of Patna in the following month of October. Meanwhile the English organized themselves, not to wait for their enemies' return, but to leave the city of Patna and go to find them at Buxar in their very entrenchment. The English ordered all their forces from Bombay, Madras, and the other factories to join them. All of them assembled in Patna and on October 5 they left the city and started their campaign.

A rumor had spread that if the emperor was unable to take Patna he planned to pillage the whole country. Therefore, once I had taken care of the business of the house and Christians in Bettiah, I went off to Patna to stay with Padre Giovanni and see the result of the military campaign. Major Munro

* This Monsieur Gentil (Marco writes "Gentile") is Jean-Baptiste-Joseph Gentil or, more fully, Guillaume-Joseph-Hyacinthe-Jean-Baptiste Le Gentil de la Galaziere (1725–92). He was an agent for the French government at the court of Shuja-ud-Daula at Faizabad from 1765–75.

** Buxar, more accurately transcribed as Baksar, is on the south bank of the Ganges about half way between Patna and Benares. Bhojpur, the town which gives its name to the region, is located about 20 kilometers east of Buxar. The battle fought at Buxar on October 22, 1764 between the English army and the coalition of the Mughal emperor, Shuja-ud-Daula, and Kasim Ali Khan made the English the masters of most of northeastern India and confirmed them as the greatest military power in the subcontinent.

said that this would be the decisive campaign and that he was going to risk all for all.

The English advanced towards the Son River, a very big river and a navigable one.* There they thought they would encounter the Moor army, but this army was not seen anywhere. They crossed the river and advanced three more days' journey and still did not encounter anyone. They finally arrived at Buxar and camped in front of the enemy lines. The English stayed there three days, inviting the enemy to come out. But the Moors, entrenched behind their picket fences, were not willing to come out. They hoped that they could outwait the English at that place without any risk and that once the English army began to retreat, they would pursue them without pause.

In fact the opposite happened. The English left 200 sepoys and a few Europeans there to continue firing at the Moors. The main body of the English army circled around to take the Moor army from behind and succeeded in doing this quite well. Meanwhile, the Moors, when they saw the fire from the English weakening, thought that they had fled. The Moors immediately advanced in order to pursue them. In fact they did massacre the few sepoys who were in front of them and set about sacking their camp. But then suddenly the main body of the English army entered the battle from behind the picket fences. They captured the Moors' cannons and kept up a hellish fire against them. Many in the Moor army were slaughtered. Confused and not knowing what to do, the Moors began to flee.

Unfortunately, there was only one bridge over which to escape from that place and this had been broken by a great

* The Son River enters the Ganges from the south about 40 kilometers to the west of Patna.

number of elephants. Many Moors were lost in that river. From one side came the fire of the English artillery. On the other side the English had 50 boats, each armed with five cannons and 100 rifles. Together they decimated the Moors who were unable to reunite. In fact the Moors left all their baggage. The English profited so well from this that there was hardly a soldier who did not take away things worth more than 10,000 rupees.

We and the [other European] persons who remained in the city of Patna were all on boats, awaiting the first news of the army and ready to flee immediately to Bengal if the English lost. Eventually the news arrived with a short note from the commander, Major Munro. The note said: "At this point I can report that the battle is ended and I am in pursuit of the enemy." In these events the emperor was taken prisoner by the English and Shuja-ud-Daula and Kasim Ali Khan fled. During this battle, 50,000 Moors remained dead on the battlefield and 630 of the English army, including both Europeans and sepoys, did the same. The battle was fought on October 26, 1764.* After this news had arrived and I saw that things were in a good state and that there was no longer any fear that the Moors would disrupt the country, I immediately departed for to Bettiah where I found that our house and the Christians had not suffered any mishaps.

The padre prefect arrived in Bettiah from Nepal and remained here until the Epiphany, after which he left for Patna. He then called me to Patna as well, saying that he was obliged to go to Bengal, called there by Padre Giovanni who had gone there to seek funds to restore the losses suffered when our house in Patna was sacked. I went to Patna, but

* As noted, the battle of Buxar, took place on October 22, 1764. It is not clear why Marco dates it four days later.

the prefect did not leave that place for Bengal. After eight days, namely on April 2, 1765, I returned to Bettiah where I remained alone, fulfilling my obligations to these Christians and the people of the country. Things have been going well and the raja is content.

Chapter 10

The English Take Bettiah

After winning the famous battle of Buxar, the English pursued the enemy as far as Benares in the territory of Shuja-ud-Daula.[1] Near Benares there was another battle. Shuja-ud-Daula himself did not dare to stop his own retreat or to again directly engage the English. Instead he hired 20,000 naked fakirs found in his territory to unleash a battle against the English. These fakirs were intrepid warriors and animated by the zeal of their religion which had been insulted by the infidels (as they called the Europeans). The fakirs prepared themselves for battle, a battle that proved to be the fiercest the English ever had. The fakirs showed no fear of the English artillery and rifle fire and advanced right up to the English bayonets. Luckily for the English, they had surrounded themselves with [defense works called] *chevaux de frise*. Otherwise they would have been undone. But the fakirs were unable to pass through these *chevaux de frise* and were obliged to stop their advance. At this point they could no longer withstand the English fire and wanted to retreat, but the English had 500 Mughal cavalry in the rear and ordered them to advance. The cavalry then massacred almost all the fakirs. This completed the perfect victory of the English who no longer have anyone to oppose them.

The English saw that they had taken more territory than they could defend over the course of time and decided to come to an accommodation with the nawab, Shuja-ud-Daula. Accordingly, they restored him to his own country on certain conditions that were advantageous to them. They involved a certain Monsieur Gentil, a French officer who was with Shuja-ud-Daula.* Monsieur Gentil initiated talks with the fugitive nawab about an accommodation with the English. Gentil's involvement succeeded to the satisfaction of both sides. Nawab Shuja-ud-Daula was obliged to swear friendship with the English. If the nawab needed the English to help him defend his country, the costs would be charged to the nawab. If, however, the English needed the help of the nawab, this would also be at the nawab's expense. It was also agreed that the nawab would give the English a number of presents and surrender to them the forts of Chunargarh and Rohtasgarh.** The English were to surrender Allahabad to the nawab, but for various reasons they did not surrender it until the year 1773.# This agreement was made in the city of Chapra## in the month of October, 1765. It was also agreed that the emperor would remain in the English camp as a prisoner and that after five years had passed, the English would take him and put him on the throne in Delhi and subjugate any rebels

* On this Monsieur Gentil, see above p. 104.

** Chunargarh or Chunar (Marco's *Cinargar*) is a famous fort and town on the Ganges about 25 kilometers south-southwest of Benares. Rohtasgarh (Marco's *Rotasgar*) is a town and fort on the Son River about 130 kilometers southeast of Benares.

The city of Allahabad is about 120 kilometers west of Benares in the present state of Uttar Pradesh. Marco gives the name in the rather unusual spelling *Eleabas*.

The city of Chapra or Chhapra (Marco's *Ciaprà*) is located on the north bank of the Ganges about 50 kilometers to the northwest of Patna.

against him. Meanwhile they assigned 5,000,000 rupees a year to him for his living expenses. Once this was done, the English withdrew to their own territory and the country was at peace.

At this point the padre prefect recalled me from Bettiah to Patna where I arrived on June 3, 1765, the season of the greatest heat. Because of the heat I got sick in Patna with a burning fever that lasted from June 5 until July 27. The course of the fever put me near death. Once I was cured, however, I left again for Bettiah on September 16. While I was crossing the Ganges in a small boat, I was caught by a storm so strong that I thought myself to be lost, as almost 3,000 boats were lost in various places of those crossings. Luckily, however, we were carried to a sand bar in the middle of the river, where we stayed for four days without being able to go either forward or back. We had to stay there in the water holding the boat with our hands so that it was not carried off by the wind and water. Once I had crossed the river, I arrived at the Dutch factory in Singia where I remained for five days while the waters receded.* After this I left and returned to Bettiah on September 30, 1765.

The raja of Bettiah now governed his country with the consent of the English. The country is partly subject to Patna, which was also controlled by the English. They then wrote to him to send them an appropriate amount of money. The raja made various excuses and delayed the payment under various pretexts. This disposed the English to make war against him.

Then Colonel Barker came to Bettiah and advanced towards the fort. Meanwhile, the raja's mother fled with the treasure

* The town of Singia (Marco's *Singhia*) in Bihar is located about halfway between Monghyr and Darbhanga. Little is known about a Dutch factory there.

and went into the mountains near Palpà.* The raja remained with his people and prepared to defend them against the English. When Colonel Barker came close to Bettiah, he wrote me a letter asking me to come out of the fort that he was going to attack. After I received the letter, I spoke to the raja and he gave me permission to leave. He also asked me to accompany his ambassador in order to make an accommodation with the English colonel. The ambassador came with me and I presented him to the colonel. The colonel, however, didn't wish to hear about accommodation and indicated that he would present himself at the fort. If the raja then came out by himself, the colonel would make an accommodation with him. This he did. He presented himself at the fort, arrayed his cannons, and had the raja informed that if he came out in person, they could make an accommodation. The raja asked him to wait until the following morning, but that he would come out. This was agreed in the afternoon and I remained with the colonel in his tent.

During the night the raja and his men fled. Then the English attacked the fort and sacked it the same night. I was very worried about our house and the Christians. I requested the colonel that some soldiers accompany me into the fort in order to guard the house. The colonel told me there was nothing to fear, but said that he did not judge it expedient to send me there at that time since everyone was in arms. After about two hours, the firing in the city stopped. Then the colonel gave me four sepoys to accompany me and protect our hospice. When we arrived at the hospice, we found it had been completely sacked. All the Christians, big and little, stripped to the skin, had taken refuge in the church. The house was full of English sepoys. It was impossible to make them

* This Palpà could not be identified. It is presumably located in Nepal.

leave. They left from one part, but then they entered another. My four sepoys were caught between two sides: that of their companions, who were sacking the place, and my own, who were opposing them.

The worst problem was that an English officer had ordered his sepoys to grab some women and they were doing their best to snatch a few. I kept all of the women around me, but since there were many sepoys, when I let go of one of the women on one side, they dragged off another on the other side. I fought in this way for more than two hours. This was February 22, 1766, at the height of the cold season. I immediately sent a message to the colonel asking him to send more men to our defense. Dawn was breaking and the colonel came himself with other officers. When he saw the pillage, he consoled me and told me not to fear. He would have everything returned to me.

I asked him to assign some trustworthy men to me to accompany our Christians out of the city. He immediately ordered an officer to give me men for this purpose. Unfortunately it was the same officer who had wanted to carry off some of the women. This officer coaxed me to wait a little and then he would assign some men to me. His real intention was to wait until the afternoon and then carry off some women into the forest through which they had to pass. I foresaw his bad intentions and had the Christians leave just after midday and accompanied them alone. I ran the risk of being admonished, and I was, but I persuaded the colonel with the same argument. Then I led the Christians quite far away and put them in a secure place. In the end they did not lose anything except their goods and ornaments. In the sack of our house, the English sepoys discharged some rifles, but only one Muslim woman who had taken refuge with some

Christians in the cemetery was killed. Other rifles fired both in the church and in the rooms did not hit anyone. Thanks be to God I was not in the house that night. If I had been, I don't know what might have happened. May God save us from this sort of encounters, particularly at night time.

The next day I petitioned the same colonel, asking him to repair the damages to our house and those of our Christians. The colonel then had 200 rupees delivered to me for present necessities and asked me to prepare an account of all that had been lost, whether broken or stolen; and also [to prepare an account] for the Christians, so they could be paid back as well. I prepared the account. It amounted to 1,900 rupees, including the damages to our house, the church and the Christians. The colonel then appointed another raja as the governor of the country and gave him orders to assign a village to our Christians. The income from this village would be used to restore the damages. I was to be in charge of distributing this income. I wrote immediately to the prefect [asking him what I should do]. He replied giving me his consent to accept the village, but only until the damages had been repaid and not further.

The colonel and the new raja had in fact written a document assigning the village [to the Mission] in perpetuity and this document had been passed on to the nawab of Patna. I kept it for only one year and a half, after which I reinstated everything according to the previous accounts. Afterwards, I delivered the document to the nawab of Patna. He, however, did not want to receive it, saying that the village had been donated in perpetuity by order of the colonel and that he did not want to fall into disgrace with that gentleman. The English governor, who was present, advised me that if, for personal scruples, I did not want to have the village in my name, I could leave it abandoned for the Christians.* When I told him that the village was too big for the Christians he offered to change it for a smaller one. To this I said: "You know our Christians. You should arrange things as you think best." The governor himself then assigned us another village called Chuhari. Our Christians still hold this village. Later the Christians from Nepal took refuge there, a story I will tell shortly.**

Meanwhile, I remained at Bettiah to take care of the mission. The many recent wars had weakened the mission and depopulated the country. Everyone was unhappy about the property they had lost and, even more, about the dramatic increase in their taxes. These grew so much that those inhabitants, or peasants, who formerly paid two within two years found themselves having to pay ten. The increased harshness of the government—a surprise to these people who were accustomed to the mildness of the Hindu government—provoked more revolutions. Factions were formed, but all of them ended in causing more harm to the inhabitants.

In January of 1757 an Englishman called Mr. Droz had come there to preside over the country, but things had not gone well. The Moor governor protested that if the English paid attention to the lamentations of the inhabitants, [they would see that] he was unable to pay the 500,000 rupees that he had promised to pay each year. For this reason things continued the same as before. This gentleman departed for Calcutta and another one came in his place. This was a Mr. Golding, a young man of much talent and a good disposition. He did whatever he could to keep the country content, but

* Probably the sense here is that Marco could release the tenants who lived in the village and then let the Bettiah Christians settle the land.

** The town of Chuhari is located about 12 kilometers to the north of Bettiah. Chuhari is still populated by the descendants of the Nepali Christians who arrived there in 1769.

without being able to reduce the taxes, so that the country kept getting more depopulated each day and the interests of the mission were going no better. The Christians, however, found themselves in a quite good situation since the gentleman used them for various commercial services. I had a close friendship with that gentleman and used it, as far as possible, to promote the good of the public, the Christians and the mission. I believed that it would be possible to accomplish much by this means. I thought that when the people of the country no longer feared being persecuted by their caste, they would be more easily converted. For that reason I did not fail to encourage them to make use of the occasion. Nonetheless, for one reason or another I did not see during those times any big increase in the number of Christians. Perhaps this was because God does not want to make use of human means, or perhaps it was because the bad conduct of the Europeans in those regions offset the doctrine taught by the missionaries.

From this, I inferred that apostolic preaching throughout the cities and the villages is the best way to make conversions among the Hindus (*gentili*). In addition, long experience had taught me that the missionary who lives a poor and lowly life will have more success than the one who lives with decorum and grandeur. Since I was alone in Bettiah, I had little time for preaching and in the city there were no other people except military men or Bengali merchants, with whom one could do nothing. Much to my regret, then, I was obliged, one could say, to lose two years of time, during which I dedicated myself particularly to translating various Hindu books. [...]

Chapter 11

Troubles Everywhere

Since I was now alone in Bettiah and Padre Giovanni da Brescia was alone in Patna, I went to Patna once every six months so we could make our confessions to each other.[1] During the five-day journey I also conducted a small mission in the villages along the route. Since the year 1762, Nepal had been besieged, or at least blockaded by the Gorkha raja named Prithvi Narayan. The subjects of Nepal were discontented with their own raja, Jaya Prakash, and wanted to depose him. They failed, however, in spite of several attempts. For this reason they invited the Gorkha raja to help them in this project. Prithvi Narayan accepted the proposal, but since he was very astute and clever and inclined to conquer that kingdom, he began to find pretexts to take possession of several remote forts located in the mountains. Then he began to close the entrance and exit from the Valley of Nepal. He quietly took possession of other posts around this valley and finally, in 1768, he entered the valley itself. He took possession of various provinces and become the lord of the countryside.

The Nepalese by then had become aware of his plan, but it was too late. He had not come simply to help, but rather to usurp the country. Prithvi Narayan deceitfully took a fortified village (*castello*) called Kirtipur* on top of a mountain. The village surrendered under a good agreement and conditions, but Prithvi Narayan, once he had it in his hands, wanted to take revenge for an arrow fired many years before. Then, during a war, they had shot one of his brothers in the eye. For this reason, he ordered that all the inhabitants, big and small, men and women, were to have their noses and lips cut off. This was immediately done without any mercy. Our padres were too late to obtain a pardon for them. This was the most barbarous act that had ever been heard of in these countries. They say that the noses and lips weighed 70 pounds.

The declared usurper, Prithvi Narayan, then advanced against the three capital cities of the valley, each with its own separate government. He reinforced the blockade and did not let anyone either enter or leave. Through duplicity, he used some persons to defeat the others. Misery and poverty continued increasing in the three cities, particularly in Kathmandu, the city of King Jaya Prakash. Four of our padres were in that city: Padre Serafino da Como, Padre Michelangelo da Tabiago, Padre Giovanni Gualberto da Massa, and Padre Giuseppe da Rovato. They had to share the common misery in spite of the fact that Padre Michelangelo had a close friendship with the son of the Gorkha raja, Prithvi Narayan. Each day this padre went to the son of Prithvi Narayan and got help from him to bring into the city all the necessary supplies for our house and for the Christians. In spite of all this, however, the effects of five years of blockade were undoubtedly felt by everyone.

I was in Bettiah and was well aware of the miseries of our fathers in Nepal. From time to time I sent to them men who

* The town of Kirtipur (Marco's *Kirtpur*) is located very close to Kathmandu.

carried provisions such as clothes, wine, sugar and dried fish. But since the passes in the mountains were formally closed, the guards wanted many documents and many gifts before they would let the men pass. Nonetheless, I did whatever I could to help the padres, and thanks to God only a few things were lost. Also, few of the messengers were harmed, except for one who was put into leg irons for six months without my knowing where he was, or how he had been arrested. Finally I found out and wrote to Prithvi Narayan, who had him freed. These expeditions cost me much expense, but there was good weather in Bettiah, and this helped furnish me with all that I needed.

Each day Raja Prithvi Narayan made further progress towards Nepal. Little by little, in a perfect and cruel siege, he reduced the three cities without the Nepalese knowing how to unite to oppose him as they should have done. In the end, Raja Jaya Prakash saw that his subjects neither wished to nor were able to free themselves from this tyrannical usurper, and he wrote to the English in Patna, begging them to free him from his enemy aggressor and promising them money and lands in Nepal.

The English, made greedy by such promises, hoped that a good foothold in that place would enable them to open a land route to China, or at least gain access to the Tibetan gold mines. They immediately sent an army of 3,000 sepoys together with sufficient Europeans for the artillery, sergeants and officers appropriate for this arduous expedition. It was commanded by Major Kinloch.* He was, I think, too impetuous and too

* In his diary, Major George Kinloch mentions meeting Marco on August 17, 1767, before the expedition left for Nepal (f. 5b): "This day I was visited by Padrey Mark an Italian Mission [*sic*], but I had little or no material Intelligence with regard to the Napaul [*sic*] Country from him." Marco's account here suggests, however, that Kinloch proceeded to Nepal

eager to reach Nepal, and he departed against the season, in other words, in the month of August exactly when the rains were strongest and there was a bad wind towards the mountains. In addition, he traveled by a route unknown to him and one of the most difficult. The rivers and fields were full of water and the difficulty of carrying supplies slowed down their progress. Prithvi Narayan, who was the master of all those mountains, had time to close all the passes. These are such that 10 men armed only with stones can repel 20,000.

When the English arrived, they found all the posts occupied. They tried to conquer them, but they lost many men and were repulsed from all the various passes that they attacked during a period of 15 days. Their supply routes were cut to prevent the arrival of their supplies. The raja of Nepal, who had promised to send them skilled men to guide them through the mountains, was unable to learn about when and where the English were advancing. All the messengers that the English sent were captured before they could get through the mountain passes. In the end the English saw that they would not be able to advance further and were forced to retreat and depart from those mountains and return to the plains. They occupied a small fort that the mountain people had in that region and remained there in the hopes of receiving help from Patna. Since the air in that place is very bad, however, within a few months most of them had died.

Commander Kinloch, himself now near death, wrote to me in Bettiah, begging me to go to see him. I replied that in that place and time, it was too great a risk because of the bad air. I excused myself in this way the first time, but he repeated his request a second time, saying that he really

---

against Marco's advice, with disastrous consequences for Kinloch himself and for the expedition.

needed to see me before dying. I assumed then that he was a Catholic and that he wished to confess without being able to explain this in his letters since secret Catholics could not state such things openly. For that reason I went to him, taking all possible precautions. I traveled in a *Dolì* (a native palanquin) and took good water from Bettiah so I never had to drink the local water. After I arrived, I stayed there only one day and two nights. The next day he left for Patna and I returned to Bettiah. He died one day later during his journey.* After I returned to Bettiah, I got a putrid and mortal fever for six months and thought I would die from it.

Only a few sepoys remained in the English expedition, because these were changed from time to time. Lacking any help from Patna, the expedition returned there and no more thought was given to Nepal.

Then Raja Prithvi Narayan, more glorious than ever, assembled his forces against Nepal. The fears of our padres who were in Nepal began to increase a great deal since Raja Prithvi Narayan had become furious against the English and against anyone who was a European. Raja Jaya Prakash began to lose hope, both for his city of Kathmandu and for his own life. Many military men of the city left in order to join the besiegers. Fear and misery grew throughout the city.

In Bettiah I had become very worried about our padres and sent messenger after messenger, but they were all either stopped or sent back without being able to reach Nepal. I also sent gifts to Raja Prithvi Narayan, but his replies were either equivocal or not encouraging. Nonetheless, I continued

* George Kinloch died in 1768. The manuscript of his narrative of the expedition breaks off in mid-sentence in the entry for October 17, 1767, and hence does not mention Marco's final visit. At the time of writing his last entry, Kinloch was already suffering from a severe fever.

to manage to have the things I sent to our padres from Bettiah reach them. I sent a bag (*fatto*)* in order to get letters [to them], but the raja was more astute and sent the bag but stopped the letters, even examining the contents of the bottles.

Around the end of September, 1768, Raja Prithvi Narayan advanced so close to Kathmandu that, with some help from persons inside, he forced the gates and entered the city. I will not say anything about the carnage unleashed when he entered, nor about how terrified our padres were. I will only mention that Padre Michelangelo had convinced Prithvi Narayan's son to send some men to protect our house as soon as they entered the city. He did this quite punctually, something that would have been difficult to manage even among our people in Europe. With the help of those men, our house and padres were saved from any harm or loss. The enemy army then advanced towards the royal palace. Raja Jaya Prakash, who was inside, escaped by some secret door and fled to Bhatgaon (another city that was not then besieged). As he fled, he received a gunshot in his arm. This did not seem to be dangerous, but a few days later he died without ever falling into the hands of his enemy. Perhaps, as they say, he took poison that he had prepared some time earlier, or perhaps some other means were used.

This then is the situation. Kathmandu, the capital city of Nepal, was in the hands of the Gorkhas, led by Raja Prithvi Narayan. He caused a great pillage both of the royal treasury and in the entire city. He seized all the important persons as his prisoners and sent them to his own fort, Nuwakot, with excellent promises. He consoled the inhabitants [of Kathmandu] for the time being, assuring them that he himself

* Marco's word *fatto* is probably derived from the Hindi-Urdu word *fota,* meaning "a bag."

would reside in the city and that he wanted to make it greater rather than to bring it down. With such beautiful promises, he won over the inhabitants and protected himself against any threatening revolution. Once everything was agreed according to his liking, he left to make another city surrender. This was Patan.* He again offered beautiful promises and subjected the city to his control. He sent all the important persons as his prisoners to another fort in his country. After this, he marched against the [third] city, Bhatgaon. He made it surrender in the same way. In the end he had the whole country and all the forts in his hands. In addition, all the important persons were his prisoners. He wanted to make permanent his conquest of the country and his residence in Nepal. He then killed all the important persons and their entire families in the most barbarous manner. He stripped them of all their possessions. He oppressed the inhabitants with gross impositions. He confiscated all their hereditary property. He made everyone work the land equally and pay taxes to the prince, as is the custom in Hindustan. To sum up, he reduced the country to misery and slavery.

Let us return now to our padres, who with great pain were spectators to so many different cruelties. God preserved and conserved them during the harsh five-year blockade, including a two-year siege, and finally, not only during the bloody assault but even more from the fury of a tyrant who raged against all Europeans, not knowing how to distinguish one European nation from another. Only the habits and ministry of these padres defended them from all these dangers.

* Patan, Kathmandu, and Bhatgaon (mentioned above) are three neighboring cities in the Kathmandu Valley. At the time, they were ruled as separate kingdoms under rajas belonging to collateral branches of the Malla dynasty.

The war had finished and the country was mostly pacified. Padre Serafino requested the prefect to give him permission to come to Patna in order to get some medical supplies. It happened that in Bettiah I had had a fever for six months and was close to death. Padre Giovanni was not always able to come to assist me. For this reason I had written to the prefect asking him to allow a padre from Nepal to come to Bettiah, at least for a while. The prefect took advantage of the coincidence [of Padre Serafino's request] and wrote to him that he should come to Bettiah for some time to take care of the things I couldn't do.

It also happened that on the first of November of that year 1768, there was an unexpected attack against the city and fort of Bettiah. This is how it happened. At that time the Englishman, Mr. Golding, was governing in Bettiah, and some of his Bengali subordinates, who governed in his name, caused many injustices and outrages. In Bettiah there was a certain Muslim, a military man but one who lived peacefully in his own house. One day one of these Bengalis had him summoned and imperiously told him to go and purchase some stores (*le stuore*) for them in various villages. The Muslim excused himself, saying that this was not his function and that he knew nothing about such commerce. The Bengali reviled him, threatening to send him by force. The Muslim departed and left the country. Eight days later he returned unexpectedly and at night attacked the fort with 6,000 men. He first attacked the camp of the English sepoys and killed them, 300 in all. He searched for the Bengalis, but only managed to seize one of them.

There was a great uproar in the city. I heard the noise but did not know what it was. Some said that there were tigers in the city. Others said that the raja had returned. Others said that the mountain men had come. I didn't know what else to do except close the gates. Around the break of dawn, I saw from the window an army that was passing in front of our house headed towards the residence of the English chief (who, luckily for him, was not in Bettiah). As I gazed at the army from the window, trying to figure out who was in it, there was a volley of gunshots at the same window. My scribe, who was next to me, was hit. From this, I inferred that this must be an enemy army. Without thinking further, I jumped over the walls of the garden and a neighboring bastion and entered the forest. In exactly that place I found all the Christians who had entered there before me. We armed ourselves against the tigers and advanced in good order into the forest. We stayed there the whole day with nothing to eat or drink.

Sometime near evening we heard a voice calling my name. We approached and they handed me a letter from the Muslim chief who had attacked the city. He told me: "I am Ajib Khan,[2] your friend. I have taken revenge against the English, my enemies, but I have nothing against you. You should return to the city. I myself have guarded your house from my people and nothing has happened to it." After reading this, I returned and met with him. He made me very welcome, but when I saw that there were 6,000 thieves assembled there together, I did not trust their promises. I foresaw that everything would end in a general pillage. Thus it was. During the night as best I could I hid all the furniture of the house and church and put the best ornaments in two baskets. Early in the morning I went to find [the Muslim chief] and asked him to allow me to go to Patna with my package (*fatto*) since I had a fever and risked dying with no one in the house to help me. He agreed to allow my departure to Patna with the package and gave me an escort up to outside the gates. It was certainly the grace of God that helped me foresee what would happen and inspired me to travel by an unknown road and get away as fast as possible.

In the morning at the usual time the men met in the council of those in charge (*del quid agendum*). All of them disapproved of my having been allowed to depart and decided to send men to bring me back, which they did, and also to capture all the Christians. Thanks to God, however, they were unable to capture any Christians. They captured only one Bengali who dressed like a Christian but was not one. He was tied to the mouth of a cannon in order to make, or so they said, a sacrifice to their gods, so that these gods would keep them in control of the country. They went to our house in order to demolish it down to the foundations, but God arranged that just when they were about to begin to knock it down, news reached them that an English army was advancing at full speed in order to expel them. They immediately abandoned the task of knocking down our house and prepared to leave in order to meet the English on the road. Ajib Khan gave battle to the English but he was killed in the battle and the others dispersed. Among the Indians it is usual that once their chief is dead, everything is finished. The English then re-entered Bettiah and things were finished. We suffered little damage.

Before turning to the story of my journey to Patna and Bengal, I want to describe another tribulation that the people suffered about two years later. This was the great famine of 1770.[3] Hindustan is a fertile country for producing food. In ancient times, food was had, one could almost say, for nothing. But to the degree that the Europeans have entered the country, food has increased greatly in price. The reason is that the Europeans wished to appear rich in order to have access to more credit for their commerce. Accordingly they displayed great generosity and since they paid little attention to what things cost, they bought things at the first price asked without making any protest. The Hindus, when they realized this, increased the prices of their goods. They saw that now they could earn as much with 10 chickens as before they could with 100. They then agreed together (as is the custom of these people) to raise the price of everything. Since the English have taken possession of these regions, the country is lost and food is more expensive than ever. Where before they sold 60 or 70 chickens for one rupee, today they sell only four or five.

The peasants are now unable to pay the land tax and have stopped cultivating. At best, those who formerly cultivated 10 measures of land, today cultivate only two. Because of the lack of cultivation, food of all sorts is very expensive, and people live in great want from one harvest to the next, so that if a harvest fails, at the least all the poor will necessarily perish. The truth of this was seen in the year 1770, when the rains failed in the month of June, the rice plants dried up, and within three months in Bengal alone [...] 600,000 people died of hunger, notwithstanding all the efforts that the Europeans and other gentlemen of the country made to assist the poor. Entire villages and cities died and no one could be found to bury the corpses. Only human sentiments—namely timidity and aversion—prevented people from eating each other. This dire condition lasted until the second harvest of the following September. That harvest was quite good and sufficient for those few who had survived. Without researching the cause of this great famine, one supposes that it was the result of bad government.

The situation in the city of Patna was almost as bad as in Calcutta.[4] In Patna, Padre Giovanni da Brescia was put in charge of carrying out of the city the corpses of the poor who died in the public square. Every day he carried out up to 350 corpses. This continued for months and the city became desolate and was on the verge of the plague that is said to have taken possession of the city after my departure. In Calcutta itself up to 500 have died each day during the month of July. August and September ought to be worse. The famine is so strong that rice costs a *paolo* per pound, and even then it is not available, nor is money. The Ganges is full of corpses.

In October, 1770, the new prefect of our mission, Padre Giuseppe da Rovato, sent a letter to his teacher in Italy, Padre Viatore da Coccaglio, containing the following heart-rending description of the Bengal famine:[5]

> *This past year the rains did not arrive in a large part of Hindustan as they usually do, namely from about June to September. The usual harvests of rice and of other vegetables, have not been made, whence this year the foodstuffs have so much risen in price, and above all rice, that is the food almost common to everyone, that used to sell even at one* paolo *per pound, and in some of the more populated regions of Hindustan, like Murshidabad,* the prices have reached even half a* filipo *per gross pound; thus in the same proportion the prices of wheat and of the other grains have also increased. For this reason, in some places more than half of the inhabitants have died; in others more than two thirds, and many lands and villages have remained completely vacant, because those few who remained alive went elsewhere to look for foodstuffs; but to many this has not served but to prolong their lives for a little time, because in the end they succumb to hunger and die of it. In the large cities were counted 300 to 400 dead and up to 500 per day. The biggest mortality has been in the months of June, July and August. Your Reverend Padre can imagine the spectacle that so great*

* Murshidabad (Giuseppe's Moscudabat) is a city in Bengal 150 kilometers north of Chandernagore. It was often the capital of the nawab of Bengal.

a famine has caused. In every street there were so many corpses of all sorts, and especially on the banks of the rivers, that it is not possible to comprehend it except by he who has seen it. The stench was extraordinary. When walking outside one always needed to keep a handkerchief over one's nose and mouth. And in Chandernagore, our hospice being on the bank of the Ganges, we were many times obliged to have the windows and the doors closed because of the stench, because some ships being anchored there and tied near to the bank, so many corpses carried by the current became entangled in the ropes that the stink was always continuous; notwithstanding the attention of the public that had destined two small boats to set free the corpses that were stopped among the ropes, because scarcely had they cleaned one part when at once other corpses carried by the current again got stuck while they cleaned the other. Everyone commonly expected a plague in consequence of such a mortality that so polluted the air. But up to now, thanks to God, this has not happened; and now the mortality has almost ceased, because the normal rains have arrived this summer and now the new harvest of rice has begun to be eaten. One hopes that it will be a good harvest, although one reduced in proportion to the few people remaining to cultivate the land.

One of the main ways that the plague has been prevented is [the scavenging by animals]. Everywhere in Hindustan, especially near the rivers, there are many big dogs similar to those that our own [Italian] peasants keep to guard their houses. These dogs have no owners and feed on corpses of all sorts. In addition, there are sciamurroné,[6] *a species of wolves that stay hidden during the day and then come out at night to feed on the corpses. There is also a prodigious number of crows and bigger birds like the vultures* (polini). *I suppose that these latter birds may really be eagles since they have all the traits of eagles. They are called* ghiddò,[7] *and there are so many of them that hundreds often appear together.*

There are moreover other birds of various sorts and among them there is one type of such an extraordinary size, that one time, having killed one, I raised one of the wings of the dead bird from the ground, and this was taller than me as I stood. Now these many big birds, dogs, and sciamarroni*—not to mention the tigers and especially the many big crocodiles—make haste to clean the thousands of corpses of all sorts that everywhere are found and especially on the banks of the Ganges, in whose waters all the gentiles put their dead. And for this reason, although the air may appear polluted by the stench, the cause of the stench is soon removed by the animals and birds, and the countries have been saved from the plague.*

Chapter 12

Back to Europe

Meanwhile I arrived in Patna, still with a fever.[1] After I had heard about the English victory, I returned to Bettiah in order to put the affairs of our house, church and Christians in order. This was necessary since in those days I had received from Rome permission to return to Europe. Once everything had been put in order, I left for Bengal on January 3, 1769. Exactly one day before my departure, Padre Serafino da Como arrived from Nepal. I turned over to him all that belonged to the Bettiah hospice and set off for Bengal. [...] It was a good journey and I arrived on the nineteenth of the same month.

When I arrived in Bengal, I found Padre Anselmo da Ragusa, the prefect, who was suffering from his usual gout. I negotiated my voyage to Europe with a French vessel named the Mascarin. I would travel as chaplain and not have to pay anything, but the ship delayed its departure during the whole month of March. The season was by then wrong for going to Europe and I decided to remain in Chandernagore until the next good season, namely the months of December or January.

Meanwhile, news about the Mission arrived. After the mentioned departure of Padre Serafino from Nepal to Bettiah, the three padres who remained in Nepal had to leave there in the same month of January and arrived in Bettiah with all the Nepalese Christians. This news really pierced my heart. I can foresee its consequences. With respect to Nepal, they might not be able to reenter the country. With respect to Rome, what would happen to the annual subsidies based on this Mission? I intended to go to Rome in order to obtain several new missionaries for reinforcing the hospices, which are greatly weakened, and in order to suggest to the Sacred Congregation of Propaganda Fide some means of improving the Mission. The news that the Mission had left Nepal made me fear not only that I would obtain nothing but also that perhaps I would not even be able to return. For this reason, I resolved to wait in India for another two years in order to hear Rome's response and the orders of the Sacred Congregation on this subject. I then wrote to Rome about how I would stay back in the Mission until the new responses arrived.

I decided to remain in Bengal, where the old padre prefect, Anselmo da Ragusa, and afterwards also the new one, Giuseppe da Rovato, assigned me the post of superior of the hospice with the power of attorney for the Mission. On July 3, 1769, three new padres (Giuseppe da Abeto and his companions)* arrived from Europe with letters assigning the prefecture to Padre Giuseppe da Rovato, who had recently arrived in Bettiah from Nepal and had brought with him the Christians of that country. The new padres also brought letters for Padre Anselmo instructing him to return to Europe. Since the prefecture had been reassigned, he departed for Europe

* Giuseppe da Abeto (d. 1771), Agostino da Marsala (d. 1773), and Eustachio da Cassine (d. 1778) were the three members of the eighteenth expedition of 1768. Little information about them is available. See Vannini 1980: 309.

on December 15, 1769, on a French vessel named Pralin, on which the Council* had granted him a free passage.

During the years before Padre Anselmo's departure, I had been sending copies of my essays and translations of Hindu texts back to our superiors in Rome, especially to Cardinal Castelli, the prefect of the Sacred Congregation of Propaganda Fide, and to Monsignor Borgia, the secretary of this Congregation.** I took advantage of Padre Anselmo's kindness to send with him some new translations for the most eminent cardinal prefect of Propaganda. In a letter dated December 2, 1769, I wrote the following to His Eminence:[2]

> *On the occasion of the departure of the former prefect of the mission to Europe, I am sending to Your Eminence, attached to this letter, four Hindu* (gentili) *books that are translated interlineally and consist of four quite different texts.*[3] *These translations should help Your Eminence to infer the topics and style of the books of these people. I could send you still others, but in Rome they cannot do much more than allow others to get to know the spirit of this country. For this reason I believe that these four translations are enough and I have not even made copies of the other ones. As for the originals, it is better that they should remain at the mission so they can be of advantage to whoever might read them.*
>
> *I also send to you, annexed here to these same pages, the literal translation of a book called the* Arjuna-gita.[4]

* The council Marco mentions here is presumably the French Council of Chandernagore.

** Cardinal Giuseppe Maria Castelli was the prefect of Propaganda Fide from 1763 to 1780. Monsignor (later Cardinal) Stefano Borgia was the secretary of Propaganda Fide from 1770 to 1789 and later its prefect from 1802 to 1804. Many of Marco della Tomba's surviving letters are addressed to Monsignor Borgia, and some of Borgia's letters to Marco also survive. See the bibliography for the complete list.

This is one of the four fundamental books of the religion of the Hindus. I have sent only the translation written in the Italian language because this text is written in the Sanskrit language. It would be useless to send it to Rome since not even I can understand it without a teacher. The translation is quite clear and [...] I have added some explanatory material to the text of the book (as I have also done in the case of the other translations) so that they can be more easily understood.

Last year I sent to you a draft of a geographical map of all the territory of our mission. It is badly drawn and made in haste. It is, however, quite correct. If Your Eminence wants to, you will be able to have it put in order by a good painter. In it you should be able to see in detail the kingdoms, provinces, and principal places of our mission. If I can find the time, I will send to you this year a copy of the same map, but extended further to the very limits of the mission. I know well that nowadays maps have appeared in Europe of all the conquests made here in Hindustan by the English gentlemen. These maps are quite exact and made according to all the rules of the English gentlemen. But the map that I sent to you, and also the map that I will send to you soon, is more detailed for the provinces where the English gentlemen have not yet entered.

In the following January, 1770, the new prefect arrived here in Chandernagore on a visit.[5] He proposed that I go to Manila as an agent of the Mission in order to obtain an account of the annual subsidies that had not been received in Bengal for more than 10 years. The lack of these subsidies had hurt the Mission. Once I had been appointed to this mission and instructed about what to do, I sailed for Manila on March 30. I left the mouth of the Ganges on a vessel named the Digue on April 23, with a quite good exit considering that it was in the wrong season.

On May 9, we were in a storm near the Andaman Island.* This lasted for 48 hours and was so strong that I didn't think it would be possible for us to get free. The rudder was smashed and the masts and the spars were broken. In addition we were very close to the rocks of that island, which offers no refuge. They claim that the people there eat men, particularly strangers. God, however, preserved us from evil on that occasion. Nonetheless, since we had remained on that voyage two and one-half months and had provisions for only one month more, we had to endure much misery and lack of supplies. We had not more than a half a bottle of water per day, which we also had to use to cook the rice, of which we received no more than a handful for each person per day.

We finally arrived at Pondicherry on July 4. There we found that the vessel was no longer in a good enough state to go to Manila. Instead, it had orders to go to the island of Mauritius to be refitted.** I then stayed at Pondicherry in order to see that the Supreme Council settled the dispute that the Jesuits had made against our church in Chandernagore. It was good luck that I was there at that time. The Jesuits in Chandernagore had been unable to win over the Council of Chandernagore and had sent letters, without the responses from us Capuchins, to Monsieur Lassa, asking him to settle the dispute by himself.# They would in fact have succeeded if I had not arrived in Pondicherry before the dispatch of his letters. Once I arrived in Pondicherry and was informed about

* The Andaman Islands (there are in fact four main islands) are located in the Bay of Bengal about 650 kilometers to the west of the southern coast of Burma. The islands are now a part of India.

** Mauritius is an island located to the east of Madagascar. At this time, Mauritius was a French territory.

This is evidently the same Jean Law de Lauriston (1719–179?) in whose army Marco served from 1759 to early 1761. See Chapter 5 above.

the package (*fatto*), I went immediately to find Monsieur Lassa, the governor of that place. I explained everything to him and had him see the copies of our responses. I told him that if he did not rip up the letters written in favor of the Jesuits, I would make a petition to the full council, in which he had only one vote. Meanwhile I explained things to all the councilors, giving copies of our responses to each one. I was quite sure that their sentiments were in our favor and in the end Monsieur Lassa withdrew the letters of reply to Chandernagore. Instead, he and the entire council signed a document, in which they ordered both sides to leave matters as they were in the past without changing anything [. . .].[6]

In the end I realized that I would not have another chance to go to Manila. I heard from Padre Salvatore da Bologna and his companion, who in those days had just arrived from Europe, that the Sacred Congregation had taken another decision about the subject of the subsidies from Manila and was promising the Mission that the subsidies would be sent directly from Rome. Given these circumstances, I returned to Bengal, departing with the new padres on a ship named Triton on September 17, 1770. We arrived in Chandernagore after a very good voyage on October 8.

Once there, this Padre Salvatore da Bologna, because of some unknown intrigue with the Jesuits, did not want to go to Patna with the padre prefect, Giuseppe da Rovato, who was preparing to leave for there. [The prefect] in fact departed with Padre Andrea da Perugia on November 3, 1770. Padre Salvatore's disobedience obliged the padre prefect to give him a command to return to Europe. He in fact left for Europe one month later, taking the route by land caravan.

Meanwhile I remained, as before, the superior and agent in Chandernagore, awaiting some replies from Rome concerning the affairs of the Mission and of Nepal. Here also is where I find myself today, in March 1773.* I have decided to depart for Europe and therefore have requested permission from the padre prefect. The padre prefect not only has given me the permission but also has given me a letter of power of attorney so that in Paris I can negotiate the affairs of the bequests that have been made to our church in Chandernagore. The capital of the bequests is now in the hands of the French East India Company. The Company's current condition does not allow it to regularly pay the interest due, and the replies from Paris about this are inconclusive.** In each case, however, we need to know the most recent resolutions so that we can arrange things to satisfy the obligations. Since I was undertaking this task and other business of the Mission, the padre prefect had no problem in granting me his permission to return. With it, I would depart for Europe and had already arranged my passage on a ship called Le Boijene. I traveled as chaplain, without having to pay anything for the voyage.[7]

This, I supposed at the time, finished my mission. I would have been content and satisfied with the spiritual fruit of my efforts, but having found myself always caught up in wars and ruin I have to say that although I worked a lot, suffered a lot and risked a lot, I cannot say that I have brought back the fruit that I hoped for. It is true that if some of my efforts were not directly related to the Mission, nonetheless they have all been at least for the Mission and because of the Mission.

* This fixes the year in which Marco wrote the first draft of this essay (*Introduzione al viaggio*). The text was revised in ca. 1775 after Marco had returned to Italy.

** The French East India Company (*Compagnie française des Indes orientales*) had, in fact, been abolished in 1769. Although Marco says that he wrote this passage in 1773, he evidently did not know that the Company was no longer in existence. The fate of the bequests of the Mission that had been entrusted to the Company is unknown.

Although the fruit of all this may be invisible to the world, I hope that it is visible to God and that even if there is no chance of hoping for a reward from Him, I can at least hope for parity in His accounts.

This then ends my short account of my first voyage and mission to India. I originally took the trouble of writing it [...] for the instruction of the new padres, so that these could see the good that is done in the Mission and the efforts that are attached to it, in short, the makeup of the state of the Mission. The future missionary must learn about and think about these things, particularly in thorny cases, so that he can avoid exposing himself (as has often happened) to the possibility of arriving in a distant mission and then not find that things correspond to his preconceived ideas. He then may lose courage and perhaps even repent ever having gone there. From the little that I have narrated here, however, future missionaries should be able, at least to some degree, to control their decisions. The only advice I can give them is to maintain a perfect resignation to divine Providence. I have never seen this fail in times of needing great zeal to do good, and it should strengthen the patience so necessary in the missionary's situation. Finally, the missionary should continually pray to obtain from God the ability to discern what is correct in important matters. It is not enough that the missionary has a fairly good idea of what ordinarily happens in the country, he must also know (to at least some degree) the country itself and the customs of the people.[8]

Once my return to Europe had been decided, the post of superior and agent of the Mission was entrusted to Padre Agostino da Marsala. I departed from Chandernagore on March 4, 1773. The winds opposed our descent down the Ganges and the river pilot did not leave the ship until the following April 11. We thus departed against the season and also arrived against the season in Europe. As a result, we had a very difficult voyage that lasted more than nine months. We finally disembarked on December 20 of the same year. The voyage was difficult because we were hit by various storms and the ship sprang leaks that made it necessary to always man two pumps. All this was recompensed, however, by good company, good health and an abundance of food. We stayed a month and a half on the Isle de Bourbon in the house of the Lazarist priests, the curates of the islands of Mauritius and Bourbon.* They welcome missionaries with great charity and courtesy and I offer them infinite praise. We also stayed for some days on St. Elena, an island of the English, who treated us civilly and gave us all the needed workers to close the leaks in our ship.

The most difficult situation was the landing at the port of Lorient. Three times we were forced to return to the high sea. The fourth time we lowered three anchors with the intention of staying there during the night. At midnight, however, the storm carried the ship and all three anchors toward the rocks with nothing we could do to stop it. In desperation, the captain cut the three ropes [to the anchors] and put up the sails. This should have hurled the ship onto the rocks that were almost touching it. Providence, however, allowed the ship to pass through the dangerous places and reach a secure place. We then easily entered the port and I disembarked.

I first went to Hennebont where I passed the Christmas holidays in our convent. At the convent I met Padre Romualdo da Senigallia and Padre Fortunato da Caldes, who were

* As noted above (Chapter 1), Marco stayed with these Lazarists of the Isle de Bourbon (now Réunion) during his first trip to India. The Lazarists were founded by the French saint, Vincent de Paul (1581–1660), in about 1625. They were prominent as missionaries in North Africa and Madagascar.

there in order to join our Mission. I gave them my travel items and clothing and also the tabernacle I had brought belonging to the Chandernagore hospice. Passage for the padres was obtained on a ship named Il Duras commanded by Monsieur Perengal and charged to the expenses of the king of France. After all this had been arranged, I left for Paris in order to attend to the tasks that the padre prefect Giuseppe da Rovato had assigned to me. I took with me a certificate in writing as the agent of the Mission. I arrived in Paris on January 25, 1774.

Chapter 13

Freemasons and Heretics

During my many years in Hindustan, I have never had any serious problems with the English and Dutch officials and traders.[1] It is true that most of them are followers of the heretical Reform, but mostly they do not interfere with our work and sometimes have helped us. Mr. Falck, the head of the Dutch factory in Patna during the 1770s, even gave our prefect, Giuseppe da Rovato, a generous contribution for the construction of our church in that city.[2] My relations with the English officials who now rule Hindustan have always been cordial. Mr. Edward Golding, the English resident in Bettiah, was a close friend. I myself have always opposed their reform, however, and have always defended our Holy Catholic Church in my conversations with them.

In Hindustan, many men among the English and Dutch followers of the reform, and also among the French Catholics in Chandernagore, belong to the congregations of the so-called Freemasons.* Our Holy Church has voiced strong opposition

* It is difficult to judge Marco's own attitude towards the Freemasons. As will be shown in the final chapter, at the end on his life Marco was accused of being sympathetic to—or even an initiated member of—the Masons by the proxy Visitor to the Tibet Mission, René Louis Foulon. My own view is that Marco was probably opposed to Freemasonry throughout

to this society. In 1738 Pope Clement XII signed the bull *In Eminenti,* the first official condemnation of Freemasonry. Even after this date, however, the society continued to grow throughout Europe, including even Italy. In 1751, Pope Benedict XIV issued another condemnation of Freemasonry in his bull *Providas Romanorum.*[3]

Pope Clement XII, in his bull of 1738, declared that the societies or conventicles of *Liberi Muratori,* or Freemasons, "are spreading far and wide and daily growing in strength." He condemned them in no uncertain terms both for the religious heresy they promote and for the dangers they bring against the peace of society:

> *These aforesaid Societies or Conventicles have caused in the minds of the faithful the greatest suspicion, and all prudent and upright men have passed the same judgment on them as being depraved and perverted. [...] Therefore, bearing in mind the great harm which is often caused by such Societies or Conventicles not only to the peace of the temporal state but also to the well-being of souls, [...] [We] have decreed that these same Societies [...] of* Liberi Muratori *or* Francs Massons, *or whatever other name they may go by, are to be condemned and prohibited, and by Our present Constitution, valid for ever, We do condemn and prohibit them.*

Clement XII added that he conceded and attributed wide faculties to the bishops, superior prelates and other Church officials "to proceed against and to investigate said

---

his life, but Freemasonry was very influential among both the French and English in India and it is not impossible that Marco, sometime late in life, adopted a more positive attitude towards it. In spite of the opposition of the Roman Church, the Freemasons even had a significant presence in Italy, including Marco's own Le Marche region, as early as the 1774–83 period during which Marco was resident in Senigallia and San Marino. See Trampus 2001: 37–47, 111–17.

transgressors and to imprison them and to punish them with the appropriate penalties, even invoking, if it proves necessary, the aid of the secular arm."

In India it is impossible to avoid association with followers of the various Masonic lodges. Not only among the English, but also among the French and Danish, most of their respective Company officials and military officers are openly, or secretly, Freemasons. These have included the English leader Robert Clive, who organized lodges in all the Company brigades; publishers and newspapermen like William Duane, John Upjohn and Joseph Cooper; barristers like William Hickey and William Jackson; English East India Company officials like Christopher Keating, Joseph Sherburne and the former resident in Bettiah, Simeon Droz; Orientalist scholars like Francis Wilford, Thomas Colebrooke and perhaps Sir William Jones; and even the architect of our fine church in Patna, Edward Tiretta.[4] The first English Lodge in India, "Star in the East," was already established in Calcutta in 1728. Others soon followed, most notably the second lodge called "Industry and Perseverance." Many publishers and scholars belong to this lodge.

In his biography of my old mentor, Padre Giuseppe Maria da Gargnano, Padre Cassiano da Macerata writes about the scandalous displays of the French and English Freemasons after the news reached Bengal of the signing of the 1748 treaty of Aix-la-Chapelle that ended the War of the Austrian Succession, a war in which the French and English had been on opposing sides:[5]

> *The English did not lose this chance to spread the sect of the* Francs Massons *also in Chandernagore, where the houses were soon seen to be full of such sectarians, who ever more impudently had the pleasure to be such, whereas the Chief*

and Governor of the colony not only was such, but also had been made by the English the propagator and receiver of the French into this new society. Efforts were made by both the parish priests and our missionaries to build a dike against this flood in public and private speeches, but instead of improvement, they had to see one day a solemn ceremony in which all the English Freemasons from Calcutta came into Chandernagore, floating up the Ganges on decorated Bazzarà *(that are a sort of fine boat of the country). There they transferred to other such boats together with the chief and all the other associated Frenchmen and then went in convoy to the other bank of the Ganges. There the French chief was given the honor of laying the first stone for the construction of a sumptuous lodge that the associates of the two nations then built there in order to hold their assemblies.*

In later years the influence of the Freemasons continued to grow as did the atheistic ideas that have led to the current troubles in France. In a long letter of January 15, 1775 that the prefect of our Mission, Padre Giuseppe da Rovato, addressed to Monsignor Mario Marefoschi, the secretary of Propaganda Fide in Rome,* Padre Giuseppe wrote about how the French laity in Patna and Chandernagore paid little attention to the Church and its sacraments and showed themselves to be worse enemies of the Church than even the followers of the Reform:[6]

Many are Freemasons, as is the present [French] chief at Patna, who so declared himself before me and who will never leave this society against which he does not want to hear anything spoken, and even less to have anyone speak to

* In fact Monsignor Marefoschi was secretary of Propaganda only until September 1770. In October of that year Monsignor Stefano Borgia became secretary and held the office until April 1789. Apparently this news had still not reached Padre Giuseppe in early 1775.

him about the sacraments. Although he is already advanced in age, he says that each person has to render account to God by himself. Others allege publicly, more than even the followers of the Reform, as I have heard many times, that each person can save himself in his own religion, whether Hindu (gentile) *or Mohammedan, citing also the authority of the Padres [of our own Religion] who say the same. A French gentleman who is now in Patna came to say in a public dinner of the English, where Father Andrea da Perugia [of our Mission] was present, that God would be unjust if he were to condemn to hell a poor Indian who does not know the true religion.*

In the same letter, Padre Giuseppe felt obliged to ask the secretary about persons who do not fulfill their annual religious obligation and are Freemasons, who then die without rejecting their society as dangerous. "Should one," inquired Padre Giuseppe, "refuse to give them an ecclesiastic burial as implied by the bull of Benedict XIV [against Freemasonry]?"

In a letter I myself wrote from Chandernagore to the Procurator of the Capuchins in December 1771, I asked him if we were required to withhold absolution from those Freemasons who claim to be Catholics. This is what I wrote:[7]

I again ask you on my own behalf to explain the sentiment of the Holy Catholic Mother Church about the so-called Congregations, or Lodges of the Freemasons, called in French, franc-maçonnerie, *because in these countries they are so common that it is difficult to find two persons of adult age who do not belong. Moreover, we are the only ones who deny them absolution, and this very often causes conflicts. We have heard that in Europe some Papal Bulls have been issued about this topic, but we do not have complete copies of them and do not know if they concern dogma or simple civil assembly […].*

Although this was only the expression of an innocent and well-intentioned doubt, I fear that it may have been the cause of the enmity that the secretary of the Procurator later showed against me when I tried to enter Rome in 1778 to explain the problems of our Mission to Their Eminences of the Sacred Congregation of Propaganda Fide and of our Capuchin Order.*

* For Marco's unsuccessful attempt to enter Rome, see below, pp. 149, 153. For his problems in obtaining permission to return to India, see below, pp. 147, 151. As noted earlier, in this book Marco's story is told from the perspective of the year 1797. I am assuming that by then he would have managed to get copies of the bulls against Masonry issued by Clement XII and Benedict XIV.

Chapter 14

Italy Again

I left Paris on March 18, 1774, and arrived in Lyon 18 days later. After Easter I left for Avignon and from there to Antibes.[1] From Antibes I took a ship to Genoa. Once there, I had to wait many days for a boat to Livorno and in Livorno I had to wait another 16 days for a ship to Civitavecchia. I arrived in Terni on July 15, 1774. There I met Padre Costanzo da Borgo San Sepolcro, who was preparing to join our Tibet Mission. I gave him an itinerary and other instructions needed for the voyage. After some delay, he left for India with Padre Carlo Antonio da Varallo. Eventually Padre Costanzo returned to Italy after serving in Patna and Bankipore,[2] but Padre Carlo died in Chandernagore only nine days after his arrival. I stayed for two weeks in Terni and then left for Assisi, the home of our blessed Saint Francis. From Assisi I traveled on to Senigallia, near my childhood home of Tomba.[3]

On August 18, 1774, I wrote to Monsignor Borgia from Senigallia, telling him about my efforts to write a reply to Monsieur Holwell's scandalous book about the Hindus and to prepare more complete versions of my own books that I had earlier sent to the Monsignor.[4] Unfortunately, for this work I needed several other books that I had left behind in Bettiah. Among them was an important book belonging to the reform movement of the Kabir Panthis, a text that is very necessary for the understanding of other Indian books.* In Bettiah I had also left behind several texts of my own that were still not finished, particularly my dictionary of the Hindustani language. I also indicated to Monsignor Borgia my own desire to return to the Mission and my willingness to join the new expedition as a supernumerary and also bring a lay brother whose expenses would be met out of my own allowance.

Finally I expressed the need for a college in Italy that could train new missionaries before they left for Hindustan. Such a college was finally established in Ancona in 1787, but it was never organized well enough to fulfill its promise.[5] Finally, together with my letter to Monsignor Borgia I enclosed a copy of a report on our Tibet Mission by Padre Anselmo da Ragusa, the elderly prefect of the Mission. This report praised my own efforts on behalf of our Mission but also described some of the sinister events that happened in that distant land.

On August 19, 1774, I wrote to Cardinal Castelli repeating the request I had made to Monsignor Borgia to return to the Mission as a supernumerary with the next expedition. I also indicated to Cardinal Castelli the importance of establishing a church in Calcutta with the permission of the directors of the English Company and the bishop of Meliapur.[6] By this time it was already more than obvious that the English Company was destined for greater success than the French Company and that Calcutta had long since eclipsed the French city of Chandernagore, which was becoming more and more deserted.

In September 1774, I received a letter from Monsignor Borgia saying that there was no room for me in the 1775

* For the Kabir Panthis (Marco's *Cabiristi*), see above, Chapter 7.

expedition for the Tibet Mission.[7] He did, however, say that if I would wait for some time, I could then apply for permission to return to the Mission, even with a lay companion, and that then "my merit" would not be overlooked. As it turned out only two padres were sent in 1775, Carlo Antonio da Varallo and Costanzo da Borgo San Sepolcro.

I wrote to Monsignor Borgia from Senigallia again in October saying that I had received a letter from the custodian of the Pondicherry Mission who mentioned the death of our Padre Agostino da Marsala in Chandernagore in December 1773.[8] This left only five padres in the Tibet Mission, two of whom were ready to return to Italy. Since there were four churches in the Mission, each of which should have been managed by at least two padres, several new padres urgently needed to be sent and I pleaded with the Monsignor to arrange for new missionaries to be sent as soon as possible. In December Monsignor Borgia wrote to me saying that the decision to send new workers to the Mission would be made in spring and promising to find me a place in the new expedition.[9] In January 1775, he wrote to me again saying that he had spoken to the procurator and the Comissario General of our Capuchin Order about the need to send new missionaries to Tibet and promised to keep me informed so I could come to Rome and from there take the best possible route to Hindustan.[10] In March, I wrote to Cardinal Castelli with another request to call me to Rome and then send me on to India together with a lay brother of our Order.[11]

In early April, 1775, I sent my book of memoirs of the Tibet Mission to Monsignor Borgia.[12] In it I tried to include all the information that was found scattered in my other books. Unfortunately, my duties with the choir and other daily tasks in the convent of Senigallia did not allow me time to finish the book as well as I would have liked. I did, however, manage to include a detailed index of all the topics and names found in the book. I wrote to Monsignor Borgia two more times in April pleading with him to let me come to Rome at the end of May and stay there during June to visit this city during the year of the Holy Jubilee and also to attend the great General Assembly of our Capuchin Order.[13] At the end of the month, I wrote to Cardinal Castelli, the prefect of Propaganda Fide, to also ask his permission to visit Rome during the month of June.[14] I told him about the books I had sent to Monsignor Borgia, including my memoir for the Tibet Mission, various Hindustani texts with interlineal translations, and my essay written in reply to the book by Mr. Holwell about the Hindu religion. All these texts were written in order to help the new missionaries in the Mission to prepare themselves for their apostolic labors in Hindustan. In mid-May, Monsignor Borgia again wrote to me advising me that the imminent General Assembly of the Capuchin Order meant that the Capuchin convent in Rome would not be able to accept outside visitors apart from those friars who had some role in the election of the new superiors.[15] He told me it would be better for me to be patient a while longer and that he would then make the necessary arrangements for sending me the "obedience" to come to Rome and from there to travel on to my ultimate destination. At this point I did something that I later had ample cause to regret.

The reverend padre custodian of Pondicherry had written requesting that I try to intercede in the General Assembly on behalf of the creation of a seminary in Pondicherry that would train native Indians to become priests who could remedy the insufficient numbers of missionaries coming from Europe. On May 19, I wrote to Monsignor Borgia, sending him the custodian's letter and asking him to arrange that the custodian's request be considered by the General Assembly. Here is part of what I wrote:[16]

Since I cannot come to Rome during the time of our General Assembly (as I would have liked) in order to propose, or request, that said Assembly, also on behalf of the Pondicherry Mission, should permit, or obtain from the Congregation of Regular Bishops, the permission to be able to receive into the profession missionaries in Pondicherry itself, as, about this, the reverend padre custodian of Pondicherry has written enthusiastically to me. This is because in every place there is a growing lack of missionaries at the same time as the conversion of the Hindus and the increase of the Faithful is speeding up. For this reason the Pondicherry Mission has closed five churches and we have closed four of our own. All this simply because of the lack of missionaries. In these circumstances, the mentioned padre custodian requests his Prefect, who is the provincial of Tours, to please propose in the Assembly the acceptance of said reception of missionaries who are quite numerous in their own schools, and who can be chosen with the advantage that they possess the language and know the climate. And then (he says) one could abstain from [having to bring missionaries from] France. It seems to me that we too, being relatively nearby, could profit from this advantage and could be in the same situation.

For this purpose I sent Monsignor Borgia the Custodian's letter as well as a letter of my own to the very reverend padre provincial of Tours Province requesting that he set about to obtain the above-mentioned permission. I also sent copies to the padre provincial himself.

In another letter to Monsignor Borgia, written on June 2, I reminded him of the letter from the Pondicherry custodian and noted that recruitment of missionaries in India itself would either require that our chapter meeting in Rome declare that the Pondicherry Mission would become an independent Province or else that the Mission obtain from His Holiness the privilege of receiving persons into the profession according to the needs of the Mission.[17] The same day I also wrote a letter to Cardinal Castelli, the prefect of Propaganda Fide, informing him about the Custodian's request and the changes it would require.[18] A decidedly negative reply to these requests came in a letter from Propaganda Fide dated July 1, 1775.[19] Monsignor Borgia wrote that he was not in agreement with the idea of opening a novitiate in Pondicherry to receive natives who wished to profess the Capuchin religion and become missionaries. He claimed that the problem of the lack of Evangelical workers in India could be solved without resorting to such novel measures.

Meanwhile, I decided to make one more attempt to persuade Monsignor Borgia to arrange an obedience for me to take up the cross of a distant mission. In a letter written on 13 July, I noted that the expedition to our Tibet Mission had been delayed for some time and that I was advancing in age and diminishing in the forces necessary for such a long journey. As an alternative, I proposed that the Sacred Congregation send me to Brasil, a territory where I already knew the language, which is Portuguese. I also told him that I had been offered some official tasks for the Picena Province of Capuchins* but had declined them in the hopes of joining a foreign mission and now needed his support to avoid having to accept some such tasks during the upcoming September chapter meeting of the province.

The answer came in a disheartening and (to be frank) sarcastic letter dated July 29 that made it clear that I had offended someone in power.[20] Here is what it said:

* The Capuchin branch of the Franciscan Order is divided into provinces that roughly correspond to geo-cultural regions. The Picena region is an alternative name for the Le Marche (The Marches) region of east-central Italy. The Piceni were an ethnic group who long inhabited the region.

> *This Sacred Congregation has seriously considered what you indicated in your letter of the 13th of the present month about your advancing age and diminishing forces. Accordingly, the Congregation has resolved to allow you to enjoy your days in a Christian life, without your having to think anything more about undertaking long and disastrous voyages, or exposing yourself to the heavy labor that employment in an apostolic mission to foreign nations would require. Therefore I offer to you this instruction for your enlightenment and regulation, and also so that you can freely accept those religious offices that one supposes will be offered to you in the provincial chapter meeting.*

As I have noted, I never fully understood, the Sacred Congregation continued to delay any decision about organizing a full-sized expedition of new missionaries for our Tibet Mission.[21] In the end only two padres were sent in the expedition of 1775: the above-mentioned Costanzo da Borgo San Sepolcro and his unlucky companion, Carlo Antonio da Varallo. I remained in Italy for another seven years. In all that time the Sacred Congregation organized only one more expedition to Hindustan, that of 1777. Only two padres joined this expedition and only one of them, Padre Gaetano Maria da Ferrara, actually sailed to India. In September or October of 1775, I moved from the convent in Senigallia to nearby San Marino.[22] From there I wrote to Monsignor Borgia at the end of October to ask about a sensitive case involving a confession I had heard and also to express my regret that I would not be able to return to the Tibet Mission, in spite of the fact that I could guide new missionaries there and knew the language of the country well.[23]

In 1778 I made one last attempt to convince Monsignor Borgia, Cardinal Castelli and the other eminences of the Sacred Congregation of the need for more and better missionaries

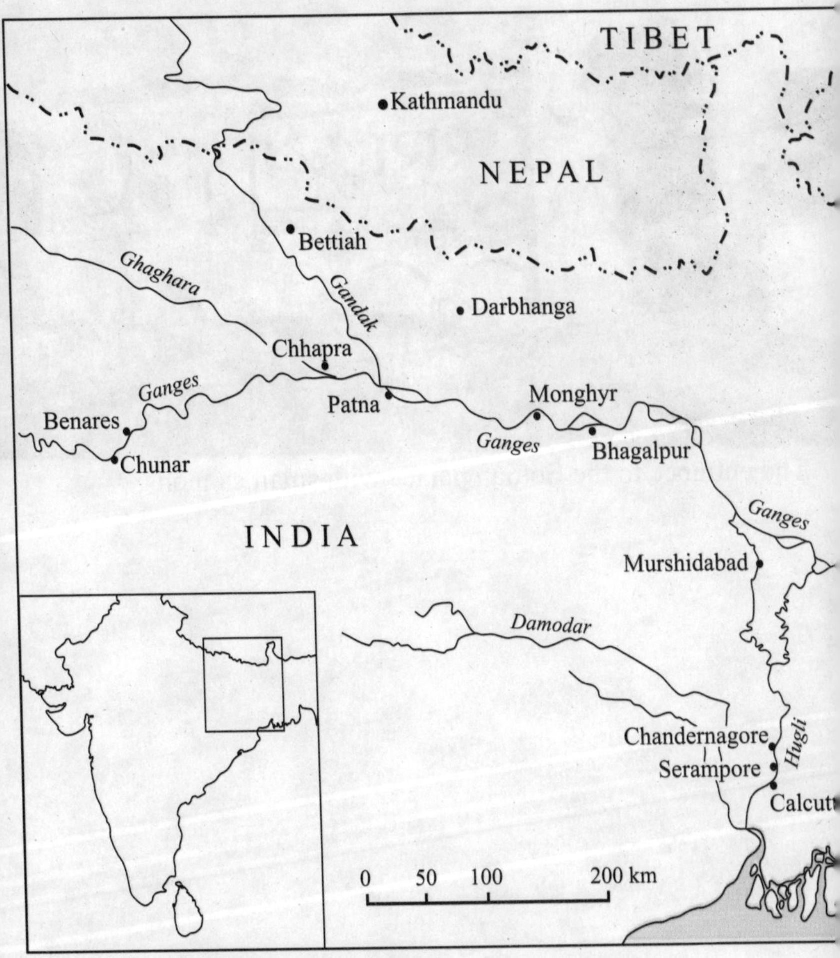

Map of the area of the Capuchin Tibet Mission.

The entrance to the Bettiah palace with small cannons.

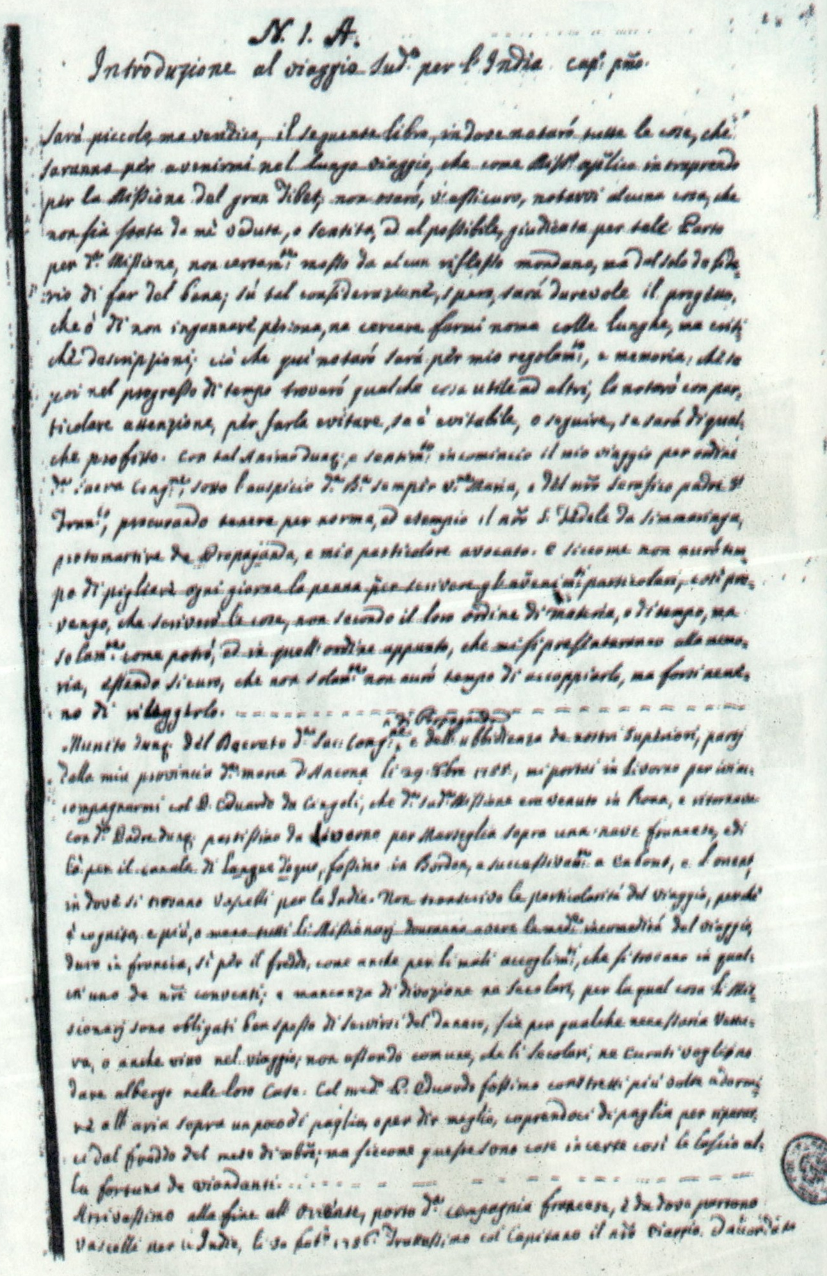

N. 1. A.

Introduzione al viaggio sud.o per l'India cap. p.mo

Sarà piccolo ma veridico, il seguente libro, in dove notarò tutte le cose, che saranno per avvenirmi nel lungo viaggio, che come Miss.o Ap.lico intraprendo per la Missione del gran Tibet; non osarò, v'assicuro, notarvi alcuna cosa, che non sia stata da me veduta, o sentita, ed al possibile, giudicata per tale. Parto per d.a Missione, non certam.e mosso da alcun rispetto mondano, ma dal solo desiderio di far del bene; in tal considerazione, spero, sarà durevole il progetto, che è di non ingannar persona, ne cercare farmi nome colle lunghe, ma esatte descrizioni: ciò che qui notarò sarà per mio regolam.o, e memoria; che se poi nel progresso di tempo trovarò qualche cosa utile ad altri, la notarò con particolare attenzione, per farla evitare, se è evitabile, o seguire, se sarà di qualche profitto. Con tal animo dunque, e sentim.ti incomincio il mio viaggio per ordine d.a sacra Cong.ne, sotto l'auspicio d.a B.ma sempre V.e Maria, e del n.ro Serafico padre S. Franc.o, procurando tenere per norma, ed esempio il n.ro S. Fedele da Sigmaringa, protomartire di Propaganda, e mio particolare avvocato. E siccome non avrò tempo di pigliare ogni giorno la penna per scrivere gli avvenim.ti particolari, così prevengo, che scriverò le cose, non secondo il loro ordine di materia, o di tempo, ma solam.te come potrò, ed in quell'ordine appunto, che mi si presenteranno alla memoria, essendo sicuro, che non solam.te non avrò tempo di accoppiarle, ma forse neanche di rileggerle.

Munito dunque del decreto d.a Sac. Cong.ne di Propaganda, e dell'ubbidienza de nostri Superiori, parti dalla mia provincia d.a Marca d'Ancona li 29 8bre 1785, mi portai in Livorno per incontrarmi col P. Eduardo da Cangeli, che d.a sud.a Missione era venuto in Roma, e ritornava con d.o Padre dunque partissimo da Livorno per Marsiglia sopra una nave francese, e di là per il canale di Languedoc, fossimo in Bordeaux, e successivam.te a Lorient, e l'Orient in dove si trovano vascelli per la India. Non trascrivo le particolarità del viaggio, perchè è cognita, e più, o meno tutti li Missionarj dovranno avere la med.a incomodità del viaggio, duro in Francia, sì per il freddo, come anche per li mali accoglim.ti, che si trovano in qualch'uno de n.ri conventi; e mancanza di divozione ne secolari, per la qual cosa li Missionarj sono obligati con spesa di servirsi del danaro, sia per qualche necessaria vettura, o anche vino nel viaggio; non essendo comune, che li secolari, ne curati vogliono dare albergo nelle loro case. Col med.o P. Eduardo fossimo costretti più volte a dormire all'aria sopra un poco di paglia, o per dir meglio, coprendoci di paglia per ripararci dal freddo del mese di 9bre; ma siccome queste sono cose incerte così le lascio alla fortuna de viandanti.

Arrivassimo alla fine all'Orient, porto d.a compagnia francese, e da dove partono vascelli per le Indie, li 30 feb.o 1786. Trattassimo col Capitano il n.ro viaggio. Dal...

The first page of Marco's 'Introduction to a Voyage to India'

Old Church in Castel Colonna (Tomba).

Ruins of the Dutch factory in Patna. By Julio Romer based on drawing by James Moffat (c. 1800).

iuseppe Maria da Gargnano baptizing Indians.
ontispiece from his biography of 1768 by Cassiano da Macerata.

Modern Bettiah Church.

The main street of Patna. By Alberto Bellon based on water color by Seeta Ram (c. 1814).

in our Mission. I sent my "Plan for the Tibet Mission" to Cardinal Castelli at the end of November.[24] In this plan I begged Their Eminences to revive the Mission and explained to them that the most pressing need was for more missionaries and not for more money. Foolishly, I also told them about my failed attempt earlier that year to come to Rome and explain to them things about the Mission that I had not dared to put in writing. In October I had managed to arrive at the very gates of Rome, only to find that I was denied entry. It is still not clear to me why in the course of so many years I was repeatedly denied the opportunity to come to Rome to present my views about the Mission in person. I had always labored for the good of the Mission and had saved the Mission more money than I had ever taken from it.[25]

In August 1779 I received a letter from the prefect of the Tibet Mission, Giuseppe da Rovato. In it he lamented that the Mission had been reduced to only five missionaries, not all of whom were up to the tasks imposed upon them. He also noted that he had not received from Rome any news or reply to his pleas for help since 1772 and that the two missionaries supposedly sent from Rome in 1777 had still not arrived. In fact only one of these missionaries, Gaetano Maria da Ferrara, ever did reach India. With his letter to me, Giuseppe da Rovato enclosed a letter to the prefect of Propaganda Fide, Cardinal Castelli, with the same complaints. I sent this letter to the cardinal himself, and myself wrote letters about this situation to Cardinal Castelli, to another cardinal, and to Monsignor Borgia.[26] In October of the same year I received via Holland two more letter packets from Giuseppe da Rovato, one addressed to Cardinal Castelli and one to Monsignor Borgia, presumably about these same matters. These packets I duly forwarded to Their Eminences.[27]

Chapter 15

The Religion of the Hindus

After I arrived in India in 1757 and began to enter into the lands on the way to Bettiah, my future residence, I saw statues of idols everywhere, some in human form, others in the form of various animals, others of monsters.[1] I saw people gathered together to make sacrifices, sometimes to a statue, sometimes to a tree, sometimes they assembled to bathe at a particular place in a particular river at a particular hour and minute, all of which were ordained and assigned by the Brahmins. I saw processions on public streets with people making noise, singing songs, and dancing around statues. I saw stones in various forms that were raised up, painted with colors, and ornamented with flowers. I saw mounds of earth with garlands on top, trees covered with rags and surrounded by many little statues. I saw men and women, each with their hands joined together, offering prayers to rivers, to mountains, to the sun, and doing various things that seemed to be acts of worship towards them.

I saw them prostrate themselves before men who wore the sacred thread around their neck and kiss their feet. I saw them worship cows, monkeys and certain kinds of birds. They were attentive to signs, to dreams, to events, to accidents. They demanded that the Brahmins tell them their destinies, the rules for their actions and movements. I heard them sing in chorus in their pagodas. At other times, I saw them stretched out on the ground with many small jars filled with colors and flowers in order to make sacrifices. In short, everywhere I looked, I saw enormous and shameless superstitions. Several times I went up to those people to tell them that they were doing evil, but I was greatly surprised to find that they did not want to listen to me. On the contrary, they began to laugh and make fun of me.

Right then and there I decided to learn everything I could about all their principles, since I was persuaded that I would never be able to dissuade them except by showing them the false origins of these principles. To this purpose I took the help of the Reverend Padre Giuseppe Maria da Gargnano (of blessed memory). I applied myself to learning the language and visited and conversed with the Brahmin scholars, enticing them with geometry and astronomy, making [terrestrial and celestial] globes[2] and [showing them how to draw] perspective for their amusement. I was always eager to profit from their company. Sometimes I took gifts to them and begged them to explain some of their books to me. Sometimes I hired them as assistants and tried to learn what I could from them. With the guide of various texts left by former padres, and particularly by Padre Giuseppe Maria, I managed to form some idea about their systems and principles.

After the events of 1761,* for three years I had in my hands all the books of the king of Bettiah, and, owing to the fortunes of the wars in that kingdom, I had in the house

* These events are described in Chapter 5. Bettiah was attacked by the forces of Nawab Kasim Ali Khan and the king of Bettiah left his books with Marco, who then was left alone with his Brahmin friend and teacher in the Capuchin hospice.

with me the same scholar who formerly had explained these books to the king himself. This scholar was a very capable Brahmin, a graduate of the academy in Benares. He had good intentions and during those three years he not only lived like a Christian but also became disposed to receive his baptism within a short time. First, however, he was obliged to go to Benares and Patna to settle some affairs. During this trip he was murdered. I do not know if this happened in some military encounter with soldiers or if it was done by those who could not accept that he had stayed in our house explaining their books to me and that he wanted to become a Christian. As for me, I already knew the language well enough not to be deceived if that scholar had wished to deceive me [...].

Having looked through all the books in these four big boxes—all the books that are usually found in this kingdom of Hindustan—and having translated line by line several of the ones that appeared to be those that these people knew best, [...][3] I managed to learn enough to be able to speak with any scholar about any subject, without fear of embarrassing myself. [...][4] Once a missionary has learned the language of the local Hindus among whom he is to exercise his ministry, the acquisition of a knowledge of the books of those people is certainly something that is quite necessary. It is a great mistake to presume that one can convince any of the Hindus simply with common conversation, having perhaps heard that they do not have enough arguments to be able to defend their own religion. This is a mistake that even I could not avoid until after I had seen the impossibility of the situation. All the missionaries unfortunately find this out, but [if they were to study the books of the Hindus] fewer of them would realize this too late.

No, the Hindus do not entirely lack arguments and principles to defend their systems. It is true that they lack the logic to argue about them, but they do have reasons to not believe our arguments if these arguments are not based on their own books, since they are persuaded that their books are divine, written by their God, and that these books should be believed literally and without interpretation. At the least, they regard these books as having more authority than whatever reasons we offer. The practice of [many][5] years has made me know firsthand that it is not prayers, tears, and loud exclamations that can touch their hearts in relation to religion. Just as the words of some Turk or heretic would not touch our hearts if he did not first convince our own scholars with our own books and scripture, so it is with the Hindus.

The Hindus have a tribe called Brahmins, who are like our ecclesiastics. These Brahmins must defend all the clauses of their religion. If we question secular Hindus about their religion, they do not reply but defer to their Brahmins, who are, as I said, a tribe of priests to their idols, scholars of their laws. All the others must believe them and obey them in things regarding religion. These Brahmins know by heart almost all their books, and immediately cite sentences that cannot be refuted except by means of some contradiction or absurdity drawn from their own books or customs. Otherwise, with a silly laugh, they shout victory. Those present all applaud, and the missionary, even if he has the best and most solid arguments, ends up discredited and frustrated. What is worse, he loses their trust and is no longer listened to.

If, on the other hand, the missionary understands the sentence of the Brahmins and replies with another sentence from their own books that contradicts it, or at least replies with some other sentence that they made (something that is not difficult for someone who has made a study of their books, which mostly consist of constant repetitions of things, so that the same sentence can be used in many situations), then they all are surprised, seeing that the missionary knows their things. The Brahmin becomes intimidated, and does not dare to cite another sentence, fearing to be contradicted and put to shame. Then the missionary has the opportunity to prove his case, and if he has a quick tongue, he causes the audience to shout: "You must be the incarnation of some god".

On such occasions, all sorts of great things are promised, but then after sending the missionary home, they say behind his back that he is a blasphemer, a kaffir, etc. This, however, does not prevent individuals in the audience from believing us, nor from talking among themselves and repeating the arguments they heard. They then will discuss these arguments among themselves, and in the end someone will be touched by the grace of God and will come to the missionary's house. He will tell the missionary about these things and will tell him about the various impressions that his arguments made in those who heard them. He will ask the missionary about his reply to various doubts and to things heard by others. He will continue to visit the missionary's house for various days, always with new objections, and in this way he will little by little be converted. This is the only way, or at least the surest, for converting the Hindus. On the other hand, those who agree to all that one tells them and immediately promise to become Christians, these sorts of persons never decide anything. For them, there is little hope. But those who appear strong in their reasons, and who every day find new objections and who do not submit to the arguments of the missionary until after they have examined them closely and compared them to those of their best scholars, these sorts of persons, although they may take their time, usually end up being converted.

The missionary, then, who is trusted and who possesses, at least higgledy-piggledy, knowledge of their things, and who takes advantage of the occasions that present themselves, is always sought out by the Hindus themselves. Either one by one or many together will go to find him, some with the idea of confounding him, some in order to outrage him with their words, and some, finally, in order to learn something from him. And then the missionary, having become all things to all men,* should reply to them all, and always draw profit from these occasions. This, however, can never succeed unless the missionary knows their systems and their stories, and knows, at least to some degree, those books that discuss their general principles. With these books, and with a little art, he can respond to specific questions.

For this purpose, I will explain here below all the most common systems of these Hindus of our Hindustan, not at the great length that they explain them, but rather in their essence. I will also explain some of their books, books that are very diffuse and full of pompous words and often repeat the same things [...]. Their books are extremely numerous, but once one understands the principal ones that discuss religion, one can refute others, higgledy-piggledy, by demonstrating their false and unsustainable principles.

It is necessary to know, first of all, that the peoples of Hindustan have existed at least since the time of Cyrus, the king of Persia, namely from about 550 years before Jesus Christ.** At that time various Persians, particularly a certain

* This phrase (in Marco's text "*fatto tutto a tutti*") is an allusion to St. Paul's first letter to the Corinthians 9.22.

** The Persian emperor Cyrus the Great ruled from 550–529 B.C. He was the first emperor of the Achaemenian dynasty. His wars and conquests are described by Herodotus. The following discussion is obviously based on mistaken ideas about the history of India and the Middle East, but it is very interesting as an example of the state of general European knowledge about the history of these regions in about the year 1775 when Marco tribe called Brahmins, who were the priests of the idols—either because of the miseries of the wars or because they did not wish to submit to the domination of the king—withdrew towards the east, lands that were then uninhabited, and began to populate them. Because of the wars, almost at the same time some Egyptian families left their country and withdrew into Hindustan and reached certain provinces beyond the river Ganges called "Tirhut" (*Tirut*), from Tirut in Africa from where they had departed.* These Egyptian families are still today called "Misra", thus retaining the name of Egypt,** and they are the first, the most ancient, and the most esteemed Brahmins of Hindustan. The Persian Brahmins founded the city of Benares, or Kashi, for their stay in India and established a university of sciences there. Similarly, the Brahmins named Misir, in other words the Egyptians, founded Tirut with an identical, or similar, university of sciences. And from these two cities the other lands of Hindustan began to be inhabited, namely the country that is found between the river Indus and the river Ganges, with the addition of that beyond the Ganges, that is, up to the Caucasus Mountains that extend from the east to the west as a united chain from the kingdom of Pegu up to the lands of Kashmir.# And this

---

wrote this passage. Some of Marco's ideas about the early connections between Egypt and India are commented on by Sir William Jones in an article written in 1784 and first published in 1789 (see Jones's text in Marshall 1970: 239–40).

* Tirhut (ancient Tirabhukti) is a region in north-western Bihar to the east of the Gandak River. The Bettiah kingdom is part of this region.

** In Arabic, Egypt is called Misr. In India many Brahmins have the surname, Misra, a word (literally meaning "mixed") that is derived from Sanskrit, not Arabic.

It is not clear why Marco places the Caucasus Mountains "beyond the Ganges". Either his geography is rather confused or he is referring to the Himalayas. Pegu is a town north of Rangoon in Myanmar (Burma).

is the country that today is called Hindustan. This country is different from that ancient India, since India began from Babylonia, today Baghdad, and extended to the east as far as the lands were inhabited. Therefore it is said that Semiramis entered India around the year 2164 before Jesus Christ, and Bacchus entered it perhaps even earlier.* Sesostris entered this country around 1720 B.C., and finally, Alexander the Great entered it.** Although many claim that Alexander did not go beyond the Indus River, it is proven that he also crossed the Ganges. It was at Benares that he had contact, also in writing, with Didame, the chief of the Brahmins of the University of Benares, as I have already noted above. Let us leave to the historians the task of discussing in more detail the antiquity of the founding of this Empire of Hindustan. For us, it is enough to suppose here (since there are no other arguments) that the Persian Brahmins and also those of Egypt, or Misir, carried their idolatries and superstitions, which were then quite simple, from their homelands and implanted them in this very Hindustan. They increased them considerably when Alexander the Great left his troops in various places of the

* Semiramis is a legendary Assyrian queen, famed for her beauty. She is said to have invaded India by crossing the Indus, but this invasion was not successful. Semiramis is sometimes identified with the historical queen Sammu-ramat, who lived sometime around 800 B.C. Stories about Semiramis are found in the classical writings of Herodotus and of Diodorus Siculus. Legends claim that the Roman god Bacchus (Greek Dionysus), the god of wine and revelry, at one time invaded India.

** Sesostris is the name of five ancient Egyptian kings of the middle kingdom. The most famous of these kings is Sesostris I who ruled from 1971–1928 B.C. A legendary king of this name is described by Herodotus, Diodorus Siculus, and Strabo. The relation between this legendary king and the historical kings named Sesostris is not entirely clear. Marco must have got the names of Semiramis and Sesostris, directly or indirectly, from these Greek and Roman sources.

country. These troops built forts and cities and stayed there for several years. And since they were from various provinces of Greece and Persia, they had various religious stories of their own. Then the Hindus (*Gentili*), who were emulators and envious of the Greek fables, began to create fables through their own fancy, not wishing to appear less than the Greeks. Such is the character of the country that when they are told a story, fable, metaphor, or metamorphosis, they immediately say that they know how to understand its meaning, a meaning that they explain in their own way, and they increase or decrease the circumstances as they like. This is a thing that is seen and heard in every conversation and discourse.

Thus to their simple idolatries and perhaps to their natural religion they added Greek fables and metaphors. In the course of time they began to believe them to be true. Above all, they believed the fables about the planetary gods, who differ little from the Greek ones. In addition, they adopted some books of various Greek philosophers that they believed *ad litteram*, as they do in the case of those of Vyasa, and of Tulsidas, who they take to be simply expositors of their divine books [...].* And here it may be observed that the Indians were ashamed to say that their books are composed by men. Since they believe that Vyasa and Tulsidas were men, although they were great contemplatives, the Indians claim that Vyasa and Tulsidas were only expositors of their divine books.

Our Indians took science from Zoroaster, the Persian noble. They know astronomy quite well. From Plato, who travelled

* Vyasa is a legendary sage who is the reputed author of the great Indian epic in Sanskrit entitled the *Mahabharata*. Tulsidas (c. 1550–1600) is the author of the famous *Ramcaritamanas,* a version of the *Ramayana* story written in the Avadhi dialect of Hindi. Marco translated one complete chapter of Tulsidas's work (the "Lanka-kand") and wrote summaries of the other chapters (see below, Chapter 16).

to those lands almost at the same time, they took the idea of the transmigration of souls derived from Pythagoras or other Egyptians. On this basis, they formed a system that claims that God, or the Supreme Spirit, emanated from himself, or else divided up the soul of Brahma, in 8,400,000 parts, that are the conscious souls that pass through the course of transmigration from body to body, that will be noble or ignoble in proportion to their actions, as they are more or less blameless, or culpable, with other paradoxes that I will here put to one side.

It was then, I think, around 550 years before Jesus Christ that the Hindus of Hindustan began to create their books, that were full of parables, fables, metaphors, paradoxes, and absurdities, and thus, higgledy-piggledy, these books were created without even the appearance of having any argument or good sense. And thus, more or less, the Hindus continued until coming into contact with other nations, especially with the Manicheans, among whom there was a certain Thomas, sent by the same Mani, who was in Hindustan around the year 300 of our redemption.[6]

Wanting to pass as a new Messiah, Mani recruited Apostles and sent them to various parts of the world. He ordered one called Thomas to Hindustan. *He perhaps wished* (as ecclesiastical history says), *to send his own false Thomas to India, and in this way to imitate Christ, who destined the Apostle Thomas to preach the gospel in India.*[*] This Thomas

* In Marco's original text the sentence in italics is underlined and written in Laţin rather than Italian. Historical legend claims that the Apostle Thomas, the direct disciple of Jesus, went to South India. His tomb is located in the city of Chennai (Madras). Marco's second (and "false") Thomas was a Christian from Persia and/or Palestine whose full name was Thomas of Cana or Cnai Thomman. He migrated to South India in the fourth century. This second Thomas was an Eastern Christian and not a direct follower of

the Manichean, afterwards called Saint Thomas the Apostle, traveled through many parts of India in order to sow his errors. These were easily accepted because they did not contradict the systems of the Indians in any way. As a general rule, the Hindus can accept almost anything as long as the maxims and doctrines of the foreigners do not interfere with their own. And this is the reason why even Mohammedanism has advanced so far among the Hindus. Also other reforms, or sects, even within Christianity, make great advances as long as they do not prohibit the Hindus from observing their ceremonies. This is what the Danish and others do, and this is enough for them to make a great number of Christian converts, or rather persons who are half-Christians and half-Hindus. Thus Thomas the Manichean did not at all oppose their ceremonies and customs. It was quite easy for him to spread his own errors among those peoples and to give a certain order to their books, so that the simplicity or extravagance of these books would no longer be a reason for them to question them. To this extreme the Devil arrives with the aid of his followers.

---

the Persian religious leader Mani (ca. 210–276) (Marco's *Manes*), although Manichean influence is strong in Eastern Christianity. The history of the St. Thomas Christians of South India is extremely complex, with many splits and schisms. The early St. Thomas Christians accepted the authority of the Eastern Orthodox bishops at Antioch, Syria, or those at the twin cities of Seleucia-Ctesiphon on the Tigris River. After the arrival to India of the Roman Catholic Portuguese from 1498, some of the St. Thomas Christians accepted the authority of the pope (some becoming Roman Catholics and adopting Latin rites and some preserving Syrian rites), while others continued to accept the authority of Eastern bishops. Later some claimed to be completely autonomous. Now most use Malayalam or Tamil for their liturgy (See Fernando and Gispert-Sauch 2004).

Chapter 16

The Hindu God Rama

The book I sent to Monsignor Borgia in 1775 included not only my account of what I had seen and done during my almost 16 years in Hindustan, but also a long exposition of what I had learned about Hindu religion. I have already described the letter of Didame to Alexander the Great and the history of the first settlement of India by the Egyptian and Persian Brahmins.* Other topics discussed in my book included the religious practices of the ordinary Hindus, the gods they worship, their seven different sects, their religious sayings and maxims, their curious and fantastic system for calculating the ages of the world, and their most sacred religious books. Here there is little point in repeating all this information. However, I do want to devote a few pages to the god Rama, one of the 10 incarnations of the great god Vishnu. I do this both because this Rama is particularly revered by the Hindus and because he is the hero of the Hindu sacred book called the *Ramayana* written by the great sage Tulsidas. I had the text of this book copied in Indian letters and made my own translation with the help of my friend, the Brahmin scholar from Benares.[1]

* See above Chapters 4 and 15.

There is a great book about this Rama called the *Ramayana*.[2] It is divided into eight big books. Here I will give a short description of it. Some believe that this incarnation was real, others that it is only allegorical. Some say that its being is eternal. Others say that the incarnation appeared 12,568,819 years ago. Others say that it appeared 880,819 years ago. Finally, others say that it appeared 2,500 years ago. This Rama is held in such veneration that even when Hindus greet each other, they say "Ram, Ram", wishing every happiness. To give a just idea of this incarnation, I must describe it at some length. First, I will explain what is written about him in the above-mentioned *Ramayana,* and then I will explain what modern speculators say about him.

There was once in this world a powerful primordial Giant, called Manu Cakshusha,* that is, the contemplative, the powerful, the devout. This giant was very devoted to the god Vishnu. He meditated on this god for 1000 years while standing on one foot in the river Gomti that passes near Benares. During that time he nourished himself only with water. He then spent another 1000 years in the same posture feeding himself only with wind, and finally he stood for another 1000 years without any food at all. Through such penance and meditation, he earned an appearance by the god Vishnu, who asked him to request whatever reward he wished. The giant requested that no one should be able to defeat him in battle. Once he had obtained this boon, the giant won wars against

* Marco writes "Manu Sachtà chetù." Manu is often used as the name of the first man in each of the 14 secondary cycles (*manvantaras*) of a major cosmic cycle called a *kalpa*. Each of these Manus has a different second name. The Manu of the current, seventh *manvantara* is called "Manu Vaivasvata". Manu Cakshusha, presuming that this is the correct equivalent to Marco's Manu Sachtà chetù, is the Manu of the preceding, sixth *manvantara*. See González Reimann 1988: 140.

all the kings of the seven parts of the world. For this reason he became dreaded and hated by all men.

One day as he was going out to hunt, he met a hermit who was precisely one of those whom he had dethroned. In order to trick him, this hermit proposed that he should offer a meal to the Brahmins. The hermit's intention was to have those same Brahmins give some curse to that giant, as in fact happened. The hermit furtively put some cow meat in the food. And then, when the Brahmins came to the table, he made a voice be heard as if it came from the sky. It told the Brahmins to avoid eating the food because there was cow meat in it (something forbidden to Brahmins). Having discovered the trick of the meat, but not knowing who was the author of this offense, the Brahmins supposed that the giant was the author. For this reason they gave him a curse, and he was changed into a wild boar with 10 heads and 20 arms. And the giant was called "Ravana." Then the giant retreated to the island of Ceylon, called by the Hindus (*Gentili*) "Lanka". He made himself king of this island, and he became a more and more violent trouble-maker. He maintained an implacable hatred for the Brahmins. Through the force of the curse, Ravana's brother, called "Kumbhakarna" became so huge that he filled a space of 2,000 miles. These giants multiplied in so gigantic a fashion that it became impossible for the earth to endure them.

Here the book describes the great outrages that these giants caused on the earth. They stopped the performance of sacrifices; they insulted the Brahmins; and they irritated the gods themselves. In the process the book contradicts itself, saying once when Ravana wished to insult King Bali, [...] Vishnu's fifth incarnation, Bali grabbed Ravana and kept him for six months under his right arm. And in the end, Bali freed him through the intercession of Tara, Bali's wife.

Sahasrabahu, also a giant of 1000 arms, held Ravana for a long time in the stables of his horses, but later he freed him through the intercession of the sage Pulastya, Ravana's grandfather.* From this one sees that Ravana was powerful only in appearance.

Given, then, the impertinences of Ravana and his giants, the Earth, taking the form of a cow, went to the god Vishnu for a remedy. Vishnu promised that he would become incarnated for this purpose; he would be born from King Dasaratha and his wife, Kausalya in the city of Kosala, namely Awadh or Ayodhya,** and that he would have four brothers.

The sage Narada, the son of Brahma, made a prophesy to Ravana of his destruction, telling him that in the city of Anegh there was a king who would have a daughter named Kausalya, who would marry King Dasaratha.[3] From them a son called Rama would be born. This Rama would kill him. When he heard this, Ravana immediately commanded that the girl be grabbed. She was put inside a basket and given to a fish called Ragò so that he would keep her in his throat.# But

* Here Marco is partly confusing two stories that are mentioned together in a passage of the *Lanka-kanda* chapter of Tulsidas's *Ramcaritmanas*, a passage that must be Marco's source. First is a story about Bali, the dwarf incarnation. Ravana is said to have gone to the underworld to defeat Bali but was tied up and put in the stables by "the children". The second story is about Sahasrabahu, a legendary king of the Haihaya dynasty, who captured Ravana and tied him up. Ravana was then released through the intercession of his grandfather, Pulastya.

** Kosala is the ancient name of the region and kingdom of eastern Uttar Pradesh where the city of Ayodhya is located. Awadh (formerly written "Oudh") is a more modern name of roughly the same region. In fact, Rama is one of four, not five, brothers, as Marco notes below.

\# It is not clear from where the name of this fish "Ragò" comes. Perhaps it is simply a variant name of the Indian fish called "*rohu.*" On the other hand, Raghu is the name of the principal ancestor of Rama's family.

that fish, wishing to amuse himself, vomited up that basket one day and put it on the bank of the sea. At that moment King Dasaratha passed by. He saw that basket, opened it, and found his future wife inside. This made him very happy and he brought her to the palace and married her. After this, Rama was born as the sage Narada had prophesied.

One may also note that when Vishnu had to incarnate himself as Rama in order to kill the giant, Ravana, all the other gods incarnated themselves as monkeys in order to serve this Rama. Up to here the narrative appears to have been taken either from the events of Moses and the Pharaoh, or from other tales of giants of those times, or else from the episode of the prophet Jonah that they could have heard from the Jews, of whom there are many on the island of Ceylon and on the coasts of Malabar and Coromandel.

From this, it can be argued that this island may have been one of the first lands that received the Christian faith. At the time of the Christian patriarch Jerome, namely around 410, many bishops and Christian monks came from those parts to visit the holy places in Jerusalem.* In the time of the Emperor Justinian I [ruled A.D. 527–565], there were on this island various churches for the Christians of Persia who went there for trade. Even today on the island of Ceylon an ecclesiastical government is preserved among the people, who are in part pagans (*Gentili*) and in part Muslims.[4] They have a chief and superior of all their priests who governs in all religious affairs, a thing that is not found among other pagans. On this island there are four dioceses, each with its suffragan, [or diocesan bishop], and its principal temple. These temples are,

* Jerome (Marco's *Geranamo*) (ca. A.D. 345–419) is most famous for having translated the Christian Bible to Latin from Greek and Hebrew. His translation is known as the "vulgate."

first, one named *Ilcipherumol*, the brother of Vishnu; second, the pagoda or temple dedicated to *Biuzurapherumol*, who they believe to be the brother of the incarnation Rama; third, Kandaswami, the son of Vishnu; and the fourth, dedicated to Vishnu himself.*

And here it is seen that these pagans do not have the same principles as the others. Some say that Adam, once he had eaten the forbidden apple, was expelled from the terrestrial paradise and condemned to stay on a mountain in the Indies. Moreover, on this island there is a great mountain, called *ab immemorabile*, Adam´s Peak, the top of Adam's mountain. Perhaps for this and other similar reasons, the book entitled, *The Science of the Court* (*La scienza de la corte*), claims that Ceylon may have been the terrestrial paradise.[5] I, however, believe that all these imaginations and others that I will tell below must have been formed after the first conquests of the Portuguese around 1505.

Now, however, let us follow the story of Rama, one that is quite ridiculous, and at the same time mysterious for the Hindus, or invented by the Devil with much skill. Rama was born in the city of Awadh or Ayodhya on the bank of the river Sarayu (Devà).** He was born on the ninth day of the

* The Kandaswami temple (Marco's *Candesuami*) may be the Nallur Kandaswami temple in Jaffna, a temple dedicated to Murugan or Murukan (Sanskrit "Skanda" or "Kumara") who is a son of Shiva, not of Vishnu. There are other Kandaswami temples, however, including the famous one at Kandy in central Sri Lanka. Marco visited Ceylon on his way back to India from Europe, but it is not certain which Kandaswami temple he visited (see next chapter). The other three temples could not be identified and the names have been left as in Marco's text.

** Ayodhya is located on the Sarayu River, a tributary of the major Ghaghara River. Marco apparently has confused the name of the region, Awadh, with the name of the city. It is not clear from where Marco got the name Devà.

waxing moon of the month Cait (March-April). All the gods went there. The Sun rejoiced and stopped for a month to contemplate him. His brothers were Bharata, Lakshmana and Satrughna. One day when Rama opened his mouth to yawn, his mother saw in it thousands and thousands of heavens, infinite gods, infinite suns, mountains, seas, rivers, forests, etc. She saw all the virtues and doctrines. At the age of 12, Rama began to do innumerable brave deeds. He killed many giants with his arrows. In the house of King Janaka at Janakapura [...], there was a daughter named Janaki, born from a pot of blood near the river Janaka. King Janaka wished to give her as a wife to the strongest man of the world, namely he who could break the bow of Mahadeva, which was very big. For this purpose he made an invitation to all the warriors, but none of them could even lift it from the ground. Rama alone took it and broke it and got Janaki as his wife, who then became known as Sita, the mother of the universe. Because of this wedding, heaven and earth rejoiced without limit.

It was on this occasion that Rama waged war against Parasurama, the sixth incarnation of the same Vishnu, without recognizing him [...]. Then the wedding was performed with much pomp in the above-mentioned city of Awadh, but their happiness did not last long. It should be noted that Rama is an incarnation of the god Vishnu who came to earth in order to kill the giant Ravana. Through a boon received from this same Vishnu, Ravana could not be killed by anyone else in battle. Vishnu was the only one who could kill him, but for this it was necessary that he have a reason to do so. Thus either through a mystery or an accident, Rama went on a hunt and brought Sita, his wife, with him.

To save her from having to go into the forest while he was following a golden deer, he left her alone in a little garden. As soon as the giant Ravana—who had been one of Sita's suitors and who had the power to change his own form and to move from one country to another in a single moment—saw Sita alone he took the form of a poor man and drew near to her in order to request some alms. As she extended her hand in order to give him some alms, he seized her and carried her to his island of Ceylon. When Rama returned to the garden with his men and did not find his wife there, he did not know where she had gone or been transported. He became very sad. He assembled all the gods, who were transformed into monkeys in order to serve him in any encounter, and sent them by the millions to the four corners of the world in order to find her (neither Rama nor the others, although they were in fact gods, knew or perceived this fact). Hanuman, the king of the monkeys [...],[6] jumped to the island of Ceylon and discovered that she was there, very sad and kidnapped by the giant Ravana.

Hanuman immediately ran to give the news to Rama, who prepared a very large army of men, bears, and monkeys and made a bridge of sand in order to lead his army to the island. During this journey, he had an encounter with 17 *cioni* of giants, who were there to prevent Rama's entry onto the island (a *cioni* is 1,000,000,000,000,000).[7] Rama defeated all of them, and the giants were obliged to retreat within their fort. This fort was built of solid gold and was 1,400 miles in circumference. After a very fierce battle, [...] the giant Ravana came out onto the field in his carriage and was killed by Rama's arrows. With these arrows, Rama cut off all of Ravana's 20 arms. He killed all the other giants in the same way. Rama took back his wife and freed the world from the tyranny of those giants [...]. Thus, in short, ends this great story described in the eight big books of the *Ramayana*. No other incarnation or story of the Hindus is so esteemed by ancient and modern writers as this one is. [...]

Tulsidas, the great expositor of Hindu books, whom the Hindus hold in great esteem, says that everything here said about Rama ought to be understood allegorically.[8] Specifically, Sita signifies good deeds; Rama signifies justice; Ravana signifies lust, and these three things are present in every man, some more and some less, and struggle among them has given the occasion to create the story. Individual persons can believe this [allegorical interpretation], but the public believes the story *ad litteram*. This Tulsidas may be the same as Thucydides, the Persian philosopher and historian who lived in 3542.* From all that has been said up to here, the missionary has a very great opportunity to convince anyone [of the falsity of such stories] using the very authority of their own books since they cannot deny either the absurdities [written in these books] or the consequences that derive from them. [...]

All these books of the *Ramayana*, and also all the law books of the Hindus, are written in the Sanskrit language.** This language is like the Latin language is to us. It is a language that they believe to be the language of the gods. Only the Brahmins, in other words only their priests, can know it. To all the others it is prohibited by law. In addition, said books

* Thucydides (460–395 B.C.) is, of course, the famous Greek (not Persian) historian of the Peloponnesian War. This Persian person could not be identified. The date Marco gives is evidently wrong, but may be one calculated from the creation. Marco writes *Tulcidide* rather than the more correct Italian form *Tucidide,* presumably to emphasize the similarity to Tulsidas.

** The *Ramayana* of Tulsidas, titled the *Ramcaritmanas,* is in fact written in the Avadhi dialect of medieval Hindi and not in Sanskrit. Marco is correct, however, when he says that the law books and many other sacred books of the Hindus are written in Sanskrit and that, in practice at least, only the Brahmins were likely to have the opportunity to learn this language.

are in poetry. And they contain such enigmas, metaphors, and allegories, that only the Brahmins and scholars can explain them. And even they explain them in their own way. The missionary needs to know the vulgar Hindustani language well in order to not be deceived in encounters [with the Brahmins]. Nonetheless, today—after much work and expense—we missionaries have managed to understand many of their books, enough to know the content of their religion and to be able to refute it.

Chapter 17

On to Lisbon and Ceylon

My patience and efforts on behalf of our Tibet Mission were finally rewarded. A larger expedition to the Mission was finally dispatched in 1782, and I received the command to join it.* Unfortunately, the expedition eventually brought as much trouble to the Mission as benefit.[1] I had four companions: Padres Giuseppe da San Marcello, Zaccaria da Verona, Arcangelo da Voltaggio, and Brother Vincenzo da Foligno. Padre Giuseppe was eventually tried for bad behavior by an ecclesiastical tribunal, put in irons, and later excommunicated. Padre Zaccaria was also tried for bad behavior and imprisoned by the Prefect. Padre Arcangelo got sick on board ship and disembarked in Cochin before ever reaching Chandernagore. Poor Brother Vincenzo died at Chandernagore only two months after arriving.

On January 21, 1782, I wrote the following in a letter to

* Unfortunately no documents relating to Marco's inclusion in this expedition survive. An important and highly revealing personal letter of August 27, 1779 from Stefano Borgia, secretary of Propaganda Fide, to Cardinal Antonelli shows that Borgia was at that time still annoyed with Marco and had quite a low opinion of the Tibet Mission itself. The letter is quoted at length in the Introduction (above, p. ???).

Cardinal Antonelli, the Prefect of Propaganda Fide, describing my passage from Rome to Lisbon.[2]

> *Now that we have arrived here in Lisbon in the best of health, thanks to God, I am writing this to tell you that my voyage from Rome to Senigallia, and from there to Livorno, was quite rapid and happy. In Livorno I waited for several days for Padre Giuseppe da San Marcello. Once he arrived we departed for Genoa, where Padre Giuseppe Felice da Milano was expecting us. A few days later Padre Zaccaria da Verona also arrived. We prepared all together for the departure, but since a direct ship to Lisbon was not available we took advantage of a Venetian ship for Cadiz. For this we had to pay 100 Genovese liras each just for the hire of the ship. Considering that the season was still not very advanced, we hoped for a happy trip. Once all the necessary things were ready, we embarked on the sixth of November and departed for Cadiz. But the winds were so contrary, and the sea so stormy, that with considerable discomfort, after thirty-four days of navigation, we were only able to reach the port of Malaga, having twice failed in the approach to Gibraltar. We disembarked, then, in Malaga. After having waited another ten days for a favorable wind that never appeared, I and Padre Giuseppe da San Marcello decided to go to Lisbon by land. We left Padre Giuseppe Felice da Milano (who because of a bad foot could not travel by land) in Malaga together with Padre Zaccaria da Verona. They were to continue the voyage to Cadiz on the same ship and after by the best means available go on to Lisbon. Meanwhile we would manage the voyage by land and could arrange for the embarkation to India in Lisbon and at the same time prepare the provisions necessary for the voyage. This, then, was our agreement and we left Malaga on the 18th of December traveling overland. This was the happiest and most successful journey that I had made. Without spending anything, we passed through Antequera, Sevilla, and Beja, a journey of about 350 miles,*

and arrived finally here in Lisbon on the seventeenth of January in the best of health. Here in Lisbon we have found all the Padres to be most hospitable. We have spoken about the ship for India, but it is believed that it will not depart until March. There is another ship about to sail for China but this does not suit us. Our other two companions have not arrived and we have had no news of them. I hope, however, that they will not be delayed much more. We have not yet been presented either to the court—which is not here but is outside in its summer residence in the country—or to the Patriarch, or to the Signore Internunzio since time has not yet permitted it. But little by little we are fulfilling all our duties, and we will in due time make a petition to the Company for the passage to India. Thus, may thanks be to God up to now all has gone quite well. For the ship from Genoa to Malaga and the provisions and other necessities, it cost for all of us about 120 Roman scudi, *without counting the expenses that the other two had in getting here to Lisbon. I hope, however, that the money assigned by the Congregation will be enough for us to reach the Mission.*

Little more remains to tell Your Eminence other than to mention the indescribable charity and hospitality that we have received in Spain and in Portugal. I should only say that both are true peoples of God, starting from those that command up to the last of those who must obey. I cannot explain otherwise the goodness of the bishop of Beja except as that of a worthy, true and excellent prelate of the Holy Church. There are many others like him but it would require too many words, and be too mortifying for our Italy, for me to tell you about all this loving hospitality.

Padre Giovanni Gualberto da Massa of our Mission passed by here some days ago and departed for Roma before our arrival. He will be able to give Your Eminence a proper report about that Mission that you can compare with the many presentations that I made about it in the past.

Before leaving Lisbon I received a letter from Monsignor Borgia encouraging me to make arrangements for the passage to India of myself and my companions.[3] I wrote back to him on April 15, 1782, and explained that we had already got the necessary passport from the Portuguese sovereign and had booked a passage to Bengal on a ship that was supposed to sail in the month of February but had day-by-day procrastinated and still had not departed. On April 14, we were told to embark and that we would sail with the first good wind. We finally did depart on April 20, 1782, after a wait of four months. Just before setting sail I wrote another letter to Cardinal Antonelli in which I quoted for him the text of our passport from the Portuguese sovereign. This document stated the following:[4]

> *The indicated padres have presented themselves to our sovereign in order to travel to the Tibet Mission. Our sovereign has kindly accorded to them a passage on the ships X and Y, (etc.). These padres have promised in return,* tacto pecore *[= swearing with one's hand on one's heart], (etc.), to always obey the orders of the same sovereign (Here I said that in our Mission his orders never arrive, but the great chancellor, pausing a moment, did not reply and continued to read) and to never oppose, neither directly nor indirectly, the interests of this sovereign or those of his nation and the just pretensions that it has over various lands and missions of Asia (some of us say that this word 'missions' was not used but I think it was).* This has been promulgated in our chancellery. Today (etc.) their passage is conceded as above specified (etc.), on the date (etc. etc.).*

* This comment shows Marco's awareness of the problem of the latent conflict between Propaganda Fide (which claimed control over all foreign missions, especially those outside of Portuguese and Spanish territories) and the Portuguese crown (which claimed control over missions even in territories where its political and military control was mostly hypothetical).

We reached the Cape of Good Hope on September 20, exactly five months after departing from Lisbon. On October 12, 1782, I wrote to Cardinal Antonelli telling him that we were about to depart again from the Cape to India.[5] The Cape was then under the control of the Dutch, but was guarded by the French. On the same day we learned that the Portuguese ship had changed its destination and we had to transfer to some French war ships that were expected to depart on the next day for the East Indies. On these ships we sailed on to Pondicherry. We still did not know how we would reach Bengal since both French and English squadrons operated along the Coromandel coast. The French did not permit just any flag to go to Bengal, and we were even facing the possibility of having to travel from Pondicherry to Bengal by land.

In fact, the French ships left us on the Island of Ceylon. There, we walked on foot all the way from Galle in the south to Jaffna in the north. After four months on the island we got a ship to the Danish city of Tranquebar, just south of Pondicherry. After 20 days there, we found a neutral ship that took us to Madras and then to Bengal.

After arriving in Chandernagore, I wrote again to Cardinal Antonelli telling him about our travels in Ceylon and the kind reception we had from our fellow missionaries on that island. Here is some of what I wrote:[6]

> *It was a great pleasure for me to be able to see the Ceylon Mission. It is a mission of priests who are followers of Saint Philip Neri and are natives of Goa.* They are priests*

* In this letter, Marco calls the mission to Ceylon (Sri Lanka) of these priests simply the "Mission of the Philippine Fathers, natives of Goa" (*Missione dei Padri filippini, naturali di Goa*). Here "Philippine" refers to Philip Neri (1515–95), not to the Philippine Islands. When the Dutch

(religiosi) who are truly full of spirit and education, and they lead the Christianity of the island with resolute patience and prudence.... There are 14 missionaries on the island and they govern some 90,000 Catholics in more than 400 churches. I would not have believed this if I had not seen it. These Christians—considering their simplicity and their innocence and the fact that they are instructed according to their capacity and possibility to learn—are certainly the best Christians in the whole world. They are very humble, obsequious to an extreme, devout, and regularly go to church. They shame not only Rome, but any country that is more devout than theirs. You will please forgive me if I say "not only Rome", but (I have to say it) Rome is the city that has most scandalized me of all the many different peoples, nations, or religions that I have seen in the world. In truth, to see with one's own eyes how well the Catholic Religion is respected and observed among so many foreign and uneducated people makes a great impression, as does to see how badly it is treated in Rome among even the most educated and high ranking people. [...]

Each of the padres in Ceylon has 30 or 40 churches to direct. Once each year, he visits all of them, administering the sacraments and other parochial tasks. During this time the padres are fed by the Christians of those churches and collect their offerings, and once each year (in a college where all the missionaries assemble to perform spiritual exercises) they turn over everything to their superior, who

---

expelled the Portuguese from Sri Lanka in the middle of the seventeenth century, they also threw out the Portuguese-sponsored Christian missionaries. In 1687, however, Father Joseph Vaz, a native Indian priest from Goa belonging to the Oratory of Philip Neri re-established a Catholic mission in Sri Lanka. Over the next century or so, most of the Catholic priests in Sri Lanka were native Indians from Goa belonging to this Oratory. The fact that the priests were ethnically and racially Indian is said to have lessened Dutch objections to their presence.

then distributes this as alms to the poor according to their needs. The missionaries normally do not return to the exact same mission but rather to another. The superior makes the distribution of assignments so that the conveniences and inconveniences of each mission are equally distributed.

In each of these churches there is a chief Christian who, when the missionary is absent during the year, should instruct all the Christians and cultivate in them their religious duties. It is truly inspiring to see how three times each week the chief Christian assembles everyone in the church to say the Rosary and many other devotions. Each Sunday he assembles them for the dry Mass, in which he step by step reads the Epistle and the Gospel, etc. in their own language; he explains things to them; he offers teachings suitable for the persons who are lower or more ignorant; he gives them admonitions, and again corrects them, and he punishes those who deserve it.*

The public rectifications are most admirable. The chief Christian must make a report to the missionary when he visits the church. The missionary preaches, corrects, admonishes, and then in a very loud voice assigns the public penances: who should be tied to a cross, who should wear a crown of spines on his head, who [should carry in procession] some candelabrums (palmatoria), *etc. The Christians submit to these things with such humility that they make one cry with tenderness.*

The patience that those Christians, and also the missionaries, display with respect to the Dutch is quite unique. They let themselves be insulted, they let themselves be oppressed for contributions of money, [and] they would even let themselves be killed before accepting anything against the Catholic Religion. They are extremely resolute, and all of the Christians valiantly combat the propositions of the Dutch,

* A "dry Mass" (*messa secca,* Latin *missa sicca*) includes all the Mass except the offertory, consecration and communion, which cannot be performed without the presence of a consecrated priest.

so that (and surely this is through the singular help of God) the Christians always end up victorious.

As I said, we arrived on this Island at a point called Galle. There we went directly to the missionary who received us with great friendship and treated us magnificently for the 15 days that we stayed in this place. When we departed he accompanied us up to Colombo and covered all our expenses. At Colombo we found the superior of the Mission. We stayed with him for a month and a half while waiting for our things that were supposed to come by sea. Here the good treatment and charity that we received when we departed by land was extraordinary. He gave us letters for all of the missionaries whom we might meet and for all the Chiefs of those churches, ordering them to treat us as if we were he himself, and all this charged to the expenses of the Mission, promising to repay them, etc., so that we were treated in the best manner, and without having to spend anything.

That superior of the Mission was then named Padre Domenico Monteiva (but every three years the superior was changed, each being nominated by the padre provost of their congregation in Goa). Padre Domenico begged me, together with the other missionaries, to obtain from Your Eminence the privilege of putting aside the impediment against matrimony in the simple second degree of blood relationship. In this country there is a real necessity for this, and because he lacks this privilege, many are married coram magistratus *[= by a civil judge] and live thus. For this reason it will be a great favor and benefit to those souls if Your Eminence can obtain for them this grace from the pope, and then send it into the hands of their provost of Goa so that it can be communicated to the superior* pro tempore *[= in turn] so that past marriages can be rehabilitated and, with caution, future ones as well. I also warmly beg you to help in this matter, since I myself have known the true necessity of this considering the difficulty of marrying persons of different* *castes, although the persons are otherwise equals.*[*] *I, then, would like that this concession with respect to the spiritual good of those people should be a small sign of recognition for the many benefits received by those missionaries.*

* It seems likely that Marco is here confusing two different problems. In Sri Lanka (Ceylon), people (particularly the Tamils) practice the custom of cross-cousin marriage (marrying the son or daughter of one's father's sister or mother's brother). In North India where Marco worked, the problem was that the number of native Christians was very small and they could, in practice, only marry within the same caste. This severely limited the number of possible marriage partners and led the Christians of Bettiah, who originally came from different castes, to join together to form a single Christian caste (see above, Chapter 9).

Chapter 18

Bhagalpur

Almost as soon as I had arrived in Chandernagore, I found myself virtually defrauded of my initial purpose.[1] I had resolved to return to the Tibet Mission with the single intention of coming to end my days in the Bettiah hospice, and in Chuhari, where I had stayed for 12 years among the Christians native to those regions, Christians who are docile and obedient, quite unlike those of Bengal and Patna. When I arrived, however, I found that the English had obliged the padres of Bettiah and Chuhari to withdraw to Patna, leaving the churches and the Christians abandoned.* [...] Two times I went to see the governor-general of Calcutta, who formerly had been my friend.** I asked him, in the name of the padre prefect, to kindly allow the padres to return to Bettiah and Chuhari so that they could care for those Christians. I said that if he had something against those padres, he should at least allow me to go there. Twice, however, he denied my request, telling me that the Supreme Council had issued a decree forbidding the padres to stay in those parts as long

* As noted earlier, Chuhari is a town located about 10 kilometers north of Bettiah where the Christian converts from Nepal were settled in 1769.

** This must be Warren Hastings, who was governor-general from 1774 to 1785.

as the padre prefect did not justify, *in forma juris* [= in legal form], his cause. For this reason, I, on the advice of the padre prefect, let my two companions leave for Patna while I stayed in Chandernagore in order to solicit, in the Supreme Council of Calcutta, the mentioned permission to return to Bettiah and Chuhari. [...]

It is true that my intention has been, and is, to carry my apostolic mission from city to city, without a bag and without a staff,* but the provinces of Bettiah and Chuhari were those best disposed to hear the word of God, because they were well-informed about our religion and had churches and a Christian population. In other provinces it would be the same, but one would have to start from nothing. The Patna hospice was standing, but there were five padres already there. Moreover, since the city was inhabited by so many English, the populace had turned a deaf ear to the word of God. As a result, it was useless for so many padres to reside there. If I was to exercise the office of missionary, there didn't seem to be any other choice than to go on tour looking for a place to build another Christian community and found another church, but in such a way that one could leave without any great loss whenever it proved necessary. The padre prefect offered me the chance to stay here in Chandernagore in charge of its hospice, but I did not leave my beloved province in order to pass my time in these fleshpots and I told him thank you but no.

The Mission in Bettiah was in fact re-established soon after this, but by that time I had petitioned the Supreme Government in Calcutta for permission to go to Bhagalpur, where I have

* This phrase (Marco writes "*sine pera, et sine baculo*") is an allusion to the Gospel of Matthew 10.9–10, in which Jesus gives instructions for his disciples to preach to the "lost sheep of the house of Israel," saying: "Take no gold, nor silver, nor copper in your belts, no bag for your journey, nor two tunics, nor sandals, nor a staff."

spent most of the last dozen or so years. Permission was given with an ample letter of recommendation from the governor of this place.[2]

In 1785 I received from Monsignor Borgia in Propaganda Fide a letter thanking me profusely for my letter of 1783 in which I had written about our travels on the Island of Ceylon and about the excellent work being done there by the Indian priests from Goa belonging to the Oratory of Saint Philip Neri.[3] Monsignor Borgia noted that the Sacred Congregation had recently decreed that we missionaries of the Tibet Mission should take control over the spiritual care of the Great Mogol province of Hindustan that had previously been managed by the Discalced Carmelites, who—for lack of an adequate number of missionaries and the great size of the province—had become unable to attend to it properly. The Monsignor wrote to me that "thus you could have space to indicate your zeal by traveling to announce the Word of God in that vast region and by attempting to establish and promote there the Holy Faith". The Monsignor wrote the same suggestion in a letter to the prefect.[4] By the time the two letters arrived, however, I was already well established in Bhagalpur.

At the end of August, 1786, I sent a long letter to Cardinal Antonelli from Bhagalpur. This city is located on the bank of the Ganges between Monghyr and Rajmahal, well within the territory assigned to our Tibet Mission. At the time I wrote, there were some 80 Catholics living in Bhagalpur without any church and without any padre. In my letter I explained to the cardinal why I had decided to stay here in Bhagalpur:[5]

> *When I arrived here, I saw the need for a padre to be in residence [to care for the already mentioned 80 Catholics and], even more, because this place borders on the lands of certain mountain people under its jurisdiction who are neither*

Muslims nor ordinary Hindus (gentili), *because they have no castes, eat everything, do not have any means of writing, and have no religion apart from some customs imitated from the Hindus. Originally they were common assassins, but today the English have subdued them, more by kind treatment than by force. They are people who are quite docile and less liars than the others.*

Here, then, I decided to stay. I was granted a piece of land where, little by little, and with the aid of my old friends, I built an adequate church and house with the necessary annexes. And here I still remain, caring for these Christians, be it understood, with the proper permissions and privileges from the padre prefect. He has designated this place as a formal hospice and has immediately made me its Superior, etc. Here, then, I remain, to my great satisfaction, content, and at peace. And even though the Bettiah hospice was reopened a few months ago, the padre prefect and I agreed that I was no longer in a position to be able to leave this hospice, which was established more through personal friendship with the government than by the initiative of the Mission. For this reason, I suggested to the padre prefect that it would not be good to immediately change over to another padre, but if the need arose this could be done after the hospice had been fully established.

In the two years and eight months that I have stayed here, I have conferred baptism on 55 persons, including both adults and children, and on two occasions the padre prefect has given confirmation to 35 persons. I would like to introduce myself among the mountain people, but they have a different language, one that I am no longer in a condition to learn. I hope, however, that the padre prefect will assign some young missionary to continue this enterprise. The two provinces of Rajmahal and Monghyr are both annexed to this place. I go to these cities from time to time, especially to offer Easter to the Christians who live there.

> *This, then, is all I can tell you with respect to this single hospice. Hindustan is tranquil under the English government and no war has appeared, except perhaps with the French. Money has become scarce, and as a result food has become abundant.*

In this same letter of August, 1786, I wrote at length about the need for the Church to allow us Capuchins to lend money at interest, in spite of our rules against usury, since this is the universal custom in this country. Here, however, there is no real need to go into this question. Suffice it to say that in 1788 I received a letter from Monsignor Borgia in Propaganda answering my letter and praising my efforts in Bhagalpur.[6] In the meantime, however, an event occurred which was to shake the foundations of our Mission.

In December of 1786, our respected prefect, Giuseppe da Rovato, died in Patna, and in 1787 Propaganda formerly designated Padre Carlo Maria da Alatri as the new prefect of the Mission. In the letter I received from Monsignor Borgia—dated September 26, 1787 but not received by me until the following year—he urged me to help the new prefect, who, he said, had been chosen because he was still in the prime of life and was able to travel to visit all the hospices and attend to all the needs of the Mission.[7] Unfortunately, as I was soon to discover, this was not enough to make him a good prefect.

The death of Padre Giuseppe was a great loss for us all.[8] He was prefect from 1769 until his death in December, 1786. For all those years he sustained the Mission with his great reputation and with his industry. All we padres cried for him, as did the lay people, big and small, but particularly the poor. From his death until the announcement arrived in 1788 naming Carlo Maria da Alatri as the new prefect, I myself served as vice-prefect of the Mission.

When I assumed this office at the end of December 1786, there were more than 500 Christians in Bettiah, served only by Padre Romualdo da Senigallia. In Chuhari there were about 200 Christians, served only by Padre Giovanni Gualberto da Massa. In Chunar and Benares there were many Christians under our care, but only Padre Giuseppe da San Marcello was there to serve them. In Bhagalpur there were 80 Christians, who were then in the care of Padre Zaccaria da Verona since I had moved to Patna to manage the affairs of the whole Mission. Two of our hospices were left without any padres to attend to them. At that time Padre Pietro della Fratta was sick and had left for Bengal with the intention of sailing back to Europe. In fact he died at Chandernagore in 1787. Before the prefect's death, Padre Carlo Maria da Alatri had also requested to return to Europe, but the prefect had denied his request in order to have someone with him during his final illness in Patna. Padre Carlo Maria did not, however, make the same request to me.

With a premonition of things to come, I had written to Cardinal Antonelli at the end of December, 1786, that it would not in fact be a bad thing for the Mission if Padre Carlo Maria were to return to Europe as he had formerly intended. For some reason, however, he decided to stay in Hindustan. Toward the end of 1787, he went to live in Nepal, and he did not return to Patna until the end of 1788, after he had received the news of his appointment as prefect of the Mission. In my letter to Cardinal Antonelli, I also suggested that Padre Giuseppe da San Marcello—who was a good linguist and knew French, Portuguese, Hindustani and English—might make a good prefect. This would have been an even more disastrous choice than Padre Carlo Maria himself, as I will explain below.

Chapter 19

The Trial of Giuseppe da San Marcello

Padre Carlo Maria da Alatri took over the post of prefect in 1788, after which I spent most of my time in Bhagalpur. Unfortunately for the Mission, the ill-considered and arbitrary actions of the prefect soon created discontent among many of the padres. In addition, the reckless and immoral behavior of Padre Giuseppe da San Marcello caused a major conflict in which the prefect predictably took the wrong side. Finally, I and three other senior padres of the Mission were forced to call Padre Giuseppe to judgment for his evil deeds. In October of 1793, we organized a trial against him and found him guilty of the vile crimes that he had committed. Before describing this trial, I need to explain some things about the history of Bettiah after the death of our old friend, King Dhrub Singh, in 1762 while a prisoner of the nawab, Kasim Ali Khan.

Kasim Ali Khan did not stay in control of Bettiah for long. In 1766, the city was attacked by English troops led by Sir Robert Barker and put under English control. At this time the English placed the palace and the land inside the fort area under the control of the padres of our Mission.[1] In 1771, the English brought back the exiled king, Jugal Kishore Singh, the grandson of Dhrub Singh, and put him in charge of the local administration. The palace and much of the land was returned to the king, but the Mission remained in control of about 60 *bighas* of land in the fort area.* The king was not satisfied and demanded the land within the fort and carried the matter to the High Court in Calcutta.

Finally, on September 6, 1786, Lord Cornwallis, the English East India Company governor-general in Calcutta, formally granted three plots of land to our prefect, Giuseppe da Rovato, and to our Mission. We Capuchins were thereby made the *zamindars*, or land-holders and tax-collectors, for these three plots. These areas were the already mentioned 60 *bighas* in the fort area, the village of Chuhari where our Nepalese converts had settled in 1769 when they were exiled from Nepal, and 200 *bighas* of agricultural land at the nearby village of Dossaya.[2] The Englishman who sponsored the grant was the Collector of Saran, Mr. Grome.** The fact that our Mission had become the zamindar of these lands put considerable power in the hands of the Superior of the Mission in Bettiah and it is precisely this power that Padre Giuseppe da San Marcello abused.

Padre Giuseppe da San Marcello had been a thorn in the side of our Mission for many years. He had left Italy with me in 1782 as part of the Mission's twenty-third expedition. Our prefect, Giuseppe da Rovato, sent Giuseppe da San Marcello to Nepal in 1786. Our prefect died shortly after in the month of December. I assumed the duties as vice-prefect

* The measure of land called a *bigha* varies in size from region to region. These 60 *bighas* were roughly equivalent to 90 acres. In present-day Bettiah, this central area of the city still has a large Christian population.

** Saran is a district of western Bihar on the north bank of the Ganges with Chhapra (also written Chapra) as its main city. The name of this Mr. Grome appears in different forms (Graem, Graham, Greene, etc.) in different sources.

until a permanent successor could be named by Propaganda. I remained in charge of the Mission until 1788 when news arrived that Padre Carlo Maria da Alatri had been named prefect *pro tempore*. With this disastrous appointment, the dark ages of our Mission began.

Giuseppe da San Marcello stayed in Kathmandu until the beginning of 1789, when the new prefect recalled him and sent him to Chunar Fort near Benares to set up a mission station to serve the Christians in the army of the English East India Company. The scandals that Padre Giuseppe created in Chunar finally forced the prefect to recall him to Patna in August 1793. The prefect pretended to punish Padre Giuseppe but, in fact, soon sent him to serve as superior of the mission station at Bettiah where my beloved friend, Padre Romualdo da Senigallia, had long been in charge. Padre Giuseppe's high-handed actions in Bettiah and his cruel treatment of Padre Romualdo immediately led to a new crisis. The Bettiah Christians sent appeals for help to the prefect and he reluctantly agreed that I and three other friars—Padres Lodovico Maria da Città di Castello, Romualdo da Senigallia and Giovanni Gualberto da Massa—should organize a trial to judge Padre Giuseppe's crimes.

The main charge in the trial was the evil treatment that Padre Giuseppe meted out to the Christian residents of our village.[3] The best way to explain why Padre Giuseppe was put on trial is to cite the document that I drew up as a record of the proceedings. We all signed this document in Bettiah on October 15, 1793:[4]

> *I the undersigned, former vice prefect and present general agent of our Mission, called the Tibet Mission, was ordered by the present very reverend padre prefect, Carlo Maria Da Alatri, in his letter dated September 17, 1793 to come to Bettiah as*

his official representative in order to proceed in Forma juris *[=in legal form] against Padre Giuseppe da San Marcello, our missionary, against whom the prefect had received many complaints by the body of Christians at Bettiah.*

This Padre Giuseppe had been sent to Bettiah by the same prefect for some temporal affairs. But since the padre radically exceeded the limits [set by the prefect], he received many grave accusations both from the padres and from the ordinary Christians and Hindus.

I arrived here in Bettiah on the past September 30, 1793. I met Padre Giuseppe at a distance of about five miles from here. He intended (as he said) to go to Chhapra in order to reclaim some things that in fact did not belong to him. I attempted to dissuade him, and bring him to Bettiah in order to show him the assignment that I had against him. But he was obstinate in intention and did not want to return.

After I had arrived here in Bettiah, the Christians and others came to me in order to complain against Padre Giuseppe. Even in the places through which I passed on my way here, I had heard how in Bettiah there was a padre who had lit a fire among the Christians and Hindus of that place, and even more among the padres themselves.

I then told all the plaintiffs here in Bettiah to put their accusations in writing, supported by sworn testimony. I would receive all these accusations and examine them in order to then make a fair report, following the orders of the prefect.

The very next day they presented to me 18 accusations written in the Hindustani language. I understand this language quite well and translate them here faithfully into the Italian language, swearing, verbo sacerdotali *[=on my word as a priest], as I also do for all this, that what I have written up to now or will write here below represents the true sense and significance of these accusations. I have preserved and keep with me the original [accusations in Hindi].*

1. The first general complaint that the Christians made was that Padre Giuseppe had made a cutchery, or place of public assembly, outside the hospice. There he summons, at his whim, the Christians and other residents of the village. He threatens them, confronts them, he himself beats them or has them beaten by his servants. He does this with unspeakable tyranny and imprudence, as the specific cases that I will cite here below will show quite clearly. I am not here to impose morals.... But for a missionary padre to sit in a public tribunal to listen to the fornications, the outrages, the quarrels and other things of these very low people: this has never been heard of, and I don't think it will ever be heard of that it might happen again in some other place or some other time. There in the cutchery accounts are rendered, the people are forced to pay money by* fas e nefas,** *that he receives with his own hands, and he forces them also to offer him presents of money or other things. To beat people in public with one's own hands is a scandal that goes against the very orders of Rome* caveant a ferula.#

This first notorious and public complaint was made in the presence of Padre Giovanni Gualberto, Padre Romualdo, and Padre Lodovico.... I have not written down the names of the plaintiffs, in other words the accusers, because the matter is public and all the Christians have a unanimous opinion in favor of the accusation, with the exception of four

* The Anglo-Indian word *cutchery* (Marco writes *cacciaria*) means a law court, both the place or building and the institution. Here it evidently refers to the place where the missionary, in his capacity as zamindar or land-owner of the village, extracted rents and other fees from his tenants and settled local disputes. The word *cutchery* is derived from the Hindi *kacahari* or *kaceri*.

** Latin for "by lucky or unlucky", i.e., "no matter what".

Latin for "Take care [against using] the stick", evidently an admonition against employing corporal punishment.

women of bad conduct (di mala vita) *who are well-known and essentially and justifiably suspected, or rather previously prosecuted, perhaps by their own husbands.*

2. Once I had arrived here in Bettiah, the daroga *(in other words the* kotwal *of the English East India Company), came to my place.** *By the express order directed to him by the Governor of Calcutta, he had to watch over the entire village of the Bettiah fort, whether they were Christians or Hindus. In the presence of Padre Romualdo, Padre Lodovico, Brother Gregorio and three of his own people, the* kotwal *told me how he had received six or seven accusations against Padre Giuseppe, but that out of respect for our status he had suspended the legal process in order to avoid the public shame to the body of Missionaries that would result from seeing a padre imprisoned and sent in custody to Chhapra. In addition, he had understood that I was supposed to arrive here in Bettiah. Therefore he made the report to me. I begged him to suspend the case since I was obliged to act against Padre Giuseppe. But if afterwards there were another complaint, then he would execute his orders. I begged him not to do it, however, without first having advised the judge at Chhapra.*

These are appearances that, if they are not remedied in time, will not only dishonor our status, but could even cause us to lose everything, both the Mission and the Christians. All the missionaries who were informed about the case thought the same. It is true (I have to say) that the padre prefect wrote to me some months ago saying that "If Bettiah is lost, the mission would be better off." In one sense this is true, because the fewer Christians there are the less work we have to do. But in another sense, there are some 600 Christians in Bettiah, without counting the catechumens. Speaking just

* The Hindi terms *daroga* and *kotwal* can both be roughly translated as "police officer". Both words are commonly used directly in English.

about this year, on the fifteenth of last August there were 100 communions, on the following September 8, there were 80 more. On the Sunday of the Rosary, the sixth of the present month of October there were 50 more in my presence, all of them confessed by Padre Romualdo.

3. Another general complaint was that Padre Giuseppe is out almost every night at the house of the four women known to be of bad conduct and suspect for good reasons. There he eats and drinks things that he brings from the hospice or that he buys (since the women are very poor). One of these women washes his feet, another fans him. Later he returns to the hospice, sometimes after midnight, entering by a private door, made for his use, or by the main door guarded by his servants. I said that I would not discuss morals here. But the scandal, rumors, suspicion, consorting, the opportunities made available [for sinning] .... Although one may not wish to believe any worse about him, Padre Giuseppe is accused by almost everyone. And some people say that they know about two children that they believe are his.

4. Padre Romualdo da Senigallia has been a missionary in this Mission for about 22 years and the superior of this Bettiah hospice for more than eight years. He was named to this post by the late prefect, Padre Giuseppe da Rovato, was confirmed by me when I was vice prefect, and has been again confirmed by the present prefect, Padre Carlo Maria da Alatri. Padre Romualdo has been a friar (religioso) *in this Mission for all these years and never has had any mark against him. Rather he has won universal esteem from the padres and the Christians, and from other, secular persons. This superior is true, humble and meek. He would have many things to say against Padre Giuseppe, who arrived here acting like he was a grenadier and behaving badly towards him. Padre Giuseppe even used violence against him, giving him a punch and then grabbing him by the throat, so that if the servant Serafino had not put himself between them I don't know how it would have ended. In this incident—one that was half public and quite scandalous—Padre Giuseppe surely became (and will always remain) excommunicated and suspended according to canon law as long as he is not absolved. Padre Romualdo did not fall [into any error], since he did nothing (according to those present at that time) except to bow his head as if prepared to suffer everything. This incident occurred on September 4, 1793.*

Right after this, Padre Giuseppe set about making Padre Romualdo really suffer. He took away from him his most faithful and diligent servants: Serafino and Giovanni Batta, two Nepalese brothers, one of them 22 years old and the other 18. Their dedication was admired by all the padres and secular people, whether for their service to the church or for all the rest of their duties.... These two excellent servants were calumniated either by some person jealous of their jobs or envious because of not being able to rob the hospice, or afraid of someone being seen by them while engaged in some bad conduct such as stopping anyone from going up to speak with Padre Romualdo and many other impertinences. I will not describe these things here since Padre Romualdo forgives everything for the love of God. I, then, declare it here because I heard this from the commune of Christians, who were almost always eyewitnesses.

The first complaint in writing was that of Fortunato, the son of our old clerk Agostino. "Padre Giuseppe," says Fortunato, "wanted to expel my wife and all the family from our house so that he could take possession of it for himself. He entered the house while my wife was sick in bed and close to giving birth. He told her that she had to leave and leave the house empty. My wife replied that since the house was her own she could not leave nor could she move to another place. Then Padre Giuseppe jumped at her to give her a punch and two blows with a cane that he held in his *hand.** *The woman—in part because of her anxiety and in part because of the beating—immediately felt the pangs of childbirth. She became gravely sick and three days later at night she gave birth. The illness continued to grow worse and 18 days later she died, and another 19 days later the newborn child also died.*

This incident was a public one, and there is no need of witnesses, since according to all laws Padre Giuseppe is guilty of two homicides. I say this in a low voice because the sentence would be the gallows. Thanks be to God that the case has been stopped from going to a secular tribunal. Meanwhile, however, Padre Giuseppe remains suspended a Divinis.** *He must make restitution for the damages and also receive his deserved punishment from us.*

Instead of recognizing his crime—and notwithstanding the lamentations of Fortunato, the husband of the woman, and those of her children—Padre Giuseppe grabbed the house and the lumber that was in it. This incident occurred on June 14, 1793. In it one can see the injustice, the wrath and the imprudence of this padre.

The second complaint in writing was that of Taddeo. As he was going to see the kotwal *of the English Company together with Antonio, Gregorio and two or three Hindus, they passed along the street in front of Padre Giuseppe, who was standing under the tree in front of the hospice. All of them together greeted Padre Giuseppe. Taddeo says: "I greeted him as well and then we continued on our journey to see the* kotwal. *While we were sitting with the* kotwal, *Padre*

* Marco's words *rotino* and *rotinate* apparently refer respectively to a stick made of cane or rattan and to blows administered with a cane, in other words "a caning." The word *rotino* is evidently an Italicization of the French word *rotin,* meaning "cane" or "rattan" (from Malay *rotan*).

** In the Catholic Church, to be suspended *a divinis* means that the priest in question can no longer say mass, hear confessions, or perform other sacred offices.

Giuseppe had me called to make me give him the toddy tax.[*] *I got up immediately and went to the bazaar in order to get six* annas.[**] *I then brought them to him in person. I gave them to him and he gave me a receipt. I then went to sit in Juri Osta's shop.*[#] *Padre Giuseppe immediately called me and said to me: 'Who are you?' I replied that by the grace of God I am a Christian. 'In that case,' replied Padre Giuseppe, 'why didn't you offer a greeting to me?' I replied that I had offered a greeting together with the others when we were passing in front of him, and I added that having offered a greeting once, wasn't this enough? Padre Giuseppe replied: 'You will have to offer me a new greeting in the cutchery.' I replied: 'Please forgive me. From now on whenever I meet you anywhere, I will always offer you a greeting.'" [Taddeo] probably wished to indicate that the cutchery was not the place for him. [Taddeo continued:] "Padre Giuseppe then said: 'You are very arrogant.' And getting up he grabbed my hand, and he had me beaten by the servant Daru with three blows of a cane. I said: 'Up to now, no padre has dishonored me, but Padre Giuseppe now has unjustly dishonored me.' " Taddeo then went to make a complaint with the* kotwal, *but Antonino stopped him.*

The third complaint in writing was that of Veronica, a serious and honorable woman. She had some angry words with another Veronica, the wife of Franco Darji,[##] *one of*

[*] The phrase used here, "*Paesà del Tarì,*" apparently uses two Hindi words, *paisa* (money) and *tadi* (palm wine or toddy).

[**] There are 16 *annas* in one rupee. Although equivalents are difficult to estimate, six *annas* in 1793 would perhaps amount to about 10 dollars U.S. in today's money.

[#] Marco writes "*Giurì ostà.*" The surname Osta is quite common among Bettiah Christians. The origin of the name Osta is unknown. The name Juri is unusual and may be either European or Hindustani in origin.

[##] The surname Dargi or Darji is derived from the Hindi word *darji* or *darzi,* meaning "tailor."

the already mentioned four women of bad conduct. This latter Veronica was tried by the late prefect, was convicted and confessed. But now she is (or at least is suspected of being) one of Padre Giuseppe's four women! This Veronica said to Veronica the plaintiff: "Fine! Tomorrow I will get Padre Giuseppe to give you a good beating." In fact, this Veronica the plaintiff was taken that night by Sadù, Padre Giuseppe's administrator (and a man who is considered to be a miserable wretch). That night this Sadù brought this plaintiff to his house and beat her with three blows of a cane and hurled the worst abuse at her. He then turned her over to Darù, Padre Giuseppe's Hindu servant, but Darù accepted the assurances of Francisca, Fedele Lavandaro's wife, and let her go. In the morning, this Veronica came to Padre Giuseppe as a suppliant. He had her brought to the cutchery, had her extended hands grabbed by two servants, and had her publicly beaten with 12 blows of a cane. And Padre Giuseppe personally gave her a kick, causing her garment to fall down so that she stood there quite naked with her hands extended in the presence of the whole cutchery: Christians, Hindus, and Muslims.*

This incident occurred on September 18, 1793. Witnesses are not needed since the thing was public. It is left to the padre prefect and to Rome to consider if this is something that a missionary padre should do. All this was caused by a woman who is a whore. How much discord, troubles and injustices have come from these four whores?

The fourth complaint in writing was that of Silvestro

* In Hindi *Lavandaro* would be *dhobi*. In several cases, Marco gives early Bettiah Christians Italian surnames translated from the names of their castes or traditional occupations in Hindi. The use of surnames for Bettiah Christians is mostly a recent practice. Early Bettiah baptismal records usually identify the baptized persons only by the given names of their parents.

Ferraro, a man of an honorable family. "In my house," says Silvestro, "there was no man present. Padre Giuseppe then forcibly entered all the rooms, without giving any warning. My daughters were there half naked because they were baking bread. At that time, Padre Giuseppe upended everything in the house. My wife said that she has never seen or heard of anyone entering the house of honest people in this manner." Silvestro says, "I was in my field, and Padre Giuseppe came to the field immediately afterwards. He had my oxen set loose and told me that I could no longer have the field." All this was because Padre Giuseppe suspected that Padre Romualdo might have deposited something in Silvestro's house. "I," says Silvestro, "wanted to appeal to the* kotwal, *but Padre Romualdo stopped me from doing so." This occurred on September 3, 1793.*

*The fifth complaint in writing was that of Giuseppe Falegname,** a man of a very honorable and good house. "My house," says Giuseppe, "is small, but 21 persons live in it. In front of my house there has always been an empty space under the* pakar *tree# where I keep my wood and where I worked. Padre Giuseppe had that empty space closed off by a wall, and now no one can have access to that space. Not even the water from the street can escape, and if there is a fire I have no way to escape. He threw out my wood, and now I am in great need of space." Giuseppe Falegname also complains about the many abuses and threats that Maria, the daughter of Carlo and the first of the four bad women mentioned above, made against him.*

* *Ferraro* is Italian for "blacksmith" or "ironworker." *Fabbro* or *Fabbroferraio* would be more correct. The Hindi equivalent is *lohar*. Among Bettiah Christians, however, most ironworkers belonged to the Thakur caste and now use Thakur as their surname.

** *Falegname* is Italian for "carpenter" (Hindi *badhai*).

\# The *pakar* (Marco writes *paker*) tree is a type of fig-tree, *Ficus infectoria*.

The sixth complaint in writing was that of Primo, one of our Christians. He says: "I had a field within the fort. Then Antu, Padre Giuseppe's chief administrator, came and took my field away from me and gave it to Niru Noniya, and he is now cultivating my field. I went there to stop him from working on my field. This Niru then appealed to Antu in the cutchery. Antu sent his servants to grab me. They took me to the cutchery, where Padre Giuseppe grabbed one of my arms and had Lazaro grab the other. He then ordered Niru himself to beat me with 20 blows of a cane, in spite of the fact that I screamed for mercy [in the name of] the padre prefect.[5] This beating made me sick for several days. This occurred on September 18, 1793, and my field has not been returned to me."*

*The seventh complaint in writing was that of Antonio, the son of Pietro. One day he got into a dispute about some carts belonging to his house. He was beaten by Padre Giuseppe with his horse's riding whip until he became unconscious.** He then fled with some others and they did not return to make the complaint until today. This incident occurred on September 22, 1793.*

The eighth complaint in writing was that of Lika Katecumeno who, Padre Giuseppe kicked and beat with a stalk of maize# for having demanded just payment for his labor. Padre Giuseppe also did this to Gomar Katecumeno because he demanded just payment for his labor. He had him given 10 blows of a cane in public in the cutchery. I have many more complaints of this sort: of beatings, of taking

* The Hindi word *noniya* (Marco's Nonià) means "a maker of, or dealer in, salt or saltpetre". Noniya is now a fairly common surname among Bettiah Christians.

** For "riding whip", Marco writes *ciabuk*, an Italian transcription of the Hindi word *cabuk*.

Marco writes: "*un fusto de Granturco*." The translation is literal but the sense is somewhat doubtful.

time is short, however, and I judge these complaints that I have already described to be more than sufficient (both the general ones and those of individual persons), I will dispense with writing down all the rest in order to turn to the things that are most essential.

I said briefly above that the most essential and general scandal is the brazen conversation that Padre Giuseppe has day and night with four women who are fundamentally suspect. First is Maria, the daughter of Carlo and wife of Giuseppe, his servant. People say that this Maria was the cause of all the troubles that occurred in the time of that excellent missionary, Padre Michelangelo, and of Padre Zaccaria da Verona. She is a truly evil woman, who even told Padre Romualdo that the sacraments are shit and said other horrendous things. The second woman, who is more than suspect, is Veronica, the wife of the late Franco Darji. This trollop was publicly caught in the act and interrogated, and she then confessed. Her trial was conducted by our late prefect of happy memory, Giuseppe da Rovato. The third woman is Dominga, the daughter of the already mentioned Maria and the wife of Marcello Mahto, another servant of Padre Giuseppe. She is still too young to have had previous trials against her. The fourth woman is Rofina, the wife of Franco, who is the brother of that same Maria, daughter of Carlo.*

These four women are almost always together in the same house that is next to the cutchery. It is rumored that these four control everything: vendettas among women, punishments, the taking away of houses, the confiscation of fields, the affronts to their enemies, and the eviction of honest people from certain places so they cannot be witnesses to their affairs. Padre Giuseppe is with them almost all the time, as I have already said.

* Mahto (Marco's *Matto*) is the Hindi name of a middle caste.

And that this is true [is shown by the fact that] Padre Giuseppe arrived here in Bettiah about mid-morning on August 30, 1793. That same evening, Padre Giuseppe went to the house of that Maria, daughter of Carlo. There in her house, Maria washed his feet and another woman fanned him. All this took place in the presence of the Christian, Simone; the Muslim, Zakir (Sakir); *and the Hindu, Rambaco. And he stayed there until well into the night. Every day he goes there and remains there until the middle of the night, and sometimes even later. Together, they eat, drink, and gossip.*

Benedetta, the wife of Ilario, has stated the following in writing: "I," she says, "was coming from the house of the Alcore and passed in front of the house of Maria, the daughter of Carlo. Hearing them talking I stopped a minute to listen to what they were saying. Maria was speaking to Veronica, the wife of Franco Darji (the woman who was tried). This Maria, speaking about Padre Marco, said: 'This son of Sodom, a great insult, through some false report had all my mother's property looted. Now he has come to throw out Padre Giuseppe. This faggot** can drag his ass nine times up the toddy palm, but not even then will Padre Giuseppe leave here.' On which Veronica replied: 'Is he the faggot who robbed your mother's jewels?' 'Yes,' replied Maria, 'that's him.'" These are the facts and words that prove what has been said up to now.*

* The word "Alcore" is probably derived from the Hindi word *halalkhor.* This word literally means "eater of *halal* meat," the meat of animals killed by the Muslim practice of bleeding to death. This meaning has been extended, somewhat illogically, to euphemistically refer to mostly Hindu persons of the very low sweeper or scavenger caste usually called Bhangis. Here Marco likely means "the house of the sweepers."

** For "faggot," Marco writes (underlined) *Garù.* This word is clearly a transcription of the Hindi word *gandu,* meaning "homosexual" or "effeminate man."

Here I must transcribe a letter that Padre Giuseppe wrote to Antù, his administrator who stays here in Bettiah. I have already said above that before arriving here I met Padre Giuseppe at a distance of five miles from Bettiah and told him that I had been sent as an official representative against him. I wanted to bring him back to Bettiah, but he didn't want to come. That said, the same day he wrote the following letter in Hindustani that I here translate in Italian verbo ad verbu *[=word for word]:*

> *Padre Marco has come to Bettiah, I do not know why. You should remain on guard and firm with regard to my affairs. Don't listen to what anyone says, not even what Padre Marco says, because his powers have no force here. He has told me that he is going to visit the padres, and nothing else. If he orders something related to my official duties, you should not let him do it. Stay firm and without fear.*
> *(Signed in Padre Giuseppe Sahab's own hand)*
> *Padre Giuseppe*
> *Gobindgunj, the 1st of October, 1793 [...]*

Here one sees the spirit of Padre Giuseppe, how he respects the orders of the padre prefect (about which I had informed him), his real falseness, verifying what the present prefect had written about him, that semel mendax, semper mendax *[=once a liar, always a liar]. In addition, I see that he has always kept, and still keeps, a mare against the express orders by the same prefect.*

Sadù—in other words, Antù, Padre Giuseppe's chief administrator—has declared that Padre Giuseppe wrote to him, while still on his journey [...], the following: "If [it is decided that] I ought to stay, then write to me. If I ought not*

* In Hindi, *sadu* means "brother-in-law." Antù is a short form of the Christian name Antonio or Anthony.

to stay, then I will destroy the fort. If they do anything more (urcus deinghè), *I will make it a wilderness."**

*(The witnesses to these words are Teclena, Damiano, Clemente Falegname, and Imandi Muratori the Muslim****).*

There is another complaint in writing that Padre Giuseppe's servants have organized a public game of chance that has already been prohibited several times because in the long run many families can be ruined because of the bets that they put out, some wagering for this one, some for the other.

Common knowledge, one's eyes, and experience prove that Padre Giuseppe is a great merchant of salt, of horses, of guns, etc., and what is worse, and incredible, is that they say that the prefect aids and abets him.

I now come, finally, to my verdict. First, Padre Giuseppe da San Marcello will be excommunicated and suspended a divinis *for the crime described in article number four above. He will stay in this condition as long as he has not been absolved and made to perform a public penance, since the incident was public and notorious. Second, he is proven and declared a criminal* in rè gravissima *[= in a very serious matter], as is learned from the above-described article number five—and the prefect will not have the power to absolve this crime, except after a long and adequate penance, proportionate to the two homicides [in which the deaths] occurred within 40 days [of Padre Giuseppe's attack], as the laws indicate.*

* In the manuscript this phrase is apparently written in Roman letters as *Urcus deinghè* (i.e., *Aur kuch denge*). It literally means "[If] they will give anything else." The phrase that follows, "I will make a desert," appears to be an allusion to the famous quote from Tacitus with which we began this book.

** *Muratore* is the Italian word for "mason or bricklayer." In Bettiah, the modern Hindi equivalent is usually *raj-mistri*. Imandi is probably Imando or Amando, an Italian name.

This case comes under the statute for Voluntary Homicide, [and absolution in such] cases is reserved for Rome alone. Nor does it appear to be possible for the prefect to absolve him because there is no need to do so. [...] In any case, it will be up to the prefect to keep Padre Giuseppe in his custody until he receives the response of the sacred Penitentiary [tribunal in Rome]. Meanwhile, for the spiritual and temporal crimes of articles four and five, Padre Giuseppe will remain deprived of all offices, or public undertakings, until the necessary absolution is received. In addition, it is declared that Padre Giuseppe was formerly suspended one other time by the present prefect, Carlo Maria da Alatri, as a notorious property owner, and, as the prefect himself writes: "Having done the accounts, Padre Giuseppe has kept about 3,000 rupees of the mission that should be turned over to this mission."

It is true that the padre prefect writes to me in his letter of October 17, 1793 that he has absolved Padre Giuseppe with a few days suspension, but with the condition of getting back this money. But since this condition has not been met in the time it should and could have been, the absolution given by the prefect is invalid. Thus even for this misbehavior, Padre Giuseppe remains still suspended for being a property owner. Nor can the prefect exempt him from this, since it is not his money, but the money of the Mission. Thus it is judged necessary to put a lien on Padre Giuseppe's goods and money and trunks, etc., which he has deposited in various houses of secular persons. It is all the more important that this be done since there is a well-founded suspicion that he might try to flee.

The very reverend padre prefect is asked, then, to immediately remove Padre Giuseppe from Bettiah because of the scandals that have occurred and can happen again. It is not only for the violence already described, and other violence that could be described, but also for the general

> *well-founded suspicions [that Padre Giuseppe has violated] the sixth commandment [against murder], and the vow of chastity, of which the proofs are all too evident.*
>
> *If the very reverend padre prefect should find some difficulty in all this, then in this case he should kindly suspend everything and leave the things in Bettiah as they were before Padre Giuseppe came here. And this should be done until there are replies from Rome, where a well-authenticated copy of this document will be sent. [...]*
>
> *In conclusion, then, the most reverent padre prefect is asked to have Padre Giuseppe turn over the accounts and also restore to the Mission the money he took (about 3,000 rupees according to the letters that you yourself have written to me).*[6] *And then Padre Giuseppe can be sent quickly to Europe, because the staff of the Mission has complained that it does not want to put up with this scandalous person in the Mission any longer. [...]*

This document recording our judgment against Padre Giuseppe da San Marcello was then personally signed at Bettiah on October 15, 1793, by Padres Giovanni Gualberto da Massa, Romualdo da Senigallia, Lodovico Maria da Città di Castello, and myself. Each padre also added a clear statement of his agreement with both the charges made against Padre Giuseppe and the verdict reached. I myself wrote a postscript to the effect that Padre Giuseppe had committed other grievous crimes including the alienation of ecclesiastical property and that this property had been furtively put in the hands of secular persons, particularly a Mr. S. Finch in Chhapra, where Padre Giuseppe had prepared a house for his life as an apostate.

Chapter 20

Our Mission Betrayed

Many of the disasters that have befallen our poor Mission in recent years have been the direct responsibility of the now deposed prefect, Carlo Maria da Alatri. Propaganda could not have made a worse choice than naming him prefect. After the sad and tragic affair of Giuseppe da San Marcello, the Mission fell into one grave crisis after another.

When the prefect Giuseppe da Rovato died in 1786, he had spent over 30,000 rupees in the construction of the church in Patna designed by the Venetian, Signore Tiretta.[1] Padre Giuseppe claimed Tiretta to be "the best architect of Bengal." Padre Giuseppe got much of this construction money from the head of the Dutch factory in Patna, a certain Mr. Falck, and from several Englishmen, despite the fact that they were all adherents of the heretical Protestant Reform. Wherever Padre Giuseppe managed to get his funds, however, he never stopped giving us missionaries our annual subsidies, and at his death he left some 2,000 rupees in my hands as procurator of the Mission. During the two years that I was acting prefect, I increased this amount, without ever stopping the subsidies, and in 1788 I turned over everything to the new prefect, Carlo Maria da Alatri. Within a short time, he claimed that all these rupees had been spent and that he could not pay us our subsidies, notwithstanding the fact that in 1793 alone I sent him another 1,000 rupees.

All this would have not brought great prejudice to the Mission if other, more essential disturbances had not occurred. All the other missionaries came to me for a solution but what could I do apart from forwarding their letters to the prefect of Propaganda Fide and sending him my own interpretation about the nature of the problems caused by our own prefect here in Hindustan? In 1793 and 1794 I sent off no less than four packets to Rome with letters from me and from the other missionaries with our just complaints against the actions of the prefect.

One of the primary disturbances concerned the continuing problems with Padre Giuseppe da San Marcello. After Padres Lodovico Maria da Città di Castello, Romualdo da Senigallia, Giovanni Gualberto da Massa, and I had pronounced Padre Giuseppe guilty of the crimes indicated in the previous chapter, we were forced to send him down the river Gandak to Patna shackled in irons so that the prefect could deal with him as he saw fit. Unfortunately, the prefect did not support our verdict against Padre Giuseppe and, in fact, defended him against us. During this journey down the river, Padre Giuseppe was freed by an English friend and business associate.[2] Padre Giuseppe then filed a court case against us four padres for cruel treatment, but luckily the English judge did not accept Padre Giuseppe's claim against us.[3] The judge, in fact, ordered Padre Giuseppe to give back to the Mission some 4,300 rupees that he had deposited into the hands of his secular friends, as I proved from original documents.[4]

Another important disturbance for the Mission was caused by the repeated transfers of the missionaries from one hospice to another and the repeated punishments meted out to them for little or no reasons.[5] These transfers put the missionaries among people they did not know and whose language they often did not speak. This caused problems both for the missionaries and for the local Christians and catechumens. Take, for example, the case of Padre Romualdo da Senigallia. He first arrived in our Mission in 1774 and since this time was stationed at Bettiah. I have already described how the prefect sent Padre Giuseppe da San Marcello to take charge of the Bettiah Mission and how Padre Giuseppe mistreated poor Padre Romualdo. After the trial of Padre Giuseppe in 1793, the prefect decided to punish Padre Romualdo for participating in the trial by sending him an order to transfer from Bettiah to Nepal where he was to practice medicine, not even bothering to ask if he knew anything about medicine or wanted to practice it. In addition, Padre Romualdo had already turned 60 years old in 1794 and could not travel easily.

Here I will mention only a few of the many other hasty and vindictive acts perpetrated by the prefect against the poor padres of the Mission. He suspended *a divinis* Padre Lodovico Maria da Città di Castello and gave him an order to return to Europe, all this because the padre had offered mass in the house of a Catholic lay person who was sick.

The prefect then sentenced Padre Lodovico, Padre Giovanni Maria da Camajore, and Padre Bonaventura da Salino to 10 days of penitential exercises under the threat of suspension, all this without giving them any reason for it. The prefect then declared Padre Giovanni Gualberto da Massa to be a heretic for having said, in jest and allegorically, that the Gospel did not function in the Indies, meaning by this that the Gospel was little observed in practice, even by nominal Christians.

The prefect also threatened to censure me and send me back to Europe.[6] This was because I refused to receive in Bettiah two scandalous whores, disturbers of the peace among the Christians, whom the prefect had sent from Patna with a letter.* The two whores, angry because of my refusal to welcome them, chose not to give me the letter and instead sent it back to the prefect. I immediately wrote a letter to the prefect and sent a messenger to deliver it to him in Patna. As it turned out, however, the letter from the two women arrived first and the angry prefect then refused to receive my letter. He spat on it, trampled his feet on it, and sent it back without ever opening it. Immediately afterward he wrote to Padre Giovanni Gualberto telling him to put me on trial on 21 truly slanderous charges that this padre found to be entirely false. [...]

These and other irregular, bullying acts disturbed and alarmed the missionaries and chilled their zeal. This caused the old and zealous missionaries to resolve to return to Europe (something that the prefect himself encouraged) and led some, especially the weak, to simply withdraw from the prefect's jurisdiction [...]. For example, Padre Zaccaria da Verona, right after his very first talk with the prefect, declared himself independent. Padre Giuseppe da San Marcello, with much more malice, did the same. Even Padre Lodovico da Città di Castello, virtually through desperation, resolved to do as much. I know well that these [padres] had been led to *spiritu impuritatis*, but it is quite true that when a priest or friar (*religioso*) in these parts—that are both irremediable and dissolute—finds himself disturbed and alarmed, he easily loses the spirit of the Lord and leaves himself ever more subject to

* The two were none other than Maria, the wife of Giuseppe, and her daughter Dominga, the wife of Marcello, some of whose actions are described in Chapter 19 above about the trial of Padre Giuseppe da San Marcello. The story of Marco's refusal to see these two women is described in more detail in Marco's letter of August 1, 1794 to Carlo Maria da Alatri.

diabolical temptations. But these things never happened in the times of the other prefects.

In spite of all the threats he made, in the end Prefect Carlo Maria da Alatri had little choice but to cancel or forget the more extreme actions he had taken.[7] The four of us padres who had taken part in the trial of Padre Giuseppe da San Marcello were first suspended but we were rehabilitated a few months later. Giovanni Gualberto da Massa, the only padre who spoke well the Newari language of the Nepalese Christians in Chuhari, was sent back to that station. I was allowed to return to Bhagalpur where I had been living during most of the time since 1784. Romualdo da Senigallia and Lodovico Maria da Città di Castello were transferred from Bettiah to Nepal. Padre Romualdo stayed in Nepal for nine months but returned to Bettiah at the end of 1994. Padre Lodovico was too sick to travel to Nepal and he retired to our hospice in Chandernagore. The prefect repented his intention to send Padre Giuseppe da San Marcello back to Bettiah and kept him detained in Patna before deciding to send him to Kathmandu towards the end of 1796.

Chapter 21

The Scourge of the Mission

Marco della Tomba's letter dated April 15, 1795 to a cardinal in Rome, probably Cardinal Antonelli, is the last document that exists written in Marco's own hand. The only surviving document from a later date is an excerpt of a letter he wrote when he was 72 years old, i.e., in about 1798, that is cited in a 1804 report about the Tibet Mission prepared by Padre Bonaventura da Salino. In spite of the absence of documents, we know that Marco continued to work in Bhagalpur from 1795 until his death in 1803 and that he continued to be at the center of the sharp squabbles among the padres of the Mission.

From the moment he took charge of the Mission as prefect in 1788, Carlo Maria da Alatri quarreled constantly with Marco and with most of the other padres in the Mission, and Propaganda Fide finally decided that it would have to intervene in the disputes and appoint a new prefect.[1] In a special meeting held in Rome on January 31, 1796, Propaganda Fide officials decided to send a Visitor Apostolic to the Mission with full powers to make whatever changes were needed. The person appointed for this task was Nicolas Champenois, the Bishop of Doliche (in Syria). Champenois was associated with the French Society of Foreign Missions

(*Société des Missions-Étrangères*). He had been in India since 1777 and from 1785 had been in charge of the See of Pondicherry. News of Champenois's appointment did not reach him in Pondicherry until February 1798.

Unfortunately, Bishop Champenois was a French citizen. By this time, the events of the French Revolution had greatly alarmed the English, and the French general Napoleon Bonaparte had already conducted his successful Italian campaign (1796–97) and was starting his campaign against the British client-state in Egypt. The French fleet was destroyed by the English Admiral Nelson in August 1798, but Napoleon managed to get himself crowned emperor on Eighteenth Brumaire (November 9–10), 1799, and hostilities with the British continued. Champenois made several attempts to get permission from the English to visit the Mission, but all his requests were refused.

On April 17, 1799, Bishop Champenois wrote to all the padres of the Tibet Mission explaining his difficulties and announcing his decision to conduct his examination of the Mission by letter. The main decisions he took were to depose the prefect, Carlo Maria da Alatri and appoint in his stead Padre Giovanni Maria da Camjore. Most of the padres accepted this as a good choice, but Carlo Maria first refused to recognize the authenticity of the bishop's letter deposing him and then, when he had to recognize it, challenged the decision claiming that Bishop Champenois had been required to visit the Mission in person, something he had not done. Meanwhile Giovanni Maria da Camjore tried to assume charge of the Mission. From January 1800 to March 1801, Padre Giovanni toured the different stations of the Mission in an effort to put things back in order. Unfortunately, his constant travel weakened his health and he died of dysentery at Chuhari near Bettiah in June 1801.

At this point Padre Marco comes back into the story. In a letter dated August 4, 1801, the Visitor Apostolic, Bishop Champenois, appointed Marco della Tomba, as interim prefect of the Mission and his friend Romualdo da Senigallia as vice prefect. As has been noted, Marco had already served as vice prefect in effective charge of the Mission in the period from 1786 to 1788. Reading between the lines of many of his letters, it is evident that he had long held hopes of being appointed prefect. By this time, however, he was already 75 years old and was more cantankerous than ever.

On May 16, 1801, the prefect of Propaganda, Cardinal Giacinto Sigismondo Gerdil, wrote to Bishop Champenois admonishing him for not visiting the Mission in person and requesting that he either do so or appoint a personal representative to do so on his behalf. Another letter with the same date was sent to the deposed prefect, Carlo Maria da Alatri, telling him to submit to the decisions already taken by Bishop Champenois. On July 14, 1802, the bishop wrote to a French secular priest already present in Calcutta, Rene Louis Foulon, requesting that he take on the task of examining the Mission. Foulon then made friends with the procurator of the Mission, Padre Angelo da Caraglio, who was living in the Chandernagore hospice, and eventually agreed to accept the appointment. On November 16, 1802, Foulon informed Marco della Tomba, who was still living in Bhagalpur, of his decision and asked him to call all the friars of the Mission for a meeting in Patna.

Unfortunately for Marco, Foulon was a disastrous choice to examine the Mission. The main problem was that Foulon was evidently under the spell of the opinions of his new friend, Angelo da Caraglio, a person with whom Marco had already crossed swords. In the passage from Marco's last known letter of 1798 to the general procurator of the Capuchin order, as quoted in Bonaventura da Salino's report to Propaganda Fide, Marco sharply criticized Angelo da Caraglio:[2]

> *For the past year Padre Angelo da Caraglio, who usurped the Chandernagore hospice with all its furniture and the church, lives there independent of anyone and charged with excommunication. He lives obstinately and does not even open the letters of the prefect* or of other missionaries. Nor does he receive any missionary in the hospice who might be sent there by a superior. And he celebrates and (what is worse* [quod pejus]) *administers the sacraments as usual. What can I say of that poor Padre Giovenale da Nizza? He got permission to return to Europe and went to Bengal to find a ship, but he could not find one because of the wars and was forced to stay for some months in Bengal. But since Padre Angelo did not wish to receive him, Padre Giovenale was unable to get shelter in our Chandernagore hospice and was obliged to find lodging here and there. Finally (it is not known whether from desperation or from bad luck), he fell into the sea and was never seen again.*

Another problem for the Mission in these years was that the Napoleonic wars in Europe had made it impossible for Propaganda Fide to send any new missionaries. Even getting letters back and forth between Bengal and Rome was difficult. The last expedition of five friars was sent from Europe on different ships in 1790. The friars arrived on various dates in 1791 and 1792. In 1803 only seven friars remained in the Mission, none of them young, and they were spread out across north India from Delhi to Chandernagore.** Padre

* In 1798, assuming this to be the date of Marco's letter, the prefect was none other than Carlo Maria da Alatri, hardly a friend of Marco.

** These were: (1) Marco della Tomba (age 77, interim prefect at Bhagalpur), (2) Carlo Maria da Alatri (age unknown, in India since 1784, residing at Patna), (3) Romualdo da Senigallia (age 69, superior at Bettiah),

Foulon, after spending over two months in Chandernagore with Padre Angelo da Caraglio, traveled on to Bhagalpur to meet with the interim prefect, Marco della Tomba.

The five or six days that Foulon spent with Marco in Bhagalpur were sufficient for Foulon to come to despise Marco. Unfortunately, we have only Foulon's side of the story, contained in his official report on the inspection of the Mission. Both Foulon's original French report and a rough Italian translation are preserved in the Propaganda Fide archives. Foulon describes his meeting with Marco as follows:[3]

> *After having been abundantly supplied with the necessary things, I left Chandernagore on December 3, 1802. After a relatively easy journey I arrived at Bhagalpur on the 24th. The Reverend Padre Marco received me quite well, and during the five or six days that I was there in Bhagalpur, I had several conversations and frequent tête-à-têtes with him. I soon got to be acquainted with him and then learn more about him. Under his very venerable exterior with very considerate manners, I was pained to see that he was a man without principles, without fear of God, a hypocrite, ambitious, false-hearted, and deceitful. I saw that the Christians entrusted to his care were in a neglected state and not educated. Sacred things were treated in the most indecent and most revolting way. In conformity with the wishes of your grace, he had drawn up the act of accusation against the Reverend Padre Carlo Maria da Alatri. He read*

(4) Bonaventura da Salino (age 57, superior at Lucknow), (5) Angelo da Caraglio (age unknown, in India since 1791, residing at Chandernagore), (6) Giuseppe da San Marcello (age unknown, in India since 1783 and from 1797 residing in Nepal), and (7) Gregorio da la Presentazione (age 60, a Carmelite friar residing in Agra). Lodovico Maria da Città di Castello had died at age 50 in 1799. See Vannini (1981, 159) and also Bishop Champenois's letter from Pondicherry to Cardinal Gerdil dated January 16, 1802.

some of it to me. He confided it to me. After a few days I informed him that Your Grace had charged me with the task of electing at Patna a new prefect, and that none of the Reverend Padres were excluded, not even Padre Carlo if he could clear himself of the accusations made against him. Padre Marco was remarkably alarmed, above all on the topic of Padre Carlo. However, he recovered from his agitation and gave me his vote for Padre Bonaventura da Salino (I have read a letter from Padre Marco to Padre Bonaventura dated in the month of October, 1802, in which he promised the prefecture to him). I left Padre Marco in Bhagalpur since I feared spoiling everything by bringing him with me to Patna. I left alone, therefore, and arrived in Patna on January 5, 1803.

In Patna, Padre Foulon was met by Padre Carlo Maria da Alatri, the deposed prefect and a longtime enemy of Marco. The only other friars who came to the meeting with Foulon were Romualdo da Senigallia, Marco's old friend, and Bonaventura da Salino, who Marco had appointed to be procurator of the Mission. The principal items on the agenda of the meeting were to decide the fate of the deposed prefect, to name a new prefect, and to decide what to do with Giuseppe da San Marcello (still in Nepal). It was agreed that Padre Carlo Maria should be returned to Europe. He accepted this decision and set sail from Bengal a few months later. The issue of who was to be the new prefect was more difficult. Padre Foulon strongly favored his new friend Padre Angelo da Caraglio, but the other friars were all strongly opposed to him and wanted Padre Bonaventura to be appointed. Foulon reluctantly accepted this decision, but later, in his final report to Bishop Champenois he reneged on this agreement and devised a scheme that would make Padre Angelo the real Prefect. Foulon was also against rehabilitating Padre

Giuseppe da San Marcello and refused to recall him from Nepal. Instead he had him excommunicated.

In his final report to Champenois, Foulon not only offered the already cited harsh assessment of his visit to Marco in Bhagalpur but also made several other accusations against him. One of the most interesting is his charge that Marco was associated with the heretical society of Freemasons. This is what Foulon wrote:[4]

> *With respect to Padre Marco, it would have been very fortunate for the Mission if he could have returned to Europe because he has been and will continue to be the scourge* (fléau) *of this poor Mission. His presence in the Mission makes one think that God left him there in order to punish it for all the iniquities and scandals committed by so many of its Evangelical workers. May it please Heaven that this not be a proof of its total abandonment. A number of persons believe what Padre Bonaventura da Salino testified to me many times, that Padre Marco is an impious man, an associate, ally and protector of impious persons. Padre Marco made accusations against [the now deposed prefect] Padre Carlo Maria da Alatri. But if Padre Marco had not had the hope of being prefect, he would probably have behaved toward me as badly as he did toward Padre Angelo da Caraglio. When he saw the Brief of Pope Pius VI, the orders of Your Grace, and the legitimate mission of Padre Angelo to take the orders and notify the various padres, and when he wrote a letter to Padre Carlo (this letter is in my hands) so that he would warn Padre Giovanni Maria da Camajore and Padre Romualdo da Senigallia to stay on their guard since Padre Angelo was wandering about the Mission carrying with him some fabricated documents, etc. etc., I was convinced by his own letters that he was as I said at the beginning: impious, an intriguer, ambitious, false-hearted, and deceitful.*

Padre Bonaventura and Padre Angelo have given me incontestable proof that Padre Marco is impious and associated with impiety. Padre Marco instigated a violent persecution against Padre Angelo. He put himself at the head of the persecutors. He wrote several letters to the Masonic club organized in Chandernagore. In them he spouted off that Padre Angelo was loathsome, a thief, an apostate, and in Chandernagore and Calcutta the letters were shown [as the letters] of an old and respectable prefect, and Padre Angelo was decried by everyone as an apostate, etc. This is not all. Padre Marco wrote two letters in the same style to the Reverend Padre Benoit of Pondicherry, and all that in order to serve the Masonic cabal that tried, and that still tries, to place in the sanctuary Padre Benjamin, an orator of the lodge [called] Turogne Perpetuel, in a word "the opprobrium of Religion." This association of Padre Marco with Impiety is quite enough proof that he himself is initiated as a Mason.

Here is another proof that was given to me by Padre Bonaventura. Padre Marco was assigned to go to Agra and Delhi. At first he accepted the "obedience," but soon he decided he didn't want to make the trip. He begged the padre prefect to name someone else instead. Padre Giovenale da Nizza della Paglia was designated, but before Padre Giovenale left, Padre Marco gave him some letters of recommendation that his friends had given to him. Padre Giovenale, when he arrived at Fatigar, delivered one of these letters to the Comte de Chaigau.[5] *The Comte received him with all sorts of demonstrations of friendship. A conversation was begun. Monsieur le Comte, believing that the Padre was initiated, revealed to him all the mysteries of the Masonry. Padre Giovenale listened to everything without interrupting, but Monsieur le Comte realized his mistake and changed the conversation. He dismissed him and saw him no more. Padre Giovenale acquired a taste for these unfortunate teachings and became Padre Marco's disciple. Padre Giovenale got lost in Calcutta, imbued with Philosophic Maxims, and died in despair throwing himself into the Ganges. This is what Padre Angelo testifies.*

All the reverend padres also unanimously testify that Padre Marco constantly squandered the possessions of the Mission. He sold its goods, things like its silver implements, etc. It is true that he bought land and a house in Calcutta, but he bought it in order to cover the sale of the silver implements of the Chandernagore Church and Hospice. He bought it also to cover a subscription that he scandalously made taking advantage of the rebellion of the Calcutta Christians against their legitimate Pastors in order to construct a Church. But although he had many Christians on his side, he was unable to succeed in his project. The land and the house that Padre Marco bought were not worth more that 2,600 rupees. Nonetheless, he produced a contract of 4,500 rupees.

Padre Marco also favored Padre Giuseppe da San Marcello's scandals. We know, on the basis of Padre Marco's own letters, that even though Padre Giuseppe was the opprobrium of the sanctuary and even though he squandered the possessions of the Chunar Mission that he had sold, this Padre Marco requested that Padre Giuseppe be named procurator of the Tibet Mission. And he would have been if Padre Carlo, because of his impious views and [thirst] for revenge, had not sent Padre Giuseppe to devastate the Christians of Bettiah, who then rebelled against [Padre Giuseppe] and obliged him to leave. After his incarceration, Padre Giuseppe was sent to Nepal where he continued his scandals, etc.

Monsignor, I assure you that I lack the courage (i ternuri) *to describe all the horrors of this Padre Marco. He will always be the scourge of this Mission if effective measures are not taken against him, since it is impossible to send him back to Europe because of his advanced age.*

Although Padre Foulon claimed that his absurdly harsh judgment of Marco was the result of their face-to-face encounter in Bhagalpur, there is little doubt that Foulon's opinion was heavily influenced by Padre Angelo da Caraglio, who had already convinced Foulon to appoint him as the new prefect of the Mission.[6] After his disastrous visit to Marco in Bhagalpur, Padre Foulon went on alone to Patna, arriving there at the beginning of January 1803. There he met with three friars of the Mission—Bonaventura da Salino, Romualdo da Senigallia, and Carlo Maria da Alatri. The three were strongly opposed to Angelo da Caraglio and Foulon was forced to give up his plan to appoint Angelo as Prefect. Instead Foulon named Bonaventura da Salino as Prefect and Angelo da Caraglio as General Procurator.

When Foulon arrived back in Chandernagore, however, he and Angelo evidently devised a plan that would give Angelo independent control over all the finances of the whole Mission and give him spiritual control over about half of the Mission stations. This plan was codified in a decree issued in Latin by Foulon on February 25, 1803.[7] Bonaventura da Salino was to remain in Lucknow with spiritual—but not economic—jurisdiction, and that too only over the Mission stations of Bhagalpur, Bettiah, Chuhari, and Lucknow. The remaining stations of Chandernagore, Patna, Agra, Delhi, Sardhana and Chunar would be under the complete control of Angelo da Caraglio. In addition, Bonaventura was to remain titular prefect only until the arrival of a new missionary from Europe, at which time Angelo would become prefect of the entire Mission with complete control over all spiritual and economic matters.

Foulon's decree was especially ruthless in its treatment of Marco della Tomba:[8]

> *We order that the Reverend Padre Procurator each month should send to the Reverend Padre Marco 20 rupees so that he can maintain a decent old age. But if he again disturbs the Mission as he has so greatly disturbed it [in the past], we excommunicate him with an automatic* (latae sententiae) *excommunication [that can be] put aside only by the pope. And he will incur the same if he writes either in favor or against our orders, writing or speaking to anyone, whether it be to the prefect, to some missionary, or to some secular person. The prefect and the missionaries will incur the same excommunication if they reply to him or have any dealings with him in any way about these present orders. And if he is so blind that he ignores these orders of ours that are endowed with pontifical authority, he will be considered excommunicated and will immediately have to be avoided* (vitandus) *both by the prefect, the procurator, and by any other missionary, if he is shown to go against [the sentence]. We order that Padre Marco should not leave his district for any reason, and if any missionary were to receive him in his own hospice both of them will incur an automatic excommunication [that can be] put aside only by the pope. However, if the Reverend Padre Marco gets sick, the missionary closest to him will go to him. And it will be allowed that the closest missionary will have the right to hear Padre Marco's sacramental confession once a year. We order that the Reverend Padre Procurator—if he finds out with certainty that Reverend Padre Marco has done something or has written something against these orders—should cease to send him anything. Reverend Padre Marco can write as much as he wishes to Rome, to the Very Illustrious and Very Reverend Dolicense Bishop Champenois and to the Reverend Padre Procurator Angelo da Caraglio.*

All this was too much for Padre Bonaventura da Salino. He resigned his devalued prefecture to Padre Angelo da Caraglio and then sailed for Europe on October 11, 1803, in order to lodge a protest against what had happened. In Rome, the heads of Propaganda Fide began a multi-session general meeting on June 4, 1804, in which the results of Foulon's visit were discussed and eventually approved.

The prefect of Propaganda Fide at the time was none other than Cardinal Stefano Borgia, with whom Marco had long corresponded. Borgia had been secretary of Propaganda from 1770 to 1789 and was prefect from 1802 to the end of 1804. As has been noted above (p. 18), in 1779 Cardinal Borgia wrote a letter to Cardinal Antonelli, soon to become prefect of Propaganda, in which he sarcastically criticized Marco's insistence on returning to India. Nonetheless, Marco always held Borgia in highest esteem and Borgia's own letters to Marco were always polite.

In a presentation about the Tibet Mission made to the 1804 general meeting, however, Borgia repeated Signore Foulon's complaints about Marco almost verbatim:[9]

> *The Visitor thus made efforts to get to know well the other padres in order to arrive at the selection of a new prefect after having also called for the votes of the same padres. Padre Marco, who aspired to this was not only deemed to not be worthy but was rather recognized as the true scourge of that Mission, a wastrel, impious, suspected of being in communication with Masons and their Lodges, and in summary, such that he should be absolutely banished, although this is something that cannot be carried out because of his advanced age. Nonetheless, in the judgment of the Visitor the strongest measures should at least be taken against him, hence he was suspended from any exercise of his ministry and his office of missionary, and will no longer do harm to the Mission.*

That Cardinal Borgia should repeat such charges with apparent approval is a sad commentary on the workings of the Propaganda bureaucracy and is a serious blot on Borgia's own reputation as an intellectually progressive, if politically conservative, leader of the Church in this period.[10]

The response to all this came from Padre Bonaventura da Salino, who was apparently allowed to present his own long report directly to the 1804 Propaganda Fide sessions sometime after the speech made by Cardinal Borgia.[11] In this report, Bonaventura laid out in detail all the irregularities of Signore Foulon's visit and decree. Most convincing is Bonaventura's argument that Foulon's blatant establishment of Angelo da Caraglio as a powerful and independent procurator of the Mission and of himself as a powerless and merely titular prefect was completely irregular and improper. Bonaventura also strongly defended Marco della Tomba and other padres who had been attacked by Foulon.

By this time, news of Marco's death at Bhagalpur—either on the March 18, or June 7, 1803—had already reached Europe, and Bonaventura did not hesitate to place a good part of the responsibility on Foulon's conduct:[12]

> *Signore Foulon declared that Padre Marco della Tomba would be declared excommunicated and was to be shunned by the others* (vitando) *if he were to speak or to write either in favor or against the Decrees of the Visit. Please hear how Signore Foulon treats this decrepit missionary, who completed 40 years in this Mission and even exercised the office of prefect to the satisfaction of the Sacred Congregation.... Could the rigor of this censure have been carried to a greater excess? Could the road have been opened wider to scandalizing the Faithful and depriving them of the sacraments? Not content with the excommunication, Foulon orders the procurator to not supply Padre Marco with anything to live*

on if he falls into these censures. Thus it happened that that missionary could no longer continue to bear so many blows and miserably lost his life. To this is what the abuse of the ecclesiastic weapons leads.

A sadder epitaph to Marco's long life in the Tibet Mission of Hindustan is hard to imagine.

The story of the Tibet Mission does not, of course, end here. Unfortunately for the Mission, Cardinal Borgia and the governing committee of Propaganda Fide decided in favor of Padre Foulon's decrees and left Padre Angelo da Caraglio as prefect of the Mission. In his modern history of the Mission, Padre Vannini (1981, 165–66) describes Angelo da Caraglio as "a man endowed with a strong persuasive personality, but guided in his actions by a blind, excessive zeal. In his opinion all but himself were bad.... His stubborn, irascible and suspicious temper made it impossible for him to foster good human relations with anyone around him." Vannini cites the opinion of Monsignor Antonino da Lodi (originally Pezzoni), a later friar and prefect of the mission who knew Padre Angelo personally: "In his exaggerated zeal—Padre Angelo feels that everyone and everything has to be reformed. He goes so far as to suspect that all, even the missionaries, are in league with the powers of evil and he thinks himself to be inspired by God to fight for the suppression of evil and the triumph of all that is good."

Cardinal Borgia died on November 23, 1804, not long after Propaganda had decided to accept Padre Foulon's decrees. Possibly in part out of respect for his role in this decision, Propaganda refused to reconsider its policy even after having received news of the continuing quarrels in the Mission provoked by Angelo da Caraglio's high-handed behavior. Already in April 1805, the Superior General of the

Capuchin Order intervened to get Propaganda to change its decision. Despite an initial rebuff from the Propaganda Fide officials, the Superior General and others continued to lodge protests. Finally, on August 27, 1805, Propaganda wrote to Monsignor Champenois, the bishop of Pondicherry who had delegated the task of Visitor to Signore Foulon, asking him to find a new solution to the problem. In 1808, Monsignor Champenois effectively divided the Mission into two parts—a western one with stations at Agra, Delhi, and Lucknow and an eastern one corresponding to the older stations of Patna, Bettiah, Chuhari, Bhagalpur, Chandernagore, etc.—and allowed the friars of the Mission to choose in which part they wanted to be stationed. Already in 1806, Padre Angelo da Caraglio had voluntarily moved to Sardhan, the principality of the Christian princess, Begum Samru. Soon after returning from Europe in 1808, Padre Bonaventura da Salino then took up the post of independent vice prefect in Bengal and Bihar and all the other missionaries opted to stay at stations within his jurisdiction. The problems of the Mission were far from over, but, for a while at least, things settled down to a semblance of peace and order.

Soon after his death, Marco della Tomba's name disappears in the archives of Propaganda Fide. Marco's numerous essays about Hindustan and Hinduism and his translations of Hindustani texts were apparently kept in the Borgia family museum at Vellatri until eventually being turned over to the Vatican Library. Some of his scholarly work is mentioned in a book by the scholar-missionary Paolino da S. Bartolomeo published in 1796, in another book by the secular Orientalist Abraham Hyacinthe Anquetil Duperron published in 1786, and in an essay by Sir William Jones first published in 1799, all three during Marco's own lifetime. After this, nothing is heard about Marco until the rediscovery of his papers in the

Vatican Library by the Italian scholar Angelo de Gubernatis in the latter part of the nineteenth century. In 1878 de Gubernatis published a selection of Marco's essays and translations. This book is still essential, but at the time it made little impact, and now it is almost impossible to find.

A few accounts of the Tibet Mission were published in the first half of the twentieth century, but it was only with the publication of the massive collection of letters and documents of the Tibet Mission by Luciano Petech from 1952 to 1956 that the Mission began to attract much scholarly attention. Petech's volumes are mostly limited to the earlier phase of the Mission up to 1745, when the friars were forced to leave Tibet proper, but Petech's Introduction also discusses some of the later friars including Marco. In the 1970s and 1980s, Fulgentius Vannini, an Italian Capuchin friar who worked in India, published four important histories of the Mission's early activities in Tibet, in Nepal, and in Hindustan. More recently, Jose Kalapura, a Jesuit scholar, has written an excellent account of the later history of the Mission and the present-day community of Bettiah Christians. Nonetheless, much research remains to be done. Particularly during the eighteenth century, the friars of the Tibet Mission lived on the crucial interface between Europe and Asia, between Christianity and the religions of Asia, between the advancing British Imperialism and the resistance of the Asian states. The Capuchin friars were certainly not neutral observers, but they were neither British nor South Asians.[13] They brought a unique perspective on the events and cultures they witnessed and wrote about. Marco della Tomba still has much to tell us.

End Notes

Introduction

1. Tacitus 1948: 80.
2. This paragraph and the next are largely based on Anthony Grafton's recent book, *What Was History? The Art of History in Early Modern Europe* (2007), and on Carlo Ginzburg's essay collection *History, Rhetoric, and Proof* (1999).
3. Grafton 2007: 42.
4. Ginzburg 1999: 73.
5. Despite the title of the Hinduism book, *Teologia dei Tibetani* (see Bibliography C, ca. 1780), the topic is Hinduism and not Tibetan religion. Likewise the translation of Matthew (see Bibliography C, ca. 1760) is into Hindustani and not into Tibetan as the library catalogue claims.
6. Some of the details of the Spinola bequest are found in Petech (1952–1956: Part 1, pp. lix–lx). The details of this bequest and the activities of the Capuchin friars working for the Tibet Mission in Mexico are questions that need further research.
7. For a discussion of some of the implications of this procedure of constructing what might be called an "unauthorized autobiography," see Lorenzen 2006: 237–40.

Chapter 1

1. *Scripto Leonis,* as quoted in Daniel 1992: 37. This passage is also found in the very popular early biography of St. Francis

known as the *Speculum perfectionis* (Mirror of perfection) (see Guerra 1998: 743). Although this paragraph (and the first half of this chapter) has been written by Lorenzen, it is quite probable that Marco had read the *Speculum perfectionis* and knew the passage in question.

2. This information is mostly based on Lupi (2003: 392–94). According to Lupi, Marco died at Bhagalpur in India on March 18, 1803. Another tradition, however, places his death in the same place and year but on June 7 (see Petech 1952–56: Part 1, pp. cxvii–cxviii).
3. Document of October 9, 1755 (ACM). The grade was "optime."
4. The text that follows from here to the end of this chapter is translated directly from Marco della Tomba ca. 1775 (*Introduzione al viaggio*): 1–4. Details of this and other texts by Marco are found in the Bibliography.
5. Monsignor Maton could not be further identified. When he is again mentioned at the end of this chapter, his name seems to be written as "Mabon" and not "Maton."
6. Marco here uses the phrase "*descendono dalle une.*" *Une* must be an Italianization of the French word *hune* meaning "topmast." Similarly, Marco uses the Gallicism *matalotti* for "sailors."

Chapter 2

1. Except for the following sentence, this paragraph and the following one are translated from Marco della Tomba ca. 1775 (*Introduzione al viaggio*): 4–5. The sentence in question is from Marco's letter of January 29, 1758. On the capture of Chandernagore (March 23, 1757), see Chaudhuri 1975: 239–43.
2. This quote is taken from a letter in Gottardo 1954: 23.
3. This paragraph is translated from Marco della Tomba's essay of ca. 1775 (*Introduzione al viaggio*): 5. In Marco's manuscript, the city of Shrirampur is given as *Selempur*. In history texts,

the old spellings of Selempur, Serampore, or Serampur are still often used.

4. This paragraph and the text that follows till the end of the chapter are translated from Marco della Tomba ca. 1775 (*Introduzione al viaggio*): 7–9.

Chapter 3

1. This chapter is translated from Marco della Tomba ca. 1775 (*Introduzione al viaggio*): 9–11. In the previous chapter (see above, p. 36), from the same source, Marco claims that he left Chandernagore on January 29, not January 2. There is no way to know which date is correct.
2. In the manuscript (ibid.: 10), Marco alludes here to an unidentified incident that he plans to discuss in a future essay on the religion of the people.
3. The word that Marco uses here, *trionfi*, is probably a mistake for *trofei*.

Chapter 4

1. This chapter is translated from Marco della Tomba ca. 1775 (*Piccola descripzione*): 77–81.
2. This word could not be identified.
3. Marco's manuscript has a blank space where the name of the animal sacrificed to Mars should be indicated.

Chapter 5

1. This and the following 10 paragraphs are translated from Marco della Tomba ca. 1775 (*Introduzione al viaggio*): 11–14.
2. This paragraph is a summary based on Marco della Tomba ca. 1775 (*Introduzione al viaggio*): 14–17. The ways in which Marco writes the names in question in the manuscript of his original essay are worth noting: *Alaberdican* (Alivardi Khan), *Suraggiadolà* (Siraj-ud-daula), *Mirza Faralican* (Mir Jafar Ali Khan), *Gagudican* (Ghazi-ud-din Khan, *alias* Imad-ul-Mulk),

Sagiudolà (Shuja-ud-daula), *Miren* (Miran, son of Mir Jafar), *Casmalican* (Kasim Ali Khan or Mir Kasim), *Alligaor* (Ali Gauhar), *Scialem* (Shah Alam).

3. This and the following paragraphs of this chapter are translated from Marco della Tomba ca. 1775 (*Introduzione al viaggio*): 17–20.
4. The word Marco uses is *currori* or *carrori*. This seems to be a variant of the Hindi word *har-kara,* meaning spy or messenger.

Chapter 6

1. This paragraph and the following 22 paragraphs are translated from Marco della Tomba ca. 1775 (*Introduzione al viaggio*): 20–24.
2. Dhrub Singh's letter and Pope Benedict XIV's reply are cited in full in English translations in Vannini 1981: 24–26; and also in Kalapura 2000. The texts in Latin are found in *Bullarium* 1752: vol. 7, p. 264.
3. Except for this first sentence, this paragraph and the following four paragraphs are translated from Marco della Tomba ca. 1775 (*Piccola descrizione*): 104–6.

Chapter 7

1. These two translations of 1762 are in the Vatican Library, manuscript Borg. ind. 4. I have not found any other extant manuscript of the *Mul-panji,* but manuscripts of the *Gyan-sagar* are found in the Kabir Chaura monastery (Benares) library and a version of the original text has been published (Yugalanand Bihari 1953: vol. 1).
2. This and the following paragraphs are translated from Marco's book of ca. 1775: 190–92.
3. The legend that Marco summarizes here, like the two texts he translated, is associated especially with the Dharamdasi branch of the Kabir Panth now centered at Damakheda in the state of Chhattisgarh. Here I have used modern transliterations for the Indian names and words mentioned by Marco. In Marco's text

the words include Naraen (Narayan), Nirangen (Niranjan), Curumb (Kurma), Bavani (Bhavani), Giorgi (Jogajit), and Cal (Kal). For "Mansarovar" Marco appears to write "Nacarnour," but both the original text of the *Gyan Sagar,* from which Marco's summary is taken, and Marco's own translation clearly indicate that the word is "Mansarovar."

4. As in the discussion of the Kabir Panth, I have used modern transliterations of Indian names whenever possible. Marco's spellings include the following: *Nanekpanti* (Nanak Panthi), *Nanek* (Nanak), *Gianik* (Janak). The names *Ain Marvan* and *Arcan* could not be identified and even the transliteration of Marco's spellings is somewhat uncertain.
5. I have slightly corrected the transliteration of the Hindi passage, but have kept a quite literal English translation of Marco's Italian translation.

Chapter 8

1. This chapter is translated from Marco della Tomba ca. 1775 (*Introduzione al viaggio*): 24–31. The long letter from Anselmo da Ragusa is included in Marco's text.
2. Literally, "guns with their wicks lit."
3. The fakir chief Ramacandra (Marco's *Ramcender*) could not be identified
4. There survive several other eyewitness accounts of the events in Patna on June 25–26, 1763 and their aftermath, most notably the massacre of British prisoners on October 5. Three British accounts are found in Firminger 1909. Giuseppe da Rovato's long letter of December 14, 1763 gives many further details about the incident. The three Capuchin friars in Patna at the time were Anselma da Ragusa, Giuseppe da Rovato, and Giovanni da Brescia.
5. This must be Jan Bacheracht (Anselmo da Ragusa's *Mr. Bacracth*). He was the Dutch *directeur* of Bengal in this period. See Winius and Vink 1994: 131. The word Marco uses for "tunics" is *cabaje* which seems to be derived from the Hindi

kaba or *kabay.* In the following sentence the word Marco uses for "cots" is *catoli* which seems to be derived from the Hindi *khatola*.

6. Two paragraphs from the manuscript are omitted here. In them Marco warns against missionaries getting caught up in wars and stresses that the missionaries should never take sides in such wars.

Chapter 9

1. This chapter is translated from Marco della Tomba ca. 1775 (*Introduzione al viaggio*): 31–35.

Chapter 10

1. This chapter is translated from Marco della Tomba ca. 1775 (*Introduzione al viaggio*): 35–39.

Chapter 11

1. This and the following 18 paragraphs are translated from Marco della Tomba ca. 1775 (*Introduzione al viaggio*): 39–43.
2. Ajib Khan (Marco's *Agibcan*) could not otherwise be identified.
3. The following material in this and the next paragraph is translated from Marco della Tomba ca. 1775 (*Piccolo Descrizione*): 75.
4. The rest of this paragraph is taken from Marco's letter of September 20, 1770 to the cardinal prefect of Propaganda Fide.
5. The following passage from this letter is translated from the text in Gottardo 1954: 107–8.
6. The Hindustani or Bengali words written here as *sciamurronè* and *sciamarroni* (below) could not be identified.
7. Gottardo (1954: 108n) identifies Giuseppe da Rovato's "*polini*" or "*pollini*" as a dialectical Italian word corresponding to "turkeys" (*tacchini*), but "vultures" must be meant since Giuseppe's word "*ghiddò*" is equivalent to Modern Standard Hindi *giddha* (vulture).

Chapter 12

1. This and the following three paragraphs are translated from Marco della Tomba ca. 1775 (*Introduzione al viaggio*): 43–44.
2. Translated from Marco's letter dated December 2, 1769 (p. 250).
3. Although Marco does not name these four translations here, they must include the ca. 1769 translations (with accompanying Hindi texts) in manuscript (BAV, Borg. ind. 4), namely those of the *Jnan-sagar,* the *Mul-panji,* and the *Lanka-kanda* of Tulsidas's *Ram-carit-manas*. There is no fourth translation in this manuscript. All these translations are published in de Gubernatis's collection (1878: 205–89, 191–203, and 129–63 respectively).
4. The manuscript of Marco's translation of the *Arjuna-gita* (Marco's *Argiunghità*) is now found in the Vatican Library (1769). It is published in de Gubernatis's collection (1878: 165–82).
5. This and the following paragraphs of this chapter are translated from Marco della Tomba ca. 1775 (*Introduzione al viaggio*): 44–47.
6. Marco specifies here that the explanation is found "in *carte* 4 of this book". Apparently this was an appendix or attachment to the original manuscript of his "*Viaggio*" essay. This appendix can no longer be identified. There is, however, a long letter from Marco to the procurator [of the Capuchin Order], dated January 15, 1771. The folios immediately following this letter (ff. 264a–288) were apparently originally attached to the letter and contain extra material sent by Marco to support his arguments about the public nature of the Chandernagore church. Much of it consists of two long disquisitions in French, one apparently written by Marco himself, the other by his Jesuit opponent. See the Bibliography for details.
7. The final two sentences of this paragraph are in the present and future tenses in Marco's text, indicating he had not yet left India when he originally wrote them.

8. A paragraph of the manuscript in which Marco mentions his plans to discuss elsewhere the geography and customs of India has been omitted.

Chapter 13

1. The documents cited in this chapter are genuine, but the rest of the text has been written by me (Lorenzen). The paragraph by Marco quoted in this chapter is the only surviving document in which he even mentions the masons. There is no evidence that Marco ever had access to Cassiano da Macerata's 1768 published biography of Marco's former mentor, Giuseppe Maria da Gargnano, but I would guess that he probably did.
2. I have not been able to identify this Mr. Falck (or Falk or Falch). The letters by Giuseppe da Rovato that mention him say at one point that he was head of the Dutch factory in Patna and at another that he was English (Gottardo da Como 1954: 136–37, 139–40). A Mr. Iman Willem Falck was the Dutch Governor in Sri Lanka from about 1765 to 1785 (Winius 1994: 137–38). Two prominent English persons in India at this time who had a similar surname were Joseph Fowke (1716–1800) and his son, Francis Fowke (1754–1820).
3. These two bulls, as quoted below, are available on the website of the Masonic Grand Lodge of British Columbia and Yukon (freemasonry.bcy.ca/anti-masonry/papal_encyclicals.html).
4. The connection of these persons with Freemasonry is mostly based on discussions in the book by Firminger (1952) and the Ph.D. thesis by Little (2003). Although no one, to my knowledge, has found any clear evidence of any connection of Sir William Jones with Freemasonry, a letter of 10 December 1784 written by wardens and members of Lodge No. 2 (Industry and Perseverance), includes a W. Jones (as well as W. T. Jones, W. Hickey and F. Wilford) among the sixteen signers (Firminger ca. 1952: 30–31). Jones arrived in India in 1783 and in 1784 founded the Asiatic Society. In one of his articles, Jones describes a meeting with Marco della Tomba

that probably took place in 1784 (Marshall 1970: 239–41). Whether or not Marco could have known all the information found in this paragraph is admittedly uncertain. Much more research on freemasonry in India is needed.

5. Cassiano da Macerata 1768: 63–64.
6. Letter of January 15, 1775 (Gottardo da Como 1954: 149–51).
7. Letter of December 20, 1771, f. 261a. The sense of the untranslated remainder of the final sentence of this quote is not clear.

Chapter 14

1. This chapter is based on paraphrases and translations of various letters written by Marco. This first paragraph is paraphrased from Marco's letter from Livorno dated May 20, 1774.
2. Vannini (1981: 310) says that Costanzo "returned home in 1779, because of old age". This is probably a mistake. He likely returned to Italy much later.
3. See Marco's letter to Stefano Borgia dated July 16, 1774.
4. Letter of August 18, 1774 to Borgia.
5. A few documents about this college are found in the Propaganda Fide archives, *Scritture riferite nei Congressi, Various Colleges*, vol. 42.
6. Letter of August 19, 1774. Meliapur or San Thomé at Madras (Chennai) was the seat of the bishop who had jurisdiction over Bengal.
7. Letter from Borgia to Marco, September 3, 1774.
8. Letter from Marco to Monsignor [Borgia], October 14, 1774.
9. Letter from Borgia to Marco, December 3, 1774.
10. Letter from Borgia to Marco, January 21, 1775.
11. Letter from Marco to Cardinal [Castelli], March 16, 1775.
12. This information is found in Marco's letter to Monsignor [Borgia] dated April 5, 1775.
13. Letters from Marco to Monsignor Borgia dated April 17, 1775 and April 27, 1775.
14. Letter from Marco to Cardinal Castelli, 27 [29?] April 1775.

15. Letter from Monsignor Borgia to Marco, May 13, 1775.
16. The following is translated from Marco's letter of May 19, 1775. The Custodian's letter apparently no longer exists. This is unfortunate since the details of his proposal are not completely clear from Marco's letter.
17. Letter from Marco to Borgia, June 2, 1775.
18. Letters from Marco to Monsignor Borgia, June 2, 1775, and to Cardinal Castelli, June 2, 1775.
19. Letter from Propaganda Fide to Marco dated July 1, 1775.
20. Translated from *Lettere,* vol. 226, ff. 280b–281a. This letter was presumably written by Borgia himself, but it seems likely that Marco's several letters had offended someone else associated with the Sacred Congregation, perhaps the Capuchin procurator, who at this time was Erardo da Radkersburg (1768–1775).
21. Letter from Marco to Monsignor Borgia, July 13, 1775.
22. Marco's five surviving letters from October 1775 to August 1779 are written from San Marino.
23. Letter from Marco to Borgia, October 30, 1775.
24. Document of November 29, 1778.
25. The story of Marco's attempt to enter Rome in October, 1778, is told in his "Plan" and also in his letter to a cardinal (either Giuseppe Maria Castelli or Leonardo Antonelli) dated November 29, 1778, to which the "Plan" was originally annexed. M. Borgia acknowledged receipt of the "Plan" in a short letter to Marco dated January 23, 1779.
26. Marco's three letters are all dated August 18, 1779. The unnamed Cardinal cannot be identified. Giuseppe da Rovato's letter to Cardinal Castelli is probably that dated January 3, 1778 (Gottardo da Como 1954: 167–68).
27. Marco's letters that accompanied these packets are both dated October 31, 1779. Giuseppe da Rovato's letters to Cardinal Castelli and to M. Borgia are probably those dated November 29 and 30, 1778 respectively (Gottardo da Como 1954: 169–73). M. Borgia acknowledged receipt of the packets in his short letter to Marco dated November 27, 1779.

Chapter 15

1. This chapter is translated from Marco della Tomba's book of ca. 1775: 110–14.
2. Marco describes making a terrestrial globe and an armillary sphere of the cosmos for the Brahmins of Bettiah in more detail in his essay (*Introduzione al viaggio*) of ca. 1775: 11.
3. Here Marco notes that he had added these translations with some explanatory notes at the end of his manuscript, presumably the same manuscript he sent to Monsignor Borgia in 1775.
4. Here Marco adds several lines insisting that he has not written anything here that is not founded on what he has read in Hindu books.
5. The manuscript in fact says "more than 17 years", indicating that it was written in 1774 or 1775 (considering that Marco arrived in India in 1757).
6. It is not entirely clear if Marco is saying that Mani was in Hindustan or Thomas.

Chapter 16

1. In his published volume of some of Marco's essays and translations, Angelo de Gubernatis (1878: 129–63) included Marco's translation of the *Lanka-kanda* chapter of Tulsidas's famous *Ramayana,* entitled the *Ramcaritmanas*. This is the only chapter of this work for which Marco wrote out a more or less complete translation, but he did make a summary of the entire text. The translation, together with a Hindi/Avadhi text in Indian script, is found in the Vatican Library manuscript Borg. ind. 4. Tulsidas's complete text is summarized, chapter by chapter, in this manuscript and also in Marco's 1775 manuscript (pp. 174–80).

   Unfortunately de Gubernatis misidentified Tulsidas's text as a *Ramayana* belonging to the Kabir Panth, an unorthodox Hindu sect. This misidentification was accepted by later scholars including C. Vaudeville and P.J. Marshall. There is no doubt whatever that the *Ramayana* in question is Tulsidas's since Marco's translation includes Tulsidas's original Hindi text. Marco in fact discusses Tulsidas in a passage located just before the beginning of his summary of this *Ramayana* in the manuscript of 1775 (p. 173, see also below). Although this passage never explicitly identifies Tulsidas as the author of this *Ramayana*, the context strongly suggests that Marco knew that Tulsidas was the author. The passage was not included in de Gubernatis's published volume. The point is important since it establishes that Marco was by far the earliest translator into a European language of a substantial part of Tulsidas's text, often called the Bible of north Indian Hinduism.

2. This and the following 11 paragraphs are translated from Marco della Tomba's book of ca. 1775: 168–70.

   Marco's spelling of some of the Sanskrit or Hindi words used is worth noting (in order of occurrence): *Ramayana* (Marco's *Ramaen*), Vishnu (*Bisnù*), Ravana (*Raun* or *Ravon*), Manu Cakshusha (?) (*Manù Sachtà chetù*), Kumbhakarna (*Curumbcarm*), Sahasrabahu (*Sahasabeta*), the muni Pulastya (*Pustamuni*), Dasaratha (*Dusarat*), Kausalya (*Cosilla*), Kosala (*Caosil*), Awadh (*Aud*), Ayodhya (*Aggiodia*), the rishi Narada (*Nard Richè*), Kandaswami (*Canesuamì*), Bharata (*Bart*), Lakshmana (*Lacciuman*), Satrughna (*Satrun*), Janaka (*Gianek*), Janakpur (*Gianekpur*), Janaki (*Gianchè*), Mahadeva (*Mahadeo*), Parasurama (*Parseram*) and Hanuman (*Anuman*).

3. The Sanskrit-Hindi equivalent of *Anegh* could not be identified.
4. Here the word *Gentili* has been translated as "pagans" rather than "Hindus" since the reference could be to either the Buddhists or the Hindus or both. It is not clear to what extent Marco, on his short visit to Ceylon (see next chapter), was aware of the difference between the Hindus and Buddhists of the island.
5. This book, if it is a book, could not be identified.

6. In fact Hanuman was not the king of the monkeys, but the king's general.
7. I could find no Sanskrit or Hindi source that mentions the *cioni*. I assume the Sanskrit word would be "*coni*."
8. This paragraph and the next are translated from Marco della Tomba's book of ca. 1775: 173–74. The text continues with a more detailed summary of the eight books of the *Ramayana*.

Chapter 17

1. This chapter is based on paraphrases and translations taken from various letters. A letter from Stefano Borgia's office to Giuseppe Ans.o Menghini Gvovic.o (?) dated September 8, 1781 discusses the inclusion of Padre Zaccaria in the Mission.
2. Translated from Marco's letter of January 21, 1782.
3. Letter from Borgia to Marco dated March 2, 1782.
4. Translated from Marco's letter of April 20, 1782.
5. This and the following paragraph are based on Marco's letters of October 12, 1782 and September 12, 1783, both addressed to Cardinal Antonelli.
6. Translated from Marco's letter of September 12, 1783.

Chapter 18

1. This and the following paragraph are translated from Marco's letter to Cardinal Antonelli dated September 12, 1783.
2. Marco's being sent to Bhagalpur is mentioned by the mission Prefect, Giuseppe da Rovato in a letter dated November 18, 1784 (Gottardo da Como 1954: 185–86). Giuseppe again mentions Marco's being stationed in Bhagalpur in his letters to Propaganda dated December 15, 1784 and March 10, 1785 (*ibid.*: 187–92). Marco himself gives some further details in his letter to Cardinal [Antonelli] dated August 30, 1786. The "Governor of this place" mentioned in this last letter is presumably Warren Hastings although the wording is somewhat ambiguous.

3. This paragraph is based on the letter from Propaganda to Marco dated October 2, 1784. The quote near the end is translated from the same letter.
4. Letter from Propaganda to Giuseppe da Rovato dated October 2, 1784 (not in Gottardo da Como). One suspects that in part Monsignor Borgia was offering Giuseppe da Rovato a method to get Marco out of the way. However, Borgia also appreciated Marco's intrepid character and ability with languages.
5. Marco's letter to Cardinal [Antonelli] August 30, 1786.
6. Letter from Propaganda to Marco dated September 26, 1787. The following paragraph is largely based on this letter.
7. There seems to be some confusion about the date of Carlo Maria's appointment as Prefect of the Mission. Petech (1952–56: Part 1, p. 112) and Vannini (1981: 311) say that Carlo Maria was appointed Prefect on November 16, 1787. The letter from Borgia to Marco dated September 26, 1787 and also a letter from Borgia to Carlo Maria himself dated September 19, 1787 mention that Carlo Maria was to be the new prefect. Perhaps the formal appointment was not made until November 16, but I did not find confirmation of this in the Propaganda Fide Archives and Petech and Vannini do not indicate their source.
8. This paragraph and the two that follow are largely based on Marco's letter to Cardinal [Antonelli] dated December 29, 1786.

Chapter 19

1. The information in this paragraph is mostly based on Vannini 1981: 262–63; Kalapura 1999: 40–41; Kalapura 2000; L.S. O'Malley and R.E. Swanzy 1932; and Leela Prasad 1981. The subject still needs more research.
2. The complete document is reproduced in the original Persian with an English translation in Kalapura 2000.
3. The name of the village is not specified. It is apparently a village attached to or very near the Bettiah hospice, probably Dossaya. The missionaries were apparently the owners or zamindars of

the village. The village is apparently different from the village of Chuhari, near Bettiah, where the Nepalese Christians were settled in 1769. The village of Chuhari was given to the mission by the English in about 1767 (See above Chapter 8).

4. Translated from the document by Marco comprising the judgment in the trial of Giuseppe da San Marcello, longer version, copied by Ludovico Maria da Città di Castello, at Bettiah on October 15, 1793.
5. For "I screamed for mercy," Marco writes, "*io gritassi il doaij.*" The word "*doaij*" seems to be a Hindi word related to either *dua* (prayer, supplication) or *daya* (mercy).
6. Here Marco slips into addressing the document directly to the Prefect, Padre Carlo Maria da Alatri, as "*V.P.*" (i.e., *Vuestro Padre*). Most of the text omitted here from the last parts of this document consists of legalistic details, many of which aimed to ensure that Padre Carlo Maria would not attempt to immediately overturn the verdict of the trial.

Chapter 20

1. The information in this and the following paragraph is mostly taken from Marco's long letter, probably written in September, 1794, to Cardinal [?Antonelli]. The information about Mr. Falck and the Patna church is found in four letters from Giuseppe da Rovato, two to Viatore da Coccaglio dated December 12, 1773 and December 13, 1774, one to Cardinal Castelli dated December 15, 1774, and one to Padre Alessandro Maria da Bergamo dated December 20, 1774 (Gottardo 1954: 136–46). I could not further identify this Mr. Falck. In the second letter he is identified as being English rather than Dutch.
2. This person may be one Signore Joseph Finch. In his letter of January 25, 1794 to Cardinal [?Antonelli], Marco describes Joseph Finch as "a Piedmontese, in whose house [Giuseppe] had all his assets, money, furniture, fine and crude merchandise, and four trunks of his things." Finch is also mentioned in Marco's letter to Cardinal [?Antonelli], dated August 20, 1794.

3. The information about the freeing of Padre Giuseppe da San Marcello and throwing out the lawsuit he brought against Padre Marco and the others is from Vannini 1981, 151. Unfortunately Vannini does not indicate his source, and I have not been able to fully corroborate the story from other sources (but see following note). Vannini may have got the story from an unpublished manuscript by Bernardo da Poppi (ca. 1976) that I have not been able to consult.
4. This information is based on Marco's letters to Cardinal [?Antonelli], dated September 1794 [?] and April 15, 1795. It is not completely clear if the lawsuit brought by Padre Giuseppe that led to this verdict is the same one referred to in the previous sentence or not. I am assuming that it was.
5. This and the following paragraph are based on Marco's letters to Cardinal [?Antonelli, dated September 1794 [?] and April 15, 1795.
6. This and the following paragraph are translated from Marco's letter of September [?] 1794.
7. This paragraph is mostly based on Vannini 1981, 152–53. Vannini does not cite his sources. Two important documents on the period after 1795 are an anonymous "Ristretto" of 1804 and a report apparently written mostly by Bonaventura da Salino in about 1803–4.

Chapter 21

1. Much of the following discussion is based on Vannini 1981, 153–70. Unfortunately Vannini does not cite the location of his sources. I have found some, though not all of the sources mentioned by him in the archives of Propaganda Fide. Vannini also claims to base some of his discussion on a modern manuscript by Bernardo da Poppi, but I have not had access to this text.
2. *SOCG*, vol. 911, f. 92.
3. Ibid., vol. 911, ff. 152b–153a. The text is in French. A loose Italian translation of this passage is found in the same volume,

ff. 102b–103a. Although I have translated this passage (and also the following one) directly from Foulon's French text, I have changed all the personal names in both passages from their French versions to the corresponding Italian ones.

4. Ibid., f. 152a. The text is in French. The loose Italian translation of this passage is found in the same volume, ff. 107b–108b. The last paragraph and a half of this passage is translated from the Italian version since the surviving version of the French text is abridged at this point.
5. I was unable to further identify either the town "Fatigar" or the Comte de Chaigau.
6. For an account of Foulon's disastrous intervention and of the subsequent misadventures of Padre Angelo da Caraglio, see Vannini 1981, 147–70. Vannini strongly takes the side of Padre Marco.
7. Foulon's decree is found in Propaganda Fide file *SOCG*, vol. 911, ff. 22a–34b. A convenient summary is found in Vannini 1981, 161–66.
8. *SOCG*, vol. 911, ff. 31a–32a. Translated from the Latin by Rubén Chauqui.
9. Ibid., vol. 911, ff. 1a–9b.
10. On Stefano Borgia, see Enzensberger 1970, 739–42; Orsatti 1996, 1–43; Lorenzen 2006, 133–35.
11. *SOCG*, vol. 911, ff. 80a–100b.
12. On the disputed date of Marco's death, see Petech, Part I, pp. cix, cxviii. The quote that follows is from *SOCG*, vol. 911, ff. 86b–87b.
13. Among the important tasks that scholars have yet to undertake are biographies of key friars of the Mission including Francisco Orazio della Penna (1680–1745), Cassiano da Macerata (1708–91), Giuseppe Maria da Gargnano (1709–61), Giuseppe da Rovato (d. 1786), and Antonino da Lodi (1777–1844).

List of Key Persons

1. Roman Catholic Clergy

Andrea da Perugia

Padre Andrea, a Capuchin of the Tibet Mission, left Europe with Padre Salvatore da Perugia in November 1769, arriving in Chandernagore about one year later. Padre Andrea is said to have robbed all the Mission's money and returned to Italy in 1777. See Vannini 1980: 309; Gottardo 1954: 165.

Angelo da Caraglio (died in 1831 or 1838)

Padre Angelo, a Capuchin of the Tibet Mission, arrived in Chandernagore in 1791. He became procurator of the Mission there. As noted here, in 1802 Angelo won the friendship and support of René Louis Foulon, the Visitor's envoy to the Mission, to become the new prefect of the Mission. Despite the opposition, Angelo became the new prefect in early 1803. He was transferred to Agra in 1806. In Agra he was supported by Begum Samru of Sardhana (see the European, Samru, below) and was largely responsible for her conversion to Catholicism and the building of the famous Catholic church in Sardhana.

Anselmo da Ragusa (1717–76)

Padre Anselmo, a Capuchin of the Tibet Mission, arrived at Chandernagore in 1750. He was named prefect of the Mission in 1758 and assumed the post in 1761. At this point he moved from Kathmandu, where he had been stationed, to Patna. From 1764 he stayed in Chandernagore. He returned to Europe in 1769.

Antonino da Monte Alboddo (1705–69)

Padre Antonino, a Capuchin of the Tibet Mission, arrived in Chandernagore in 1739 and became the Superior of the Patna hospice. He returned to Europe in 1755. He finally arrived in Rome in August, 1756. There he refused the post of prefect of the Tibet Mission which had been conferred on him a month and a half earlier. He did not return to India.

Bonaventura da Salino (1746–1811)

Padre Bonventura, a Capuchin of the Tibet Mission, arrived in Chandernagore in 1792. As noted here, he was briefly named prefect of the Mission in late 1802 but gave up the post in disgust a few weeks later and went back to Italy where he defended Marco and the Mission from the bad decisions of the Visitor's envoy, Renato Foulon. Bonaventura returned to India in 1808 and again became prefect in 1809. He sailed for Italy again in 1811 but died on route near Bahia, Brazil.

Stefano Borgia (died 1804)

Cardinal Borgia was one of the most influential clerics in Rome during this period. From 1770 to 1789, he was the secretary for Propaganda Fide, first as Monsignor and later as Cardinal. From 1802 to 1804 he was prefect of Propaganda. He was a learned man and corresponded with many European scholars and Orientalists. He was also a collector of exotic objects and manuscripts from Asia and elsewhere. Marco thought of him as his patron and wrote many letters to him, now found in the Propaganda Fide archives. Some of Borgia's letters to Marco are found in the same archive. Borgia's own attitude to Marco was not always favorable. See the bibliography here for his correspondence with Marco.

Carlo Maria da Alatri (died about 1809)

Padre Carlo Maria, a Capuchin of the Tibet Mission, arrived in Chandernagore in 1784. He was named prefect in 1787 and assumed the office in 1788. He soon quarreled with Marco and most of the other padres of the Mission. He was deposed by Bishop Champenois in 1799. He sought to regain the post after the death of Giovanni Maria da Camajore in 1801. He was again deposed on the advice of the Visitor's envoy, Renato Foulon, at the end of 1802. He sailed for Europe early in 1803.

Nicolas Champenois (1734–1811)

Bishop Champenois was associated with the French Society of Foreign Missions. He arrived in India in 1777. He was appointed the titular Bishop of Doliche (in Syria) in 1785 and put in charge of the See of Pondicherry. He was named Visitor to the Tibet Mission in 1796 but was unable to travel to British-controlled Bengal because he was a French citizen. Eventually, he named a French secular priest named Rene Louis Foulon already resident in Bengal as his envoy. As noted here, this appointment had disastrous consequences for the Mission and for Marco.

Costanzo da Borgo San Sepolcro

Padre Costanzo, a Capuchin of the Tibet Mission, arrived in Chandernagore in 1775. He eventually returned to India but it is not certain exactly when. A few letters from him are found in the Propaganda Fide archives. The Vatican Library has a manuscript dated 1787 that is signed by Costanzo and contains the Hindi text and a (new) Italian translation of Giuseppe Maria da Gargnano's 1751 "Dialogue between a Christian and a Hindu about Religion."

Daniele da Morciano (1706–65)

Padre Daniele, a Capuchin of the Tibet Mission, arrived in Chandernagore in 1739 and stayed there until 1749 when he left for Europe. For some reason he stopped in Mauritius and stayed there until 1753, when he returned to Bengal. He left for Manila in 1765 or 1766 but was lost in a shipwreck on the way there.

Fortunato da Caldes

Padre Fortunato, a Capuchin of the Tibet Mission, arrived in Chandernagore with Romualdo da Senigallia in 1774. Fortunato soon became a major headache for the prefect of the Mission, Giuseppe da Rovato. A 1776 document sent from Giuseppe to Monsignor Stefano Borgia in Rome describes the many problems caused by Fortunato and begs Borgia to order Fortunato to return to Italy. Fortunato did finally return in 1785. See Gottardo 1954: 196–99; Vannini 1980: 309–10.

René Louis Foulon

Padre Foulon was a secular priest of French origin who was named by Bishop Champenois, the Visitor appointed to inspect the Tibet Mission, to be his envoy. Foulon inspected the Mission in 1802 after establishing a friendship with Angelo da Caraglio, the procurator of the Mission, in Chandernagore. As noted here, Foulon met Marco in Bhagalpur and almost immediately developed a strong hatred against him. Foulon's attempt to impose Padre Angelo as prefect was strongly opposed by the remaining padres of the Mission, and Foulon's attempt to totally silence and isolate Marco probably did much to hasten Marco's death.

Giovanni Gualberto da Massa (1729–96)

Giovanni Gualberto, a Capuchin of the Tibet Mission, arrived in Chandernagore in 1761. Like Serafino da Como, he was stationed in Nepal and moved to Chuhari with the Nepalese Christians in 1769. He returned to Italy in about 1780, but came back to India and Chuhari in 1784. He was one of the four judges (along with Marco, Romualdo da Senigallia and Lodovico Maria de Città di Castello) in the 1793 trial of Giuseppe da San Marcello. He died at Chuhari in 1796.

Giovanni Maria da Camajore (died 1801)

Padre Giovanni Maria, a Capuchin of the Tibet Mission, arrived in Chandernagore in 1791. He was stationed at Chuhari. He was named prefect of the Mission in 1799 and died a little over two years later.

Giuseppe Alfonso da Palermo

Padre Giuseppe Alfonso, a Capuchin of the Tibet Mission, arrived in Chandernagore in December, 1762. He was made Superior of the Chandernagore hospice at the end of 1763. He returned to Europe in 1766 or 1767.

Giuseppe da Rovato (died 1786)

Padre Giuseppe, a Capuchin of the Tibet Mission, arrived in Chandernagore in 1762. He stayed first in Patna and then from 1764 until 1769 in Nepal. From then until his death in 1786 he was mostly in Patna. He was named prefect of the

Mission in 1768, assumed office in 1769, and held it until his death. He was a good administrator and wrote many letters back to his teacher, his friends, and his superiors in Rome. Many of these letters survive, and most have been transcribed and published by Gottardo da Como (1954).

Giuseppe da San Marcello (died 1810)

Padre Giuseppe, a Capuchin of the Tibet Mission, arrived in Chandernagore in 1783. After the death of the prefect, Giuseppe da Rovato, in 1786, Giuseppe da San Marcello provoked serious conflicts among the friars of the Mission. The most important conflicts were those caused by his high-handed behavior as administrator of the Mission lands in the town of Bettiah. Marco organized a trial against him in 1793. From 1797 until his death in 1810, Giuseppe lived in Kathmandu.

Giuseppe Maria da Gargnano (1709–61)

Padre Giuseppe Maria (originally Bernardino Bernini) was one of the best-known Capuchins of the Tibet Mission. He arrived in Chandernagore in 1739. Giuseppe Maria belonged to an aristocratic family associated with the city of Brescia in eastern Lombardy. He is said to be the author of many translations of Hindu religious texts into Italian, but none of them survives. He also wrote a "Dialogue between a Christian and a Hindu about Religion" in both Hindustani and Italian. Two manuscripts of this text still exist. Giuseppe Maria's Capuchin friend and colleague, Cassiano da Macerata, wrote a hagiographic biography about him in Italian that was published in Verona in 1767. He spent time in Patna, Lhasa, Nepal and Chandernagore before being stationed in Bettiah in 1749. He died there in 1761.

Lodovic Maria da Città di Castello (1750–99)

Padre Lodovico Maria, a Capuchin of the Tibet Mission, arrived in Chandernagore in 1792. In 1793 he participated in the trial of Giuseppe da San Marcello organized by Marco and signed the judgment along with Marco, Giovanni Gualberto da Massa, and Romualdo da Senigallia. He was rather sickly and died at Chandernagore at 49 years of age.

Michelangelo da Tabiago

Padre Michelangelo, a Capuchin of the Tibet Mission, arrived in Chandernagore in 1761. He was stationed first at Bettiah and then, from 1764 to 1768, stayed at Nuwakot in Nepal. He then returned to Bettiah and was mostly there until he went back to Europe in 1785.

Odoardo (or Eduardo) da Cingoli (1702–56)

Padre Odoardo was one of three Capuchins of the Tibet Mission who went to India in 1735. He stayed mostly in the Mission hospice at Chandernagore in Bengal as Procurator of the Mission. He returned to Italy in 1753. As Marco tells us, Odoardo died in Lorient in 1756 while waiting to again set sail for India. See Lupi 2003: 373-74 and Vannini 1976: 468.

Onofrio da Monte Cassiano (1716–62)

Padre Onofrio, a Capuchin of the Tibet Mission, arrived in Chandernagore in 1753. After the fall of Chandernagore in 1757, he became a chaplain in the renegade French army of Jean Law de Lariston and was Marco's predecessor in this post. Onofrio is briefly mentioned in Law's memoirs (1913: 198).

Romualdo da Senigallia (1734–1815)

Padre Romualdo, a Capuchin of the Tibet Mission, arrived in Chandernagore in 1774. For most of his many years in

India, Romualdo was stationed at Bettiah and Chuhari. His home town, Senigallia, is near to Marco's home village of Tomba. During Marco's second visit to India the two became good friends. Marco describes him as a gentle soul who was well liked by his colleagues. Romualdo later became one of the victims of the high-handed conduct of Padre Giuseppe da San Marcello as described in Chapter 19. Romualdo died in Bettiah in 1815.

Salvatore da Bologna (died 1789)

Padre Salvatore, a Capuchin of the Tibet Mission, left Europe for India together with Padre Andrea da Perugio in November 1769, arriving in Chandernagore about one year later. Salvatore had already been a missionary in Tunis. In India his health deteriorated, and he returned to Europe in 1771 only a few months after having arrived. See Vannini 1980: 309; Gottardo 1954: 165.

Serafino da Como (1725–1804)

Padre Serafino, a Capuchin of the Tibet Mission, arrived in Chandernagore in 1761. He was in Nepal until 1769, when he took his Nepalese Christians to Bettiah and then to nearby Chuhari. He returned to Italy in 1772. In 1784 he was sent to the Le Marche region where he became a professor in the Pesaro seminary. See Petech 1954–56: cxix.

Tranquillo d'Apecchio (1708-1768)

Padre Tranquillo, a Capuchin of the Tibet Mission, arrived in India in 1739 in the same expedition as Daniele da Morciano. Tranquillo was named Prefect of the Mission in 1746, assumed office in 1748, and relinquished it in 1758. He was in Lhasa from 1741 to 1745. He spent most of the rest of his time in Kathmandu and then in Chandernagore where he died.

2. Indians, Nepalese, and Armenians

Ahmad Shah Abdali (died 1773)

Ahmad Shah Abdali, also called Ahmad Shah Durrani, was an Afghan chief who invaded India several times in the 1750s. He is often considered to be the founder of modern Afghanistan and ruled in that region from 1747 to 1773. In 1756 his troops sacked Delhi, but he returned to Afghanistan in 1757.

Dhrub Singh (Bettiah raja, lived 1715–62)

The Bettiah raja, Dhrub Singh (Marco's Dhurup Singh), was a Bhumihar Brahmin by caste. He became acquainted with the Capuchin friar, Giuseppe Maria da Gargnano, in the 1740s and encouraged the establishment of a Capuchin hospice in Bettiah. He was ousted as raja by Mir Kasim in 1762 and died soon after.

Jaya Prakash Malla (King of Nepal, ruled 1735–68)

King Jaya Prakash was a Malla king of Nepal. Collateral lines of this dynasty also controlled the neighboring small kingdoms of Patan and Bhatgaon in the same Kathmandu Valley. The valley was conquered by the Gorkha king Prithvi Narayan in 1768. The Malla kings generally had good relations with the Capuchins of the Tibet Mission who stayed in Kathmandu. After the arrival of Prithvi Narayan these relations soured and the Capuchins and a couple hundred converts left Kathmandu for Bettiah in 1769.

Jugal Kishore Singh (Bettiah rajah, died 1783)

The Bettiah rajah, Jugal Kishor Singh, was the son of Dhrub Singh's daughter Bonga Babui. He was put in charge of the Bettiah kingdom in 1762 by Mir Kasim. After the defeat of

Mir Kasim in 1764, the English left Jugal Kishore on the throne. In 1766, however, Jugal Kishore failed to pay the revenue the English demanded and they took direct control of the kingdom. In 1771 the English restored Jugal Kishore to the throne but kept most of the power in their own hands.

Khojah Gregory alias Gorgin Khan

This Armenian (Marco's Gregorio) was the commander-in-chief and chief minister of Nawab Mir Kasim or Kasim Ali Khan from 1760 to 1763. Many Armenian merchants and military adventurers migrated to India in the sixteenth, seventeenth and eighteenth centuries. See Seth 1992: 383–418.

Margar Johanness Khalanthar

The Armenian named Margar (Marco's Marcat), was an important general in the army of Mir Kasim commanded by another Armenian, Khojah Gregory alias Gorgin Khan. Margar played a leading role in the capture of Patna in 1763. As Marco notes, Margar helped the Capuchins who were captured in the aftermath of the Patna battle. See Seth 1992: 413–14.

Mehndi Ali Khan (Deputy nawab in Bihar and Patna)

Mehndi Ali Khan (Marco's Mendialican) is mentioned in the 1763 diaries of Surgeon Anderson and Surgeon Fullarton, two survivors of the Patna massacre perpetrated by Samru, as Mindy Ally Cawn or Mindialy Cawn (Firminger 1909: 64–70). Dutta and Jha (1976: 108) say that Nawab Mir Kasim, in about 1762, "appointed Mir Mahdi Khan, a nephew of Asad-ullah Khan, to remain in charge of the districts of Sasaram and Chainpur."

Mir Jafar (Nawab of Bengal, 1757–60 and 1763–65)

Mir Jafar (Marco's Mirzafaralica, i.e., Mir Jafar Ali Khan) was an important official and general in the administration of his predecessor as nawab, Siraj-ud-Daula. Mir Jafar quarreled with Siraj-ud-Daulah and allied himself surreptitiously with the English in the battle of Plassey (Palasi) in 1757. With English help, Mir Jafar became nawab. In 1760 he was deposed by the English, who made his son-in-law, Mir Kasim, the new nawab. After Mir Kasim fought against the English and was defeated, Mir Jafar was again made nawab.

Mir Kasim or Kasim Ali Khan (Nawab of Bengal 1760–64)

Mir Kasim (Marco's Casmalican, i.e., Kasim Ali Khan) was the son-in-law of Mir Jafar. After the English made him nawab in 1760, he proved to be an unexpectedly efficient ruler and eventually rose in rebellion against the English. He joined a military alliance with the Mughal emperor, Shah Alam II, and the nawab of Awadh, Shuja-ud-Daulah, but they were defeated at the battle of Buxar (Baksar) on October 22, 1764. Mir Kasim died in poverty several years later.

Miran

Miran was the son and heir of Mir Jafar. Miran arrested the previous Bengali nawab, Siraj-ud-Daulah, after the battle of Plassey in 1757 and had him killed at Murshidabad. Miran died in 1760, hit by a bolt of lightning.

Prithvi Naryan Shah (1723–75)

Prithvi Narayan (Marco's Pirtinaraen) was a Gorkha (Marco's Gorcà) king who started a gradual conquest of the Kathmandu Valley in about 1761. In 1767, at the request of the Malla king of Kathmandu, Jaya Prakash, the British sent troops to Kathmandu under the command of George Kinlock.

In 1768 Kinloch's troops were defeated by Prithvi Narayan, who then took control of Kathmandu. In 1769 the Capuchin missionaries were forced to leave Nepal with their converts.

Siraj-ud-Daulah (Nawab of Bengal, ruled 1756–57)

Nawab Siraj-ud-Daulah was the son of the daughter of the previous nawab of Bengal, the very able Alivardi Khan (ruled 1740–56). Shortly after becoming nawab, Siraj-ud-Daulah attacked and captured the fortified settlement of the English East India Company at Calcutta. The English returned in 1757 led by Robert Clive. The army of Siraj-ud-Daulah was defeated in the battle of Plassey (Palasi). The English then arranged the appointment of Siraj-ud-Daulah's general Mir Jafar as the new nawab of Bengal. Marco arrived in Bengal shortly after these events.

Shah Alam II (Mughal Emperor, formerly Prince Ali Gauhar, ruled 1759–1806)

Prince Ali Gauhar's father, Emperor Alamgir II (ruled 1754–59), was murdered by his chief minister (*wazir*), Imad-ul-Mulk, in 1759. Ali Gauhar then became emperor, taking the name Shah Alam II. He was part of the coalition of the nawab of Awadh, Shuja-ud-Daulah, and the nawab of Bengal, Mir Ali Khan, against the British. After the defeat of this coalition at Buxar (Baksar) on October 22, 1764, Shah Alam II became a virtual puppet of the English.

Shri Kishen Singh (Claimant to Bettiah throne)

Shri Kishen Singh (Marco's Kissumsingh) was the son of Prithi Singh, a younger brother of Raja Dalip Singh (died 1715) of Bettiah. Dalip Singh was the father of Dhrub Singh, who was the raja of Bettiah until 1762 (see this list). Shri Kishen Singh was thus Dhrub Singh's cousin.

Shuja-ud-Daulah (Nawab of Awadh, ruled 1754–75)

Shuja-ud-Daulah (Marco's Sagiadolà) was the third virtually independent nawab of the rich Awadh region in what is now the state of Uttar Pradesh. He was also wazir, or chief minister, to the Mughal emperors Alamgir II (1754–59) and Shah Alam II (1759–1806). Together with Mir Kasim, the nawab of Bengal, and the Mughal emperor, Shah Alam II, Shuja-ud-Daulah fought and lost the 1764 battle of Buxar (Baksar) against the English. The following year, however, he made a pact with the English that obliged him to pay for the upkeep of British troops in his own territory. He continued to rule the Awadh region, at least nominally, until his death.

3. Europeans

Thomas Adams (1730–64)

Adams was a military officer in the army of the English East India Company, ending his career as a Brigadier General. He was named Commander-in-Chief of the Company forces in Bengal and campaigned against Mir Kasim in 1763. Poor health forced him to resign his commission, and he died at Calcutta early in 1764.

Sir Robert Barker (1729–89)

Barker (Marco's Colonel Barchèr) headed the army in India from 1770 to 1774. He resigned in 1774 after a dispute with the governor-general of Fort William (Calcutta), Warren Hastings.

Dom Carlos (King of Naples, lived 1716-1788)

The king of Naples, whom Marco calls Dom Carlos, eventually became Carlos (Charles) III, the Bourbon king of Spain. He was king of the two Sicilies (Sicily and Naples) from 1735 to 1759, and king of Spain from 1759 to 1788. He was a relatively progressive, but not a particularly able, ruler.

John Carnac (1716–1800)

Carnac was an important, and controversial, English military officer (final rank of brigadier general) in this period. He fought with the Mahrattas in 1765. In 1767 he returned to England, but he was back in India in 1771 and became a member of the Bombay council. He participated in the aggressive policies that led to the defeat of the English Bombay army at Wadgaon in 1779. For this he was dismissed from the Company's service.

Robert Clive (1725–74)

Clive was an English East India Company official who commanded the capture of Chandernagore. He arrived in India at a young age as a clerk in the Company's service in Madras. In 1751 he became a captain in Company's army. After the capture of the East India Company's fortified station at Calcutta in 1756 by Siraj-ud-Daulah, Clive organized an expedition from Madras that retook Calcutta and defeated Siraj-ud-Daulah in the battle of Plassey (Palasi) in 1757. Clive was governor of Bengal from 1757 to 1760 and again from 1765 to 1767.

Lord Charles Cornwallis (1738–1805)

Cornwallis was governr-general of the English East India Company government in India from 1786 to 1793. Earlier he had commanded the losing British forces during the American War of Independence. From 1798 to 1801 he was in charge of the British government in Ireland.

Simeon Droz

According to Firminger (ca. 1952: 18n), Simeon Droz was Assistant at Patna in 1765, Secretary to the (Calcutta) Council in 1767, Sheriff of Calcutta in 1768, Chief at Patna in 1769, Secretary to the Council of Revenue for Bihar in 1771, and a member of the Patna Council in 1772. He was also an active Freemason. In 1778 he was Grand Junior Warden of the Provincial Grand Lodge of Bengal, and in 1779 he was Deputy Provincial Grand Master.

Edward Golding

We learn from Marco that Golding replaced Simeon Droz sometime after 1757 in order to "preside over the country" (Bettiah). Not much is known about Golding from published sources. Marco knew him in Bettiah, and they were on good personal terms.

Charles Grome

In the 1780s, Charles Grome was the Collector of Saran, a region of western Bihar with Chhapra as its main city. Little is known about him and even the spelling of his name is in doubt. Kalapura (2000) calls him "Mr. Greene," while L. Janaki (1981) calls him "Charles Graeme." His name appears in the land grant of the village of Dossaya near Bettiah to the Capuchin Mission. See also Yang 1989.

John Zephaniah Holwell (1711–98)

Holwell was a surgeon employed by the English East India Company in Bengal. In 1760 he briefly held the office of governor of Bengal. His three-volume book entitled *Interesting Historical Events, Relative to the Provinces of Bengal and the Empire of Indostan* . . . (1765–71) was re-published in a French translation in 1768. Marco probably made use of this translation for his essay that criticizes Holwell. Holwell was sympathetic toward Hinduism and critical of Christianity. Voltaire made use of Holwell's book to support his own criticisms of Christianity. See Marshall (1970: 1–105) for an excerpt of Holwell's book.

Major George Kinloch (died 1768)

In 1767–68, Major Kinloch (Marco's Kilnok) botched the invasion of Nepal to help the Malla king, Jaya Prakash, against the Gorkha king, Prithvi Narayan. This led to Kinloch's illness and death. He met Marco in 1767, before his expedition had left for Nepal, and after his disastrous retreat to the plains bordering Nepal in 1768 he became sick and called for Marco, evidently to receive the Catholic last rites. The manuscript of Kinloch's diary of the expedition up to October 17, 1767, is available on microfilm (Document of 1767).

Monsieur Lassa (1719–9?)

This person's real name was Jean Law de Lauriston. It is not clear why Marco calls him M. Lassa. After the fall of Chandernagore Jean Law organized a small army of mostly French soldiers who wandered about north India as mercenaries. They were employed by the Mughal emperor and fought with the emperor and his allies against the English. From 1759 to 1761 Marco was a chaplain in this army. After surrendering to the English, Law returned to France and eventually wrote his memoirs. These are now available in published form (Law 1913).

Sir Hector Munro (1726–1805)

In 1764, the then Major Munro (Marco's Menerò or Meneraun) was the victorious English general in the battle of Buxar (Baksar). In 1780, however, he was defeated in southern India by Haidar Ali Khan. Munro retired in 1782.

Pierre Renault

In the 1750s Pierre Renault (Marco's M. Renold) was the French chief of Chandernagore, the French city and trading port on the Hugli River in Bengal, not far north of Calcutta (Kolkata). Renault's role in the defense of Chandernagore in 1757 is well described by S. C. Hill (2006).

Samru, originally Walter Reinhardt

Samru—also called Sumroo, Somer, and Sombre (Marco's Sombroù)—was a European military adventurer with a colorful history. His real name was Walter Reinhardt. He is thought to have been raised in western Germany near Trier. After his participation in the notorious massacre of English military prisoners in Patna in 1763, he moved further to the west. Near Delhi, he met and employed a young Muslim woman named Zeb-un-Nissa, who became his loyal concubine. Zeb-un-Nissa was later converted to Christianity. In about 1777, Samru obtained a large fief (*jagir*) from the Mughal emperor in the region between Aligarh and Muzaffarnagar (to the east of Delhi). He made the town of Sardhana near Meerut his residence. After his death, Zeb-un-Nissa, by then known as the Begum of Sardhana, built a famous Roman Catholic church there. On Samru and the Begum, see Banerji 1925 and Shreeve 1996.

Edward Tiretta alias Count Tiretta of Trevisa Abbe Coste

Tiretta was a colorful adventurer who appears prominently and notoriously in the famous memoirs of Giovanni Giacomo Casanova, the legendary Don Juan. Tiretta met Casanova in March 1757. According to Casanova, one of Tiretta's lady friends gave him the nickname "Count Sixtimes." Tiretta left for Bengal in later 1759 or early 1760. In Calcutta he became a successful civil architect for the East India Company. He established what is now known as the Tiretta Bazaar in Calcutta in 1783. Tiretta was a Freemason and in 1775 was nominated as Senior Warden of the second Calcutta lodge, called "Industry and Perseverance" (Little 2003: 136–37; Firminger ca. 1952: 5–6n).

Henry Vansittart (1732–70)

Vansittart was the governor of Fort William (Calcutta) in Bengal from 1760 to 1764. His published *Narrative of the Transactions in Bengal* (1766) is an essential document for the history of this period in Bengal and Bihar.

Bibliography

All manuscripts are from the Propaganda Fide Archives and are written in Italian unless otherwise specified. See the "List of Abbreviations" (above) for the abbreviations used. The manuscripts of each section are arranged chronologically.

A. Letters and Other Writings In Manuscript by Marco della Tomba

Letter of 16 September 1757 to Monsignor [Borgia]. *SCIOC*, vol. 29, ff. 83–84.

Letter of 29 January 1758 to Monsignor [Borgia]. *SCIOC*, vol. 29, ff. 23–24.

Letter of 6 November 1758 to Monsignor [Borgia]. *SCIOC*, vol. 29, ff. 188–89.

Letter of 25 November 1758 to Monsignor [Borgia]. *SCIOC*, vol. 29, ff. 190–91.

Letter of 9 June 1761. Letter to Cassiano da Macerata in which Marco mentions Giuseppe Maria da Gargnano's death. A passage is quoted in Cassiano da Macerata 1767: 210.

Letter of 15 December 1761[?2] to Cardinal Spinelli. *SCIOC*, vol. 30, f. 78.

Translation of 1762. *Gyan Sagar*. Hindi text in Devanagari script and Italian translation side by side. BAV, Borg. ind. 4, CD 20b–127a.

Translation of 1762. *Mulpanji*. Hindi text in Devanagari script and Italian translation side by side. BAV, Borg. ind. 4, CD 8b–20a. Several of final folios are blank.

Document of ca. 1768. "Breve raccolta dei principj d.a Religione dei Gentili settentrionali del Fiume Gange." *SOCG*, vol. 832, ff. 108a–130a. This text is evidently a draft of parts of Marco's *Libro in cui. . . .* (see his "Book of ca. 1775" below).

Document of ca. 1768. Untitled. *SOCG*, vol. 832, ff. 132a-b. Describes time in Bettiah. Mentions translation help of three Brahmins.

Letter of 13 January 1762 to Eminent Cardinal. *SCIOC*, vol. 30, ff. 145–46.

Translation of 1764. *Lanka kanda* of the *Ramcaritmanas* of Tulsidas. The Italian title is *Ramaen, Libro Lanka*. Hindi text in Devanagari script and Italian translation side by side. BAV, Borg. ind. 4, CD 127b–154b. The translation is mostly complete but some sections are only summarized and others are not translated.

Letter of 10[?] March 1769 to Cardinal of Propaganda. *SOCG*, vol. 832, ff. 147–48.

Letter of December 2, 1769 to Cardinal Prefect of Propaganda Fide. Biblioteca Apostolica Vaticana [BAV], Borg. lat. 524, pp. 248–51. Also in de Gubernatis 1878: 183–188.

Letter of 20 [?10] December 1769. Addressee is high church official but his name is not indicated. BAV, Borg. ind. 4, ff. 5a–6a (CD 6b–7b). Also excerpted in de Gubernatis 1878: 188–89.

Translation of 1769. *Arjuna-gita*. Italian title "*Traduzione interlineale di un Libro Bed dei Gentili detto Argiun Ghità in lingua sancrita, oppure Dialogo fra Baghien, Do dei Gentili e Ragiun uomo discepolo.*" BAV, Borg. lat. 524, pp. 240–47. The original text, said to be written in Sanskrit, is not included. At the end of the text, appears the date, 2 December 1769.

Letter of 20 February 1770 to Cardinal Prefect of Propaganda Fide. *SOCG*, vol. 832, ff. 136–37.

Letter of 20 September 1770 to Cardinal Prefect of Propaganda Fide. *SOCG*, vol. 832, ff. 138, 140.

Essay of ca. 1771. "*Breve raccolta dei principj d.a Religione dei Gentile settentrionale del Fiume Gange.*" *SOCG*, vol. 832, ff. 108–135. This seems to be another version of some of the material found in more finished form in BAV manuscripts Borg. lat. 524 and 525.

Letter A of 15 January 1771 to Cardinal Prefect of Propaganda Fide. *SOCG,* vol. 836, ff. 294a–295b.

Letter B of 15 January 1771 to Procurator [of Capuchin Order]. *SOCG,* vol. 836, ff. 262a–263b. The following folios in this volume are documents that Marco sent with this letter to support his arguments about the public status of the Chandernagore church. This material includes the following:

(1) Some papal bulls written in Latin (ff. 264a–265a).

(2) A note on the bulls by Marco in Italian, signed but not dated (f. 265a);

(3) Marco's own "*Observations sur la Reponse que Mousieur Paussevin Curé a faite au Mémoire que j'ay presenté a Monsieur le Directeur en Janvier 1770,*" written in French and dated 3 April 1770 (ff. 266a–279a).

(4) A text that begins "*A Monsieur Chevalier, Directeur a Chanderngor,*" written in French, apparently written by Marco, but not signed or dated (ff. 280a–283b).

(5) "*Response au Memoire que le R. Pere Marc Supérieur des R. R. P. P. Capucins de Chandernagor presente a Monsieur le Directeur en Janvier 1770,*" written in French and signed by several persons (not all the names are legible) beginning with M. Possevin but not dated (ff. 284a–288a).

Letter C of 15 January 1771. Copy of previous letter (without document copies). *SOCG,* vol. 836, ff. 290–91.

Letter of 20 December 1771 to Procurator [? of Capuchins.]. *SOCG,* vol. 836, ff. 260–61.

Letter of 30 November 1772 to Cardinale Castelli. *SCIOC,* vol. 33, ff. 350–51.

Essay of ca. 1774. "*Breve discussione sul nome di 'Paramessor' (Vero Dio).*" BAV, Borg. lat. 525, ff. 7–11.

Essay of ca. 1774. *Luoghi Santi dei Gentili dell'Indostano.* Vatican Library, manuscript Borg. Lat. 525, ff. 1.4v.

Essay of ca. 1774. "*Notizie sull'India.*" BAV, Borg. Lat. 525, ff. 13–22. Date of the donation is given as 25 June 1774.

Essay of ca. 1774. "*Osservanzioni sopra le Relazione che fà*

Monsieur Holwell, Inglese, degli evenimenti [sic] istorici ed interessanti toccanti le Provincie del Bengala e dell'Imperio del Gran Mogol e dell'Indostano." BAV, Borg. lat. 537, sec. XVIII, ff. I-IIIv., pp. 64, ff. I-Vv. On first folio there is note from Stefano Borgia dated 12 February 1775 saying this text was donated by Marco della Tomba.

Essay of ca. 1774. *Scala numerica dei Gentili dell'Indostano con la quale numerano le Incarnazioni dei loro Dei.* BAV, Borg. lat. 525, f. 23.

Letter of 20 May 1774. *SCIOC,* vol. 34, f. 115.

Letter of 16 July 1774 to Monsignor [Borgia]. *SCIOC,* vol. 34, f. 161.

Letter of 18 August 1774 to Monsignor [Borgia]. *SCIOC,* vol. 34, f. 187.

Letter of 19 August 1774 to Cardinal Castelli, Prefect of Propaganda Fide. *SCIOC,* vol. 34, f. 192.

Letter of 14 October 1774 to Monsignor [Borgia]. *SCIOC,* vol. 34, ff. 246–47.

Book of ca. 1775. *Libro in cui si descrivono diversi sistemi della Religione dei Gentili dell'Indostano e Regni circonvicini.* BAV, Borg. lat. 524, pp. 110–203. Glossary, pp. 210–236.

Essay of ca. 1775. "*Introduzione al viaggio per l'India (1755–1774).*" BAV, Borg. lat. 524, pp. 1–47, text summarized on pp. 208–209

Essay of ca. 1775. "*Nota breve su un Libro Indostano del Museo Borgiano.*" BAV, Borg. lat. 524, p.255.

Essay of ca. 1775. "*Piccola descripzione dell'India orientale, o Industan.*" BAV, Borg. lat. 524, pp. 73–106, 238.

Letter of 16 March 1775 to "Cardinal". Found in Prop. *SCIOC,* vol. 34, f. 483.

Letter of 5 April 1775 to Monsignor Stefano Borgia. *SCIOC,* vol. 34, ff. 508–509.

Letter of 17 April 1775 to Stefano Borgia. *SCIOC,* vol. 34, ff. 527–28.

Letter of 27 April 1775 to Stefano Borgia. *SCIOC,* vol. 34, ff. 533–34.

Letter of 27 [?29] April, 1775 to Cardinal Castelli. Excerpted in de Gubernatis 1878, 189–90. Whole text in BAV, Borg. ind. 4, ff. 2a–3b (CD 3b–4a).

Letter of 19 May 1775 to Stefano Borgia. Found in Prop. *SCIOC*, vol. 34, ff. 537–38.

Letter of 2 June 1775 to Stefano Borgia. Found in Prop. *SCIOC*, vol. 34, ff. 548–49.

Letter of 2 June 1775 to Cardinal Castelli, Prefect of Propaganda Fide. *SCIOC*, vol. 34, ff. 564–66.

Letter of 13 July 1775 to S. Borgia. *SCIOC*, vol. 34, ff. 574–75.

Letter of 30 October 1775 to S. Borgia. *SCIOC*, vol. 34, ff. 641–42.

Document of 29 November 1778. *"Piano della missione del Tibet per la Sac.a Cong.ne di Propaganda"* In the present book, this text is referred to as "The Plan of 1778". The text is addressed to a Cardinal. *SCIOC*, vol. 35, ff. 736a–740b.

Letter of 29 November 1778 to Cardinal. *SCIOC*, vol. 35, f. 735a-b.

Letter of 18 August 1779 to Cardinal [Castelli]. *SCIOC*, vol. 35, f. 741.

Letter of 18 August 1779 to Cardinal [unidentified]. *SCIOC*, vol. 36, f. 144.

Letter of 18 August 1779 to Monsignor [Borgia]. *SCIOC*, vol. 36, ff. 137–38.

Letter of 31 October 1779 to Monsignor [Borgia]. *SCIOC*, vol. 35, f. 751.

Letter of 31 October 1779 to Cardinal [Castelli]. *SCIOC*, vol. 36, f. 195.

Document of ca. 1780, apparently in Marco's hand. Italian National Library collection called "S. Maria della Scala," manuscript bundle 35 (K), a few pages only. The text gives the names and locations of several cities associated with the Tibet Mission. The date of the manuscript is quite uncertain.

Letter of 21 January 1782 to Cardinal Antonelli, Prefect of Propaganda Fide. *SCIOC*, vol. 37, ff. 36–37.

Letter of 15 April 1782 to Monsignor S. Borgia. *SCIOC*, vol. 37, ff. 109–110.

Letter of 20 April 1782 to Cardinal Antonelli. *SCIOC*, vol. 37, ff. 111–12.

Letter of 12 October 1782 to Cardinal [?Antonelli]. *SCIOC*, vol. 37, ff. 230–31.

Letter of12 September 1783 to Cardinal [?Antonelli]. *SCIOC,* vol. 37, ff. 436–37.
Letter of 30 August 1786 to Cardinal [?Antonelli]. *SCIOC,* vol. 38, ff. 412–415.
Letter of 29 December 1786 to Cardinal [?Antonelli]. *SCIOC,* vol. 38, ff. 475–76.
Letter of 30 November 1787 to Cardinal [?Antonelli]. *SCIOC,* vol. 38, ff. 676–77.
Document of 12 October 1793. Trial of Giuseppe da San Marcello, short version. *SOCP,* vol. 69, ff. 54a–55b.
Document of 15 October 1793. Judgment in the trial of Giuseppe da San Marcello, long version, composed largely by Marco but copied by Ludovico Maria da Città di Castello. *SOCP,* vol. 69, ff. 48a–53b.
Letter of 20 December [1793?]. Marco's comments on the back of a letter by Giovenale da Nizza. *SOCP,* vol. 69, f. 25b.
Letter of 20 December 1793 to Cardinal Prefect of Propaganda Fide. Marco's copies of letters originally written by others are added after f. 35b. *SOCP,* vol. 69, ff. 34a–35b.
Letter that is undated but probably of January 1794 (Marco signs as missionary of 37 years and age 67, which should mean 1793, but Romualdo's (f. 28a, 29a) letter to which Marco's comments are apparently added is dated 3 Jan. 1794). *SOCP,* vol. 69, ff. 28b, 29a-b.
Letter of 7 January 1794. Marco's comments added to letter of Giovanni Gualberto da Massa. *SOCP*, vol. 69, f. 27b.
Letter of 25 January 1794 to Cardinal [unidentified]. *SOCP,* vol. 69, ff. 44a–45b.
Letter of 10 August 1794 to Carlo da Alatri. Found in Prop. Fide file *SOCP,* vol. 69, f. 41a–42b.
Letter of Dated 10 August 1794 probably to Prefect of Propaganda Fide. *SOCP,* vol. 69, f. 43a-b.
Letter of 20 August 1794 to Cardinal [=?]. *SOCP,* vol. 69, ff. 46a–47b.
Letter that is undated but probably of September 1794 (mentions Marco's age as 69 years) to Cardinal [=?]. *SOCP,* vol. 69, ff. 122a–125a.

Letter of 20 September 1794 to Carlo da Alatri. *SOCP,* vol. 69, ff. 126a–127a.

Letter of 15 April 1795 to Cardinal. *SOCP,* vol. 69, f. 116a–117b.

Letter that is undated but probably of 1798 (mentions Marco's age as 72 years). The letter was written to the General Procurator of the Capuchin Order. The original is lost but an excerpt is found in Bonaventura da Salino's report of 1804. *SOCG,* vol. 911, ff. 92a-b.

B. Letters in Manuscript Addressed to Marco della Tomba

Letter of 15 November 1766 from Propaganda Fide. *Lettere,* vol. 208, f. 320a-b. Answers Marco's letter of 29 Jan. 1766 (lost).

Letter of 22 November 1766 from Propaganda Fide. *Lettere,* vol. 208, f 344a-b. Answers Marco's letter of 25 Oct. 1765 (lost).

Letter of 27 December 1768 from Serafino da Como. *SOCG,* vol. 832, ff. 133a–34b. An extract of this letter is published in Petech 1954–1956, part 2, pp. 230–32.

Letter of 23 December 1769 from Propaganda Fide. *Lettere,* vol. 214, ff. 362b–363b. Answers Marco's letter of 10 March 1769.

Letter of 26 May 1770 from Propaganda Fide. *Lettere,* vol. 216, ff. 240b–241a.

Letter of 26 January 1774 from Propaganda Fide (S. Borgia). *Lettere,* vol. 224, ff. 19b–20a.

Letter of 23 February 1774 from Propaganda Fide (S. Borgia). *Lettere,* vol. 224, f. 98a-b.

Letter of 18 July 1774 from Anselmo da Ragusa. *SCIOC,* vol. 34, ff. 188–89.

Letter of 3 September 1774 from Propaganda Fide (S. Borgia). *Lettere,* vol. 224, f. 473a-b. Marco's name mistakenly given as Francisco Maria della Tomba.

Letter of 3 December 1774 from Propaganda Fide (S. Borgia). *Lettere,* vol. 224, ff. 580b–581a.

Letter of 21 January 1775 from Propaganda Fide (S. Borgia). *Lettere,* vol. 226, ff. 27b–28a.

Letter of 13 May 1775 from Propaganda Fide (S. Borgia). *Lettere,* vol. 226, f. 162a-b.

Letter of 1 July 1775 from Propaganda Fide (S: Borgia). *Lettere,* vol. 226, ff. 249a–250b.

Letter of 29 July 1775 from Propaganda Fide (S. Borgia). *Lettere,* vol. 226, ff. 280b–281a.

Letter of 23 January 1779 from Propaganda Fide (S. Borgia). *Lettere,* vol. 234, ff. 39b–40a.

Letter of 27 November 1779 from Propaganda Fide (S. Borgia). *Lettere,* vol. 234, ff. 700b–701a.

Letter of 2 March 1782 from Propaganda Fide (S. Borgia). *Lettere,* vol. 240, f. 175a-b.

Letter of 2 October 1784 from Propaganda Fide (S. Borgia). *Lettere,* vol. 244, f. 806a-b.

Letter of 26 September 1787 from Propaganda Fide (S. Borgia). *Lettere,* vol. 250, ff. 574a–575a. Reply to Marco's letter of 30 August 1786.

Letter of 18 November 1789 from Propaganda Fide. *Lettere,* vol. 255, ff. 634a–636a.

Letter of 14 August 1793 from Carlo Maria da Alatri to Marco and others. *SOCP,* vol. 69, f. 43a. Copy transcribed by Marco with his own commentary.

Letter of 12 November 1793 from Carlo Maria da Alatri to Marco and others. *SOCP,* vol. 69, f. 37b. Copied by Marco with his own commentary.

Letter of 6 February 1794 from Lodovico Maria da Città di Castello. *SOCP,* vol. 69, f. 40a–b.

Letter of April 1794 from Lodovico Maria da Città di Castello. *SOCP,* vol. 69, ff. 38a–39b.

C. Other Relevant Letters and Documents in Manuscript

Document of 1751 in Hindustani and Italian by Giuseppe Maria da Gargnano. *Jababasval aik kristian aur ai hindu ke bic mo iman ke upar.* BAV, Borg. ind. 11. Another manuscript of this text in Hindustani with a different Italian translation by Costanzo da Borgo San Sepolcro and dated 1787 is found in BAV, Borg. ind. 16.

Document of 9 Oct. 1755. General Archives of the Capuchin Missions [ACM], *Esami de Missionari,* vol. 1 (1724–1757), p. 234. Exam result of Marco as missionary.

Document of 1757 by Cassiano da Macerata. *SCIOC,* vol. 40, ff. 675a–682b. A report on the Tibet Mission. Cassiano returned to Italy in 1754.

Letter of 26 December 1758 from Giuseppe Maria da Gargnano to Cardinal Prefect of Propaganda. *SCIOC,* vol. 29, ff. 184–85. An extract from this letter published (dated in wrong month) in Petech 1954–1956, part 2, pp. 202–203.

Document of ca. 1760 by Cassiano da Macerata. *Matteus (S.) apostolus, S. Evangelius Jesus Messiae* . . . Manuscript no. 490 in the Biblioteca Mozzi-Borgetti in Macerata. The Gospel of Matthew translated in Roman script into Hindustani (not Tibetan as the library catalogue claims). The date is very uncertain but the translation is likely to have been made shortly before or after Cassiano left India in 1754.

Letter of 1763 from Giuseppe da Rovato to Viatore da Coccaglio. ACM, file AD. 121. Published in Gottardo 1954, 39–41. Mentions Marco and the events of 1763 in Bettiah.

Letter of 14 December 1763 from Giuseppe da Rovato to Viatore da Coccaglio. ACM, file AD. 121. Published in Gottardo 1954, 25–39. Events of 1763 in Patna.

Letter of 22 November 1766 from Prop. Fide to Anselmo da Ragusa. *Lettere,* vol. 208, f. 333a-b. Says Marco should bring a Tibetan (i.e. Hindu?) scholar back with him.

Document of 1767. George Kinloch's account of his expedition to Nepal. From the British Library (MS Eur F. 128/140 1767), available on microfilm through Adam Matthew Publications of Marlborough, England.

Letter of 29 December 1769 from Giuseppe da Rovato to Erardo Radkersburg. *SCIOC,* ff. 114–117. In Gottardo 1954, 86–99. Mentions Marco.

Letter of 12 February 1770 from Giuseppe da Rovato to the "Nunzio Pontificio alla corte di Francia." *SCIOC,* vol. 32, ff. 477–78. In Gottardo 1954, 100–104. Refers to Marco, though not by name.]

Document of ca. 1773 by unknown author. *SCIOC,* vol. 40, ff.

661a–668b. Another copy in *SOCG*, vol. 842, ff. 102a–107a. A short history of the Tibet Mission. It mentions Marco.

Document of ca. 1773 by Serafina da Como. *SOCG*, vol. 836, ff. 239a–244b. A report about the state of the Tibet Mission. It mentions Marco. An extract of this report is published in Petech 1954–1956, part 3, pp. 298–303.

Document of 15 June 1773 by Cardinal Buonaccorsi. *Acta*, vol. 143, ff. 201a–224b. Another copy is found in *SOCG*, vol. 836, ff. 222a–37b. A report to Propaganda Fide by the Cardinal. The content is based on Serafino da Como's 1773 report (see previous). It mentions Marco.

Letter of 13 December 1773 from Giuseppe da Rovato to Padre Viatore da Coccaglio. ACM, file AD 121. Published in Gottardo 1954: 136–37.

Letter of 12 December 1774 from Giuseppe da Rovato to Padre Viatore da Coccaglio. ACM, file AD 121. Published in Gottardo 1954: 137–40.

Letter of 15 December 1774 from Giuseppe da Rovato to Cardinal Castelli. *SCIOC*, vol. 34, ff. 312–13. Published in Gottardo 1954: 141–43.

Letter of 20 December 1774 from Giuseppe da Rovato to Padre Alessandro Maria da Bergamo. ACM, file AD 121. Published in Gottardo 1954: 143–46.

Letter of 15 January 1775 from Giuseppe da Rovato to Monsignor Marefoschi, Secretary of Propaganda Fide. Published in Gottardo 1954: 146–52. Mentions freemasons.

Letter of 3 January 1778 from Giuseppe da Rovato to Cardinal Castelli. *SCIOC*, vol. 35, f. 524. Published in Gottardo 1954: 167–68.

Letter of 29 November 1778 from Giuseppe da Rovato to Cardinal Castelli. *SCIOC*, vol. 35, f. 742. Published in Gottardo 1954: 169–70.

Letter of 30 November 1778 from Giuseppe da Rovato to Monsignor Borgia. *SCIOC*, vol. 35, ff. 743–44. Published in Gottardo 1954: 171–73.

Letter of 27 August 1779 from Monsignor Stefano Borgia to Cardinal Antonelli. *Lettere*, vol. 235, ff. 96a–97a. Describes some of Marco's misdeeds.

Cassiano [Beligatti] da Macerata. ca. 1780. *Teologia dei Tibetani.* Manuscript no. 372 of the Biblioteca Mozzi-Borgetti, Macerata. Despite the title, this book is about Hinduism. The "Tibetans" of the title presumably refers to inhabitants of the territory of the Tibet Mission, i.e. Bihar. Date is very uncertain.

Letter of 8 September 1781 from Propaganda Fide to Giuseppe Ans.o Menghini Gvovic.o. *Lettere,* vol. 238, ff. 762a-b.

Letter of 2 October 1784 from Propaganda Fide to Giuseppe da Rovato. *Lettere,* vol. 244, ff. 804b–806a. Recommends sending Marco to Mogol Mission territory.

Letter of 18 November 1784 from Giuseppe da Rovato to Viatore da Coccaglio. ACM, file AD 121. In Gottardo 1954, 185–86. Mentions Marco in Bhagalpur .

Letter of 15 December 1784 from Giuseppe da Rovato to Cardinal Antonelli. *SOCG,* vol. 876, ff. 134 and 139. Another copy in ibid., ff. 136–37. In Gottardo 1954, 187–89. Mentions Marco in Bhagalpur.

Letter of 10 March 1785 from Giuseppe da Rovato to Cardinal Antonelli. *SOCG,* vol. 876, ff. 141–42. In Gottardo 1954, 190–92. Mentions Marco in Bhagalpur.

Document of 16 April 1787 by Cardinal Archinto. *SOCG,* vol. 876, ff. 114a–133b. A report to Propaganda Fide on the History of the Tibet Mission. It mentions Marco.

Letter of 19 September 1787 from Propaganda Fide to Carlo Maria da Alatri. *Lettere,* vol. 250, ff. 552a–553b.

Letter of 8 September 1793 from Carlo Maria da Alatri to Giuseppe da San Marcello. *SOCP,* vol. 69, f. 37a-b. Copied by Marco with his own commentary.

Letter of 14 September 1793 from Carlo Maria da Alatri to Giuseppe da San Marcello, *SOCP,* vol. 69, f. 36a-b. Copied by Marco with his own commentary.

Letter of 26 December 1794 from Angelo da Caraglio to an "Eminent Signore." Mentions Marco and Samru.

Letter of 16 January 1802 from Nicolas Champenois to Cardinal Gerdil. In Latin. *SCIO,* vol. 1, ff. 69a-b, 71a. Mentions Marco in Bhagalpur as the Prefect of the Tibet Mission.

Letter of 29 July 1802 from Nicolas Champenois to Cardinal Gerdil. In Latin. *SCIO,* vol. 1, ff. 125a–126a. Mentions Marco.

Document of 25 February 1803 by Louis René Foulon. In Latin. *SOCG*, vol. 911, ff. 22a–34b. A decree issued by Foulon after completing his official visit to the Tibet Mission. Marco prominently mentioned.

Letter of 10 and 12 March 1803 from Louis René Foulon to Nicolas Campenois. In French. *SOCG*, vol. 911, ff. 150a, 151b–153b. A rough Italian translation is found in ibid., ff. 102a–110a. A letter-report on the Tibet Mission. Marco is prominently mentioned.

Letter of 22 February 1804 from Nicolas Champenois to Cardinal Borgia. In Latin. *SCIO*, vol. 1 ff. 241a–242a. Mentions Marco's death.

Document of September 1804 by Cardinal Borgia. *SOCG*, vol. 911, ff. 1a–21b. A report on the Tibet Mission presented to Propaganda Fide and largely based on R. Foulon's report as Visitor. Marco is prominently mentioned.

Document of October [?] 1804 by Bonaventura da Salino. *SOCG*, vol. 911, ff. 80a–101b. A Report on the Tibet Mission. Marco Prominently mentioned.

Hilarion ab Abtei. 1908. *Manuscript on History of Patna Mission.* A handwritten copy of this big book in English is found in the archives of the Bishop's house in Patna. The author is also called Fr. Hilarion Valentin. He was prefect of Bettiah Mission in about 1920 and earlier.

Hosten, Henry, S. J. ca. 1930. *Materials for the History of the Capuchins in the Tibet Mission.* Vol. 27 of *The Collected Works of the Rev. H. Hosten.* The manuscript in English is found in the Vidyajyoti College of Theology Archives in Delhi.

D. Published Editions of Works Written before 1800

Alam, Muzaffar and Seema Alavi. 2001. *A European Experience of the Mughal Orient: The I'Jaz-i Arsalani (Persian Letters, 1773–1779) of Antoine-Louis Henri Polier.* New Delhi: Oxford University Press.

Breve relacion de la prodigiosa, y nueva Conquista espiritual del Reyno del gran Tibet, y otros confinantes . . . . 1745. Printed in Madrid and reprinted under license in Mexico: Imprenta de la

Viuda de D. Joseph Bernardo de Hogal. The probable author is Francisco da Ajofrín (see Melchor 1966 below). A copy is found in the St. Bonaventure University library, Allegany, NY. See also *Carta*...(below).

Bullarium Ordinis FF. Minoram S.P. Francisci Capuccinorum. 1752. Vol. 7. Rome: Typis Joannis Zempel Austriaco-Viennensis.

Carta familiar de un Sacerdote: Respuesta a un colegial, amigo suyo, en que le dá cuenta de la admirable conquista espiritual del vasto Imperio del Gran Thibét; y la Mision que los Padres Capuchinos tienen allí, con sus singulares progresos hasta el presente. 1772. Madrid: D. Joachin Ibarra, Impresor de Cámara de S. M. The "*Breve relación*" of 1745 (see above) is included in this *Carta familiar.*

Cassiano da Macerata, O.F.M. Cap. ca. 1757. *Giornale di Fr. Cassiano da Macerata nella Marca di Ancona, Missionario Apostolico del Thibet e Regni adiacenti, dalla sua partenza da Macerata seguita gli 17 agosto 1738 sino al suo ritorno nel 1756, diviso in due libri*. Most of the first volume is published in Petech (1954–56), part 4. The original manuscript of the first volume is Manuscript no. 362 in the Biblioteca Mozzi-Borgetti, Macerata. The second volume is lost or never written and has never been published. A quite similar text, though different and also incomplete, is found in manuscript in Prop. Fide file *SCIOC*, vol 33, ff. 675–705.

Cassiano da Macerata, *Padre*, O. C. 1767. *Memorie Istoriche delle virtú viaggi e fatiche del P. Giuseppe Maria de Bernini da Gargnano Cappuccino della Provincia di Brescia e Vice Prefetto della Missione del Thibet*. Verona, Italy: Moroni Press. An unpublished rough English translation by Henry Hosten is found in the Vidyajoti College (Delhi) library.

[Cassiano da Macerata, attributed]. 1771. *Alphabetum Brammhanicum sev Indostanum Universitatis Kasí*. Romae: Typis Sac. Congregationis de Propag. Fide.

Cotton, Evan (ed.). 1926. "An Account of Our Party at Patna Attacking the City, the 25th June, 1763," *Bengal: Past and Present* 31, 157–86. Contains the narratives of the Ensign Hugh M'Kay, Dr. William Anderson, and Dr. Fullarton.

de Gubernatis, Angelo. See Marco della Tomba in this section.

Didier, Hugues (trans. and presenter). 2002. *Les Portugais au Tibet: Les priemières relations jésuites (1624–1635).* 2nd ed. rev.; Paris: Editions Chandeigne.

Firminger, Walter K. 1909. *The Diaries of three surgeons of Patna, 1763.* Calcutta: Calcutta Historical Society. Contains the narratives of Dr. William Anderson, Dr. Peter Campbell and Dr. Fullarton, with a long introduction by Firminger.

Gottardo da Como, O.F.M. Cap. 1954. *La Missione Tibet-Hindustan negli scritti del P. Giuseppe da Rovato, O.F.M. Cap., Prefetto Apostolico del Tibet (1761–1786).* Thesis for Pontificium Institutum Propagandae Fidei. Asmara.

Guyon, Claude-Marie (Abbé). 1744. *Histoire des Indes orientales ancienne et modernes.* Paris: Vve Pierres, 1744. There is an English translation published in 1757. This is book used by Marco della Tomba in his "Piccola descrizione..."

Holwell, Jonathan Zephania. 1766–1771. *Interesting Historical Events Relative to the Province of Bengal and the Empire of Indostan.* 3 parts. London: Beckett and De Hondt. A substantial part of volume 2 is republished in Marshall 1970, pp. 45–106 (see secondary sources below).

Jones, William. 1789. "On the Gods of Greece, Italy and India." *Asiatick Researches,* volume 1, chapter 9. Also in Marshall 1970, pp. 196–245 (see below). First written in 1784. Describes meeting with Marco della Tomba.

Law de Lauriston, Jean (1719–179?). 1913. *Mémoire sur quelques affaires de l'Empire mogol, 1756–1761.* Paris: E. Champion.

Luca 1987?

Marco della Tomba. 1878. *Gli scritti del Padre Marco della Tomba, missionario nelle Indie orientali.* Edited by Angelo de Gubernatis. Florence: Le Monnie.

Petech, Luciano (ed.). 1952–1956. *I Missionari italiani nel Tibet e nel Nepal.* In seven parts. Rome: La Libreria dello Stato. The whole collection comprises volume two of the series *Il Nuovo Ramusio*, edited by various scholars.

Seir Mutaqharin. See Tabataba'i below.

Tabataba'i, Ghulam Husain. 1789. *Siyar al-Muta'akhkhirin.* Translated from the Persian in four volumes by M. Raymond as *A Translation of the Seir Mutaqherin; or, View of Modern*

Times. . . . Calcutta: James White. Covers the period up to 1782.

Vansittart, Henry [Governor of Bengal, 1760–64]. 1766. *A Narrative of the Transactions in Bengal, from the Year 1760, to the Year 1764*. 3 vols. London: By the author, 1766. Also reprinted, Calcutta: K. P. Bagchi, 1976.

E. Published Secondary Sources

Antonini, Chiara Silvi. 1984. "Della 'Piccola descrizione dell'India Orientale o Industan' di Marco Della Tomba," in *La conoscenza dell'Asia e dell'Africa in Italia nei secoli XVIII e XIX*, volume 1, ed. Ugo Marazzi, tomo 1, pp. 397–409. Napoli: Istituto Universitario Orientale.

Brown, Rebecca M. 2006. "Inscribing Colonial Monumentality: A Case Study of the 1763 Patna Massacre Memorial," *Journal of Asian Studies* 64, 1: 91–113.

Capuchin Mission Unit. 1923. *India and Its Missions*. New York: Macmillan.

Celestine, Peter, O.F.M. Cap. 1982. *Early Capuchin Missions in India: Pondicherry, Surat, Madras, 1632–1834*. Sahibabad: Capuchin Publications.

Chaudhuri, Nirad. 1977. *Clive of India: A Political and Psychological Essay.* Bombay: Jaico.

Clemente da Terzorio [or Clemens a Terzorio]. 1934. *Le Missioni dei Minori Cappuccini, sunto storico*. Vol. 9, *Indie Orientali, Parte Seconda, 1745–1935, Nepal-Bengala-Indostan missioni, Agra-Patna-Allahabad-Lahore-Ajmer-Simla-Bettiah*. Rome: Curia Generalizia. Whole series of 10 vols. published from 1913 to 1938.

Cotton, Evan. 1931. "The Patna Massacre of 1763." *Bengal Past and Present* 41: 5–23.

Criveller, Gianni. *The Chinese Priests of the College for the Chinese in Naples and the Promotion of the Indigenous Clergy (XVIII-XIX Centuries*. Hong Kong: no publisher indicated (pp. 40).

Cuthbert, Father, O.S.F.C. 1929. *The Capuchins: A Contribution to the History of the Counter-Reformation*. 2 volumes. New York: Longmans, Green and Co.

D'Arelli, Francesco (ed.). 1996. *Le Marche e l'Oriente: Una tradizione ininterrotta da Matteo Ricci a Giuseppe Tucci.* Atti del Convegno Internazionale Macerata, 23–26 ottobre 1996.

Daniel, E. Randolph. 1992. *The Franciscan Concept of Mission in the High Middle Ages.* St. Bonaventure, NY: The Franciscan Institute.

Datta, Kali Kinkar and Jatashankar Jha (eds.). 1976. *Comprehensive History of Bihar,* Vol. III, Part I. Patna: Kashi Prasad Jayaswal Research Institute.

Dent, Paul, S.J. ca. 1930. *A Brief History of Patna Mission.* Mimeo. A few copies are found in the archives of St. Xavier's School in Patna.

D'Souza, Rev. Daniel Anthony. 1982. *The Growth and the Activities of the Catholic Church in North India (1757–1858): A Historical Study.* Mangalore: Rev. Vitus Prabhudas, St. Anne's Friary.

———. 1993. *Capuchin Missions in India.* Brahmavar, Karnataka: Capuchin Publications.

———. n.d. *A History of the Catholic Church in North India.* [up to 1757] Mangalore: Fr. Desmond Rebello, Assisi House, Jail Road.

Fatica, Michele. 1997. *Matteo Ripa, Carlo VI, la Compagnia di Ostenda e il progetto di fondazione a Napoli di un Collegio dei Cinesi.* Naples: Istituto Universitario Orientale (p. 29).

[Felix of Antwerp, O.F.M. Cap. (or Felix Finck)]. 1922. *Brief Account of the Capuchin Mission in Tibet.* Bettiah: Catholic Mission Press.

Fernando, Leonard and G. Gispert-Sauch. 2004. *Christianity in India: Two Thousand Years of Faith.* New Delhi: Penguin Books India.

Filibeck, Elena de Rossi. 1996. "Il contributo di Cassiano Beligatti alla conoscenza del Tibet." In *Le Marche e l'Oriente: Una tradizione ininterrotta da Matteo Ricci a Giuseppe Tucci,* edited by Francesco D'Arelli, pp. 261–272. Atti del Convegno Internazionale Macerata, 23–26 ottobre 1996.

Firminger, Walter K. ca. 1952. *The second Lodge of Bengal in the olden times: being a history of the early days of Lodge Industry and Perseverence, no. 109 of England, 1761–1812*. Mysore: K.A. Korula at the Wesley Press.

———. *The Diaries of three surgeons of Patna, 1763*. Calcutta: Calcutta Historical Society, 1909.

Fortescue, John William. 1911. *A History of the British Army*, Vol. 3 (1763–1793). London: Macmillan.

Grafton 2007

Ginzburg 1999

González Reimann, Luis. 1988. *Tiempo cíclico y eras del mundo en la India*. México: El Colegio de México.

Guerra, José Antonio (ed.). 1998. *San Francisco de Asís: Escritos, Biografías, Documentos de la época*. 7th edition. Madrid: Biblioteca de Autores Cristianos.

Hartmann, Anastasii [Bishop]. 1939–1948. *Monumenta Anastasiana – Documenta vitam et gesta Servi Dei Anastasii Hartmann, O.F.M. Cap*. 5 vols. Eiditon mere privata – Apud Curiam Provinciae Helveticae Ord. Min Capuccinorum, Lucernae (Luzern) Switzerland.

Hill, S. C. [2006]. *Three Frenchmen in Bengal*. Whitefish, MT: Kessinger Publishing. First published in 1903.

Hosten, H., S. J. 1912. "Padre Marco della Tomba and the Ashoka Pillars near Bettiah," *Journal and Proceedings of Asiatic Society of Bengal*, New Series, 8, 3: 109–113.

[Kalapura, Jose, S.J.] John, Jose K. 1999. "Religion and Community: The Bettiah and Ravidas Christian Communities in Bihar, 1930–1980." Ph.D. thesis (approved in 2000) in Centre for Historical Studies, Jawaharlal Nehru University.

[Kalapura, Jose, S.J.] John, Jose Kalapura. 2000. "Kings, Fort, Zamindaris and Missionaries: The Founding of Bihar's Oldest Christian Community, 1745." *Proceedings of the Indian History Congress, Kolkata*, pp. 1011–1028.

Launay, Adrien. 2001. *Histoire de la Mission du Thibet*. 2 vols. Paris: Missions Étrangères de Paris. Originally published in 1903. The main focus of these volumes is a nineteenth-century French mission.

Iriarte, Lazaro, O.F.M. Cap. [or Lazaro de Aspurz]. 1982. *Franciscan History: The Three Orders of St. Francis*. Chicago: Franciscan

Herald Press. Translated from the original Spanish edition of 1979.

Little, Nigel Ken. "Transoceanic Radical: The Many Identities of William Duane." Ph.D. thesis, Murdoch University, 2003.

Lorenzen, David N. 1991. *Kabir Legends and Ananta-Das's Kabir Parachai.* Albany: State University of New York Press.

———. 1999. "Who Invented Hinduism?" *Comparative Studies in Society and History* 42: 630–59. Also republished in my *Who Invented Hinduism?* (2006b below, pp. 1–36).

———. 2002. "Marco della Tomba and the Kabir Panth," in *Images of Kabir*, edited by Monika Horstmann, pp. 33–43. New Delhi: Manohar.

———. 2003. "Europeans in Late Mughal India: The Perceptions of Italian Missionaries." *Indian Economic and Social History Review* 40,1: 1–31. Republished in Lorenzen 2006b above, pp. 187–226.

———. 2006a. "Marco della Tomba and the Brahmin from Banaras: Missionaries, Orientalists and Native Scholars", *Journal of Asian Studies* 65, 1: 113–41.

———. 2006b. *Who Invented Hinduism? Essays on Religion in History.* New Delhi: Yoda Press.

———. 2006c. "Marco della Tomba in Hindustan," in Lorenzen 2006b above, pp. 227–40.

———. Forthcoming. "Marco della Tomba". In *Dizionario bibliografic degli italiani.*

Lupi, Renato Raffaele. 2003. *Missionari Cappuccini Piceni: Schede biblo-biografiche.* Ancona: Archivio provinciale cappuccini Ancona.

Marcellino da Civezza (d. 1906). 1857–1895. *Storia Universale delle Missioni Francescane,* 11 vols. Roma: Tipografia Tiberina.

Le Marche tra Ottocento e Novecento: tai del Convengo, Pesaro, 20 novembre 1992. Pesaro: Amministrazione provinciale di Pesaro e Urbino, [1995].

Marshall, Peter J. 1970. *The British Discovery of Hinduism.* Cambridge: Cambridge University Press.

Meersman, Achilles, O.F.M., 1964. "Some Documents concerning the Founding of the Capuchin Church in Chandernagore, Bengal." *Collactanea Franciscana* 34: 177–81.

Melchor de Pobladura, O.F.M.Cap. 1966. "El verdadero autor de la 'Carta familiar', Mexico 1765: Francisco de Ajofrín (1719–1789)," *Collectanea franciscana* 36, 56–86.

Nardella, Umberto. 1984. "La conoscenza dell'Hindi e Urdu in Italia nel secoli XVIII e XIX." In Aldo Gallotta and Ugo Marazzi (eds.), *La Conoscenza dell'Asia e dell'Africa in Italia nei secoli XVIII e XIX,* volume 3, tomo 1, pp. 5–72. Naples: Istituto Universitario Orientale.

Neill, Stephen. 1985. *A History of Christianity in India, 1707–1858*. Cambridge: Cambridge University Press.

O'Malley, L.S. and R.E. Swanzy. 1938. *Champaran*. Patna: Government Printing. In series "Bihar and Orissa District Gazetteers." First written by O'Malley in 1907 and revised by Swanzy in 1932.

Paci, Libero. 1978. "L'Ambiente religioso maceratese del settecento." *Studi maceratesi* 12 (*Il Settecento nella Marca*), pp. 33–89. Centro di Studi Storici Maceratesi.

Petech, Luciano. 1996. "I cappuccini marchigiani e il Tibet." In *Le Marche e l'Oriente: Una tradizione ininterrotta da Matteo Ricci a Giuseppe Tucci,* edited by Francesco D'Arelli, pp. 247–60. Atti del Convegno Internazionale Macerata, 23–26 ottobre 1996.

Prasad, Leela. 1981. *Opposition to British Supremacy in Bihar: 1757–1803*. Patna: Janaki Prakashan.

Rocco da Cesinale, *P.* [or Cocchia Rocco, da Cesinale]. 1867–1873. *Storia delle Missioni dei Cappuccini,* 3 vols. Parigi-Roma: [P. Lethielleux], 1867–1873. (volume 3, Roma: Tipografia Barbèra, 1873).

Seth, Mesrovb Jacob. 1992. *Armenians in India, From the Earliest Times to the Present Day, A Work of Original Research*. New Delhi: Asian Educational Series. Originally published in 1937.

Shreeve, Nicholas. 1996. *Dark Legacy.* Crossbush, England: Bookwright.

Spear, Percival. 1975. *Master of Bengal: Clive and His India.* London: Thames and Hudson.

Stoneman, Richard (trans.). 1991. *The Greek Alexander Romance.* London: Penguin Books.

Tacitus. 1948. *Tacitus on Britain and Germany.* A translation of the "Agricola" and the "Germania" by H. Mattingly. West Drayton: Penguin.

Trampus, Antonio. 2001. *La massoneria nell'età moderna*. Rome-Bari: Gius. Laterza & Figli.

Upright Lives: Documents Concerning the Natural Virtue and Wisdom of the Indians (1650–1740). 1981. Introduction by Thomas Hahn. The Augustan Reprint Society: Publications Numbers 209–10. Los Angeles: William Andrews Clark Memorial Library, University of California, Los Angeles.

Vannini, Fr. Fulgentius, O.F.M. Cap. 1966. *Bishop Hartmann*. New Edition; Allahabad: St. Paul's Press.

———. 1976. *The Bell of Lhasa*. New Delhi (and Capuchin Ashram, Udyognagar, Agra 282 007).

———. 1977. *Christian Settlements in Nepal During the Eighteenth Century*. New Delhi. (and Superior/ Capuchin Ashram/ Udyognagar/ Agra 282007 or St. Fidelis Ashram, Mahanagar, Lucknow 226 006).

———. 1981. *Hindustan-Tibet Mission*. New Delhi (and Superior/ Capuchin Ashram/ Udyognagar/ Agra 282007 *or* Superior, St. Patrick's Church/ Sec. III Rajendra Nagar/ Sahibabad 201006/ Ghaziabad District).

Verma, Dinesh Chandra. 1976. *Plassey to Buxar: A Military Study*. New Delhi: K. B. Publications, 1976.

Winius, George D. and Marcus P. M. Vink. *The Merchant-Warrior Pacified: The VOC (The Dutch East India Company) and its Changing Political Economy in India*. Delhi: Oxford University Press, 1994.

Yang, Anand A. 1989. *The Limited Raj: Agrarian Relations in Colonial Saran District, 1793–1920*. Berkeley: University of California Press.

———. 1998. *Bazaar India: Markets, Society, and the Colonial State in Gangetic Bihar*. Berkeley: University of California Press.

Yugalanand Bihari (ed.). 1953. *Kabir Sagar*. 11 vols. Bombay: Shrivenkateshvar Steam Press. First published in about the 1910s. Volume 1 contains the *Gyan Sagar*.